Doug is masterful at translating all things "quality" in the healthcare arena. This book provides clear understanding of how to design, implement, manage, and sustain programmatic quality management in a way that is easily adopted by any healthcare organization. Doug demonstrates a great ability to simplify and organize the complexity of healthcare systems for greater understanding among those who lead and operate within them. This book demystifies the complexities of healthcare operations and provides, in abundantly clear language, a path forward to sustainable quality improvement.

Mark Epstein MD, MBA
Chief Medical Officer RS21
7/10/2023

It is with great pleasure that I wholeheartedly endorse Doug's book on *Hospital Quality*. Doug points out many key points that will be painfully obvious to healthcare workers, administrators, C-suites, and stakeholders. For over 25 years I have been a Lean Master consultant in healthcare, applying Lean concepts in almost all areas. Time and time again quality is talked about, the emphasis is on "talked about." One healthcare senior vice president told me that his entire staff was so completely esoteric on quality that they looked at everything and inch deep and a mile wide. So, there you have it; at times quality is the storefront window display versus really delivering quality care and quality outcomes.

As Doug appropriately points out from Shigeo Shingo, "Sustainable results depend upon the degree to which an organization's culture is aligned to specific guiding principles rather than depending solely on tools, programs, or initiatives." The most difficult thing I have seen is getting quality into the DNA of the culture. Living it, talking to it, thinking about it, every day and in every way.

Hospital systems are complex from a compliance standpoint. Every Lean training class I have done I ask the participants (usually 18–25+), raise your hand if you have policies and procedures. Ultimately, every single person raises their hand. I then ask, "How many of you follow those policies and procedures?" (many of them required by quality regulations), almost no one raises their hand. How is that possible?

As Doug points out correctly, the moment there is an interaction between staff and patient is where quality begins. To effectively be successful with quality in any organization, you cannot dictate quality or demand it. You must interact with the front line and at the immediate point of contact with the customer, in any setting. Quality is not a given; it is earned through practice and refinement. Toyota lost focus on quality in the mid-2000s trying to be the number-one sales automobile supplier in the world. They succeeded, but there was a severe consequence: their quality faltered. They had to regroup and get back to their Lean principles.

This book contains the necessary foundational structure to build a quality process. It is a process. Many people reading this book will know what PDCA (plan-do-check-act) or PDSA (plan-do-study-act) is. Masaaki Imai points out in his book *Gemba Kaizen* that there is no process you cannot do PDCA or PDSA; you must do SDCA (standardize-do-check-act)! This book is a key guide to building that quality foundation. It is straightforward and captures all the elements a quality leader will need.

I have gotten to know Doug for years; we have grown together regarding Lean and Six Sigma and how each can help improve *all* healthcare processes. Our conversations are challenging and create a hunger for more knowledge. I highly recommend *Hospital Quality* by Doug Johnson.

Michael Hogan
Lean Master
05/24/2023

The moral responsibility to provide high quality care in an increasingly complex healthcare industry challenges the best healthcare organizations. Fierce competition for resources and the multidisciplinary nature of healthcare can leave organizations less focused and structured than needed to achieve their quality goals. *Hospital Quality* is a fantastic resource for providing a practical and straightforward path to attain quality objectives. Douglas Johnson captures his decades of learning during his practice as a system, process, and quality professional. It is truly scalable to each organization's current capabilities and can be used to stand up an entirely new program or as a reference to assist established programs in accelerating performance.

Troy Greer, FACHE, MBA, MSHA
CEO of Boone Health in Columbia, Columbia, MO, USA

Hospital Quality

In healthcare, quality management refers to the administration of systems design, policies, and processes that minimize, if not eliminate, harm while optimizing patient care and outcomes. Whether you are a hospital with 1,000 beds or 25, the fact remains that every hospital must navigate and manage the many complexities associated with a quality management system.

Why is quality management important in healthcare? There are numerous reasons why it is important to improve quality of healthcare, including enhancing the accountability of health practitioners and managers, resource efficiency, identifying and minimizing medical errors while maximizing the use of effective care and improving outcomes, and aligning care to what users and patients want in addition to what they need.

Hospital Quality: Implementing, Managing, and Sustaining an Effective Quality Management System demonstrates a practical approach to managing and improving quality. Whether you agree with the premise that these activities are complex or not, this book will outline a standardized approach that any organization can adopt to meet their needs while accommodating the foundational concepts of quality improvement by accreditation agencies. It also outlines how to set up and manage a quality management program as a part of continuous process improvement initiative, as well as the purpose and managing of a patient safety organization.

The purpose of this book is twofold. If you're a senior healthcare manager or director tasked with setting up a quality management system, this book will provide tools and techniques you can immediately apply. If you're a healthcare professional preparing for the CPHQ certification exam, this book will take you beyond study guides by explaining what you need to know and the why behind each concept.

Hospital Quality

Implementing, Managing, and Sustaining an Effective Quality Management System

Doug Johnson

Routledge

Taylor & Francis Group

A PRODUCTIVITY PRESS BOOK

Cover image credit: www.shutterstock.com

First published 2024
by Routledge
605 Third Avenue, New York, NY 10158

and by Routledge
4 Park Square, Milton Park, Abingdon, Oxon, OX14 4RN

Routledge is an imprint of the Taylor & Francis Group, an informa business

ISBN: 978-1-032-41505-5 (hbk)
ISBN: 978-1-032-41500-0 (pbk)
ISBN: 978-1-003-35840-4 (ebk)

DOI: 10.4324/9781003358404

Typeset in Adobe Garamond Pro
by Apex CoVantage, LLC

Contents

Acknowledgments xii
About the Author xiii

    Introduction 1

1 An Introduction to Quality 3
    1.1   Defining Quality 3
    1.2   Examples of Quality 4
    1.3   Quality Culture 4
    1.4   Cost of Poor Quality 5
    1.5   Summary 7
            1.5.1   Key Concepts 7
            1.5.2   Areas You Can Geek Out On 7

2 Quality Regulation and Benchmarking 8
    2.1   Regulation 8
    2.2   Centers for Medicare and Medicaid Services (CMS) 9
    2.3   CMS Five-Star Rankings 13
    2.4   QualityNet/HARP 18
    2.5   Other Benchmarking Agencies 18
    2.6   Other Regulations Important to Quality Departments 18
    2.7   Health Insurance Portability and Accountability Act (HIPAA) 21
    2.8   Clinical Laboratory Improvement Amendments (CLIA) 22
    2.9   Summary 22
            2.9.1   Key Concepts 23
            2.9.2   Areas You Can Geek Out On 23

3 Managing Quality 24
    3.1   The Original Mission 24
    3.2   The "Quality Director" as Defined by Job Descriptions 25
    3.3   The Paradigm of Managing Healthcare Quality 27
    3.4   Quality Governance Structure 29
    3.5   The Quality Committee 34
            3.5.1   The Quality Committee Structure 34
    3.6   The Medical Executive Committee (MEC) 40
    3.7   The Governing Board 41

3.8 Summary 43
    3.8.1 Key Concepts 43
    3.8.2 Areas You Can Geek Out On 43

4 Quality Measurement and Analytics 44
    4.1 Basics of Quality Measurement 44
    4.2 Quality Measurement and Analytics 47
        4.2.1 Exercise 48
    4.3 SMART Goals 54
        4.3.1 Exercise 55
        4.3.2 SMART Goals for Individual Tasks 57
    4.4 In-Process versus Outcome Measures 57
    4.5 Trending Data 60
    4.6 Control Charts 62
    4.7 Pareto Chart 66
    4.8 Cascading Measures 68
    4.9 The Quality Oversight Scorecard 72
    4.10 Updating the Quality Oversight Scorecard 78
    4.11 Summary 80
        4.11.1 Key Concepts 80
        4.11.2 Areas You Can Geek Out On 80

5 Quality Improvement 82
    5.1 Process Improvement Techniques 85
        5.1.1 Lean 85
        5.1.2 Six Sigma 86
        5.1.3 ISO 9001 89
        5.1.4 Plan-Do-Study-Act (PDSA) 89
        5.1.5 Root-Cause Analysis 94
    5.2 Change Management 96
    5.3 Summary 99
        5.3.1 Key Concepts 99
        5.3.2 Areas You Can Geek Out On 99

6 Quality Training 101
    6.1 Role of the Quality Professional in Training 101
    6.2 Employee Engagement 103
        6.2.1 Motivation 103
        6.2.2 Assessing the Current State of Employee Engagement 106
    6.3 Catch-Ball Sessions 107
    6.4 Standard Work 109
    6.5 Training within Industry 111
    6.6 Summary 113
        6.6.1 Key Concepts 113
        6.6.2 Areas You Can Geek Out On 113

7 Project Management 115
    7.1 Project Management in Quality 115

7.2   Action Item Tracking Tool 119
7.3   Action Item Standard Work 120
7.4   Summary 120
    7.4.1   Key Concepts 122
    7.4.2   Areas You Can Geek Out On 122

8   Accreditation 123
8.1   Role of the Quality Professional in Accreditation 123
8.2   Managing the Activities of the Accreditation Agency 124
8.3   Manage Survey Action Plans 125
8.4   Survey Readiness and Preparation 125
    8.4.1   Leadership Commitment 125
    8.4.2   Manager Accountability 126
    8.4.3   Survey Readiness Oversight 126
    8.4.4   Requirements Oversight 127
    8.4.5   Organizational Assessment 128
    8.4.6   Staff Education 128
    8.4.7   Survey Audits 129
8.5   Sample Case Study 136
    8.5.1   Pre-Survey Activities 137
    8.5.2   Post-Survey Activities 137
    8.5.3   Staff Recognition 138
8.6   Summary 138
    8.6.1   Key Concepts 139
    8.6.2   Areas You Can Geek Out On 139

9   Sustaining Quality 140
9.1   Role of the Quality Professional in Sustaining Quality 140
9.2   Daily Operations 140
9.3   Standard Work for the Quality Professional 143
9.4   Summary 147
    9.4.1   Key Concepts 148
    9.4.2   Areas You Can Geek Out On 148

10   The Quality Plan 149
10.1   Components of the Quality Plan 150
10.2   Summary 152
    10.2.1   Key Concepts 152
    10.2.2   Areas You Can Geek Out On 152

11   External Reporting 153
11.1   National Healthcare Safety Network (NHSN) 153
11.2   Hospital Consumer Assessment of Healthcare Providers and Systems (HCAHPS) 154
11.3   QualityNet/HARP (CMS) Portal 155
11.4   Using Vendors for QualityNet Data 157
11.5   Updating Information in QualityNet 158
11.6   COVID-19 Reporting 159

11.7   Summary...160
        11.7.1   Key Concepts..160
        11.7.2   Areas You Can Geek Out On...160

12 Patient Safety Organization, Quality Incidents, and Mortality Reviews.................161
12.1   Patient Safety Organization (PSO) 161
12.2   Quality Incident Events...163
        12.2.1   Serious Reportable Events (SRE)......................................164
        12.2.2   Sentinel Events (SE) 165
        12.2.3   Never Events (NE) 165
        12.2.4   Patient Safety Indicators (PSI) 165
        12.2.5   Hospital-Acquired Infections (HAI)................................165
12.3   Quality Incident Summary..165
12.4   Mortality Reviews 167
12.5   Summary..169
        12.5.1   Key Concepts..170
        12.5.2   Areas You Can Geek Out On...170

13 Managing Hospital-Acquired Conditions (HAC) and Harms 171
13.1   Role of the Quality Professional in HACs and Harms...................171
13.2   Summary..173
        13.2.1   Key Concepts..173
        13.2.2   Areas You Can Geek Out On...174

14 Managing the Quality Team 175
14.1   Developing the Quality Team 175
        14.1.1   Interviews 175
        14.1.2   Summarize the Findings..176
        14.1.3   Prioritize Your Key Themes...176
        14.1.4   Present Your Findings to the Group..................................176
        14.1.5   Provide a Plan 177
        14.1.6   Personality Assessment..177
        14.1.7   Outline the Work of the Department 178
        14.1.8   Assign Primary and Secondary Owners.............................179
14.2   One-on-One Meetings 179
14.3   Huddle Meetings..181
14.4   Calendar for Reporting...184
14.5   Support, Support, Support 186
14.6   Summary..186
        14.6.1   Key Concepts..186
        14.6.2   Areas You Can Geek Out On...186

15 Summary: Bringing It All Together 187
15.1   Quality Professional Next Steps...187
15.2   Sample Scenario 188
15.3   Summary..190

Appendix..**191**
    Chapter 2 Appendix.. 191
    Chapter 4 Appendix.. 193
    Chapter 8 Appendix.. 194
    Chapter 10 Appendix.. 199
    Chapter 12 Appendix.. 204

Glossary of Acronyms **216**

Index **219**

Acknowledgments

My career in healthcare has taken me to many places I never dreamed I would go. Over the last 30 years, I have had many experiences and progressed through numerous roles exposing me to challenges and opportunities along the way. There was always someone who believed in my abilities and challenged me to strive beyond what I thought I was capable of. Some of the people who had a direct impact on my career were:

Bruce Alexander
Clay Holderman
David Scrase, MD
Donna Agnew
Donna Garcia
Er Ralston
Harvey White, MD
Jerome Goss, MD
Mark Epstein, MD
Michael Hogan
Paul Neis
Peter Snow
Rae Woods
Troy Greer

Each one of these people coached, mentored, and challenged me to strive to reach the next phase of healthcare career progression. We may spend our lifetimes studying and learning, but I am convinced it is the people we encounter and work with who truly guide us and instill the confidence to move forward.

A special thank you goes out to my parents, who continue to believe in me and taught me, through their example of hard work, to always "do the best I can do."

To my wife, Lynn Ann, who continues to support me and trust me to be the best version of myself. She's my daily confidant in brainstorming and developing ways in which we can improve the quality of healthcare throughout the United States.

About the Author

**Doug Johnson** has been in healthcare over 30 years. He is a registered nurse, certified professional in healthcare quality, and Lean Six Sigma black belt and earned his BSN summa cum laude. His healthcare career began in patient transport and has progressed over numerous areas including the cardiovascular lab, health plan operations, the emergency department, operating departments, nursing units, urgent care, billing processes, electronic medical records, patient throughput, regulatory and accreditation requirements, quality, database management, data analytics, and software development.

Doug has outstanding interpretive skills in quantitative and qualitative analyses, identifying root causes of poor process control and inefficiencies. His vast experience in the multifaceted business of healthcare has equipped him to design, improve, and provide sustainable solutions in all areas of healthcare operations.

His company, DcJ Solutions (www.Innovate2Accelerate.com) offers quality management consulting and training through proven tools and techniques to allow your organization to implement, manage, and sustain a quality management program using existing and permanent staff. He developed a team of experts in both healthcare operations and information technology design. By combining the skills of healthcare operations, process improvement, and technology, this team is well aligned to create meaningful solutions for healthcare organizations.

Introduction

When I speak to people outside healthcare and tell them I manage quality in healthcare, I get that polite smile and nod that abruptly end the conversation. What are they thinking? Why the sudden lack of interest in what that means or how that works? Quality and healthcare should go hand in hand. I believe people assume and expect quality exists in healthcare. After all, we don't go to see a physician because we want them to harm us. The mere fact that someone is in a position to "manage quality" informs them that their assumed expectation of quality may not exist. The fact is, there are people managing quality in most industries, but there are few that focus solely on that for their career.

If quality typically happens at the level of product development (advances in surgical implements) or at the level of providing service (caring for patients), what does a hospital quality department actually do? I like to think of quality professionals as technical business consultants or extremely important support personnel. This book will help give you the expertise you need to create, deliver, and sustain quality in your organization.

This book focuses on the methodology and practices necessary to help lead organizations to provide exceptional quality healthcare. I have 30 years of experience working in healthcare. Much of that was focused on process improvement and quality. The impetus of creating this book, however, did not come from a passion to share my experiences and knowledge related to quality in healthcare. It came from the significant struggles I have witnessed across the industry to provide a quality program in healthcare. The "quality professional" has little or no purposeful education outside past experience, fragmented educational inputs, and self-teaching. This means every quality professional has their own methods of developing and achieving a quality program that is unique to that person and, therefore, unique to each hospital. Accreditation standards under the Centers for Medicaid and Medicare Services (CMS) require that healthcare organizations have quality programs in place. These programs require hospitals to have a named person responsible for that agenda. This leaves organizations scrambling to find qualified candidates to fill the role of quality professional in their organizations. Regardless of the size of the hospital – they could have 5 beds or 800 beds – they must have a quality program in place. Given the nature of the methods by which most quality professionals obtain their knowledge and practices, these hired quality professionals create individualized programs that are new to the organization each time they are introduced. A quality professional who remains at their post for ten or more years may have the ability to create some stability for the organization in their methodologies; however, we all know that, in this time of excessive turnover and transition of employees, most organizations are lucky to retain a quality professional for two years. You may get some quick wins in this period of time, but true quality in healthcare is a journey, not simply a destination.

Who would want to go to a hospital knowing that quality was just a "nice to have" privilege in the hopes that it existed? The manner in which healthcare quality is applied, defined, and managed, however, is extremely variable. One might ask, "What about all the quality measures CMS has imposed on hospitals and the penalties created for those that don't do well? Does that not define quality for healthcare?" The answer would be, yes, these are noble measures to improve, follow, and live by, but they are significantly weak when measuring the quality of an organization. They drive organizations to chase the outcome or the "grade," rather than focusing on the day-to-day operations that lead to those improved results. This is akin to cramming for an exam as opposed to mastering the material for application. We in healthcare have all spent our careers understanding and learning the skills and techniques necessary to provide high-quality and effective care. Why do we allow regulation to come in and tell us what quality is and how we should measure it? This drives organizations just to get past the test rather than focusing on the very thing we aspired to do in the first place – providing exceptional patient care to our community of fellow human beings.

This book is aimed at the healthcare professional who would like to initiate the management of a quality program. It contains the immediate structure needed for implementation to get you started. My intent is to eliminate all the multiple sources of information and research that must be assimilated when starting your path in healthcare quality and provide real-world education and steps to start your journey. As I previously stated, there are as many methods of managing quality in healthcare as there are quality professionals doing the job. There is, however, little information on the real-life concepts of understanding quality, why we do it, how we implement programs, and how we manage them. Those already in quality professional roles may have other methods, ideas, and techniques to achieve the concepts I outline in this book. This is a blueprint that contains all the necessary elements of managing a quality program accompanied by my recommended methods to achieve them. You can follow the education in this book exactly as it is given, or you can utilize sections or techniques to add to the practices you've already established while on the job.

My purpose for each chapter in this book is to outline the key concepts related to healthcare quality management. I describe the concepts with some educational background, provide examples, and, in some cases, tools to follow. This book is not a deep dive into each concept but rather an overview to enable you to seek additional resources if that area interests you. I am convinced that there is no single reference material that teaches quality professionals how to do their jobs for their particular organizations. At the end of each chapter, I summarize the key concepts and provide additional resources in case you want to "geek out" on a specific topic. It is up to you, the reader, to determine if you are interested in going further into any specific material.

I am always excited to receive other's experiences and feedback on this subject. If you have suggestions to improve this book, please share those so future publications can be enhanced.

Chapter 1

An Introduction to Quality

1.1 Defining Quality

What is quality? *Quality* tends to have as many definitions as there are people giving them. The reason, I believe, is because each person's definition of *quality* is a personal one. Our experiences, perceptions, background, and upbringing all add to our definition of the word. Consider this analogy.

> A high school student has fairly good grades and plays sports. He lives in a middle-class neighborhood with his parents and has never lived anywhere else.
>
> Now consider a middle-aged female, married with kids and working full time. Her parents have had significant health issues lately, and she is juggling to support them and her children, husband, and job.
>
> What would the responses be from each of these people if asked their definition of *quality*? We can only speculate, but do you think they would be similar? The high school student may define *quality* using his experiences in sports by saying something like "Quality is consistent performance while at bat." On the other hand, the woman's perception of *quality* may be "consistent and reliable customer service leading to good results." Can we determine which one should be used to define *quality* or determine if one is better than the other? No, each is specific to the perceptions of the individual, and each provides valuable insight into our pursuit of quality. In this respect, we must realize that there is no definition of *quality* that is wrong. The definition matches the perceptions and feelings of every individual.

If you agree, and you are willing to believe there are some significant differences in the way each individual views quality, how can a definition of quality in healthcare be standardized? We build our service offerings on the needs of our customers, and our customers are no different than the analogy provided here. If each individual has their own perception of quality in healthcare, it makes it quite challenging to meet those expectations when each comes with their own definition.

Although we don't demand that our customers agree on a standardized definition of quality, we must, at the very least, get input from our customers and combine key themes that relate to their definition of quality. In the previous example, although the two definitions are unique, one shared theme is "consistent." By obtaining and creating a definition utilizing these key themes,

DOI: 10.4324/9781003358404-2

3

we can communicate to our customers how we perceive and define healthcare quality. This transparency enables us to close the gap between our customers' perceptions and what we are actually trying to achieve as it relates to healthcare quality.

1.2 Examples of Quality

What companies do you think of when you think of a "quality organization"?

Figure 1.1 shows some recognizable company brands – what quality things do these companies do to create quality?

Figure 1.1 Well-known company brands.

It may be difficult to think of quality in isolation. Through your experiences with services or brands like those in Figure 1.1, you may be able to better perceive the reasons these brands represent quality or don't. For example, Starbucks may bring the idea of customer service and friendliness as a component of quality. Coke may bring the idea of consistency – always tastes the same wherever you get it. Toyota may bring the idea of reliability and longevity as it relates to quality. Finally, Apple may provide feelings of reliability and usability as it relates to quality.

If your customers applied these same concepts to healthcare, what would they perceive? Would they see customer service and friendliness? Like Coke, would they see consistency in that service? Would they have the same experience at every one of your emergency departments, regardless of the location? Is there a status with your healthcare brand like the status associated with Toyota? And lastly, do your customers believe they can rely on your healthcare system every hour of every day, much as they can rely on the technology of Apple when they need it?

1.3 Quality Culture

With all of these perceptions and definitions of *quality*, one might believe quality is just as intangible as culture. David Mann discusses this concept in depth in his book *Creating a Lean Culture*.

Although he is specifically referencing the process improvement components of Lean as it relates to culture, one thing is very similar to our definition of quality. He states that culture is a hypothetical construct. That is, culture is a label or idea – a concept we make up to organize and get a handle on what we have seen or experienced. Is *quality* much the same? We create the concept based on our experiences and history. Mann, however, goes on to state that the target of achieving culture (quality) is futile – rather, we must define our management system to create the kind of culture we want to achieve. In this same way, quality is a direct result of the processes, management systems, and intentional design of systems that result with the quality we want to achieve.

Another source for quality culture is the Shingo Institute.[1] The purpose statement of the Shingo Institute at Utah State University is "Based on timeless principles, the Shingo Institute shapes cultures that drive operational excellence." From the work of Dr. Shingeo Shingo, this organization understands the impact of organizational culture on sustainable quality. Sustainable results depend on the degree to which an organization's culture is aligned to specific guiding principles rather than depending solely on tools, programs, or initiatives. The Shingo model provides a powerful framework that will guide the reader in transforming an organization's culture and achieving ideal results. More information on the Shingo model can be found at https://shingo.org/shingo-model/.

1.4 Cost of Poor Quality

Many forget one of the key components of quality: how quality relates to the bottom-line financial performance. Most of us, in our lifetime, have seen many companies go out of business. More often than not, we are not surprised when they close their doors. We haven't seen their financial profit-and-loss statements or spoken with the president of the company who explained their difficulties prior to closing, yet we are quite confident when we utter the words "They will be out of business soon," or "It's not a surprise they are out of business." How can we make such statements? They come from our experiences with the business. Directly related to the service we received when we went there, the cost of their products, the reliability of their product, poor customer service, reduced inventory – did I need to return it because it broke or was not as advertised? All these warning signs are specifically related to the processes, management systems, culture, and design that either make or break an organization.

The concept of quality in business is not a one-and-done thing. Companies that were once thought to be the pillar of quality and service met their demise in, quite frankly, a very short period of time soon after they took their eye off the concept of quality service. Some examples on a national level are Toys R Us, Borders bookstore, Saturn, Sports Authority, and Blockbuster. I am sure you can think of many more, especially on a local level.

If you're not sold on the fact that poor quality leads to the demise of your bottom line, there are many external forces that will gladly take your money if you do not manage the business properly. This is demonstrated in the Centers for Medicaid and Medicare Services' (CMS) value-based purchasing model. Healthcare organizations are penalized or "incentivized" based on their defined outcome–based quality measures. CMS withholds payment percentages for Medicare throughout the year and only gives that money back if the health system meets certain thresholds in quality outcomes. Readmissions, value-based purchasing measures, inpatient quality reporting (IQR), meaningful use, and hospital acquired conditions all contribute to the percentages withheld. The total withheld can equal 8% of total spending when adding all the programs together. This seems like a small percentage, but when we consider hospitals bill Medicare on average $72,479,691 each year, 8% of that is $5.7 million.

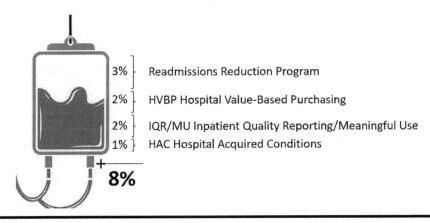

Figure 1.2   CMS quality penalties.

Another consideration of poor quality is the cost of managing the extra work and overhead associated with a poor quality outcome. Literature suggests[2] a stage-3 pressure injury, for example, leads to an additional $32,292 in costs for additional care, and those same complications usually result in an average legal settlement of $300,000. Five hospital-acquired pressure injuries in a year could cost the organization as much as $1.6 million.

Other costs of poor quality are related to customer satisfaction and experience. How many customers fail to continue using your services when they have had a bad experience? How many people do they tell about their bad experience? How does positive and negative feedback affect potential customers? Think of your emergency department's "left without being seen" patients. Do you actually think those patients leave and forget about the poor customer service while telling no one? The fact is they may never come back again, and they are likely to tell at least one other person about the negative experience. Take, for example, a hospital I worked with that had over 300 patients a month leave without being seen. This calculates to 3,600 patients a year. If they told just one person about their experience, over 7,000 people are likely to have a somewhat if not significant negative perception of the facility. Many will never return unless, of course, you are the only shop in town, and customers utilize your services because they don't have a choice. This brings a whole new level of complexity to customer satisfaction, but that's a topic we aren't covering here. The point is there is a law of exponential expansion applied here. The growth is proportional to the quality present, or, more simply, there is a constant doubling time. The bad news is that it spreads like wildfire.

Another key factor to consider when discussing the cost of poor quality is employee satisfaction and retention. In 30 years of healthcare experience, I have never met one healthcare employee who came to work to do a bad job. In fact, most healthcare workers are intrinsically motivated to contribute to society by giving back their skills and talents to make others' lives better. Working in an environment where processes do not coincide with quality of care can lead to a significant dilemma in an employee's moral thought process. Processes such as poor and inefficient electronic medical records, poor staffing, toxic leadership, and inadequate supplies (just to name a few) leave employees who are, by nature, motivated to do a great job faced with an environment that does not. It is not "if" but "when" these <u>exceptionally intrinsically motivated employees looking to provide exceptional, high-quality patient care</u> end up looking for an environment elsewhere that will help them achieve that goal.

1.5 Summary

Defining *quality* can become very subjective. Always remember, that it is your customer who defines quality. We provide a service, and they will be the judge of the level of quality the service reaches.

Quality culture, as intangible as it may seem, can be shaped in your organization. It is through leadership, processes, management systems, and intentional design of systems that result in the quality we want to achieve. Behavioral principles need to support your quality culture and be defined in the organization.

Finally, poor quality does create costs to organizations. Sometimes those costs are more difficult to correlate directly to quality, but evidence tell us it does directly impact the ability of your company to stay in business.

1.5.1 Key Concepts

- To define healthcare quality, you must solicit information and feedback from your customers.
- Although measures exist to determine quality in healthcare, customer perceptions trump any measures that prove otherwise.
- Culture is intangible yet very real in organizations that embrace culture and those that do not.
- The cost of poor quality has a multifactorial impact on the success of your business.

1.5.2 Areas You Can Geek Out On

- The Shingo Model "Way of Thinking": https://shingo.org/shingo-model/

Notes

1 https://shingo.org/.
2 Readmit, mortality, and HAC: https://onlinelibrary.wiley.com/doi/10.1111/iwj.13482; bedsore costs: https://nycbedsorelawyer.com/how-much-is-an-average-bedsore-lawsuit-settlement/; adverse events and LOS: www.americandatanetwork.com/wp-content/uploads/2015/01/A-Business-Case-Identifying-Excess-Cost-and-Length-of-Stay-of-Adverse-Patient-Safety-Events1.pdf; Cost for HAC: www.jointcommissionjournal.com/article/S1553-7250(20)30105-7/pdf.

Chapter 2

Quality Regulation and Benchmarking

This chapter discusses the overall regulation and accreditation components of managing healthcare quality. Since most quality departments in hospitals are also responsible for managing accreditation and some regulatory functions, the intent of this chapter is to provide some overall understanding of these topics. As with any of the topics of this book, you can spend significant amounts of time studying all of the details for accreditation and regulation. My hope is that this sets you on paths that interest you for further study.

2.1 Regulation

The US Department of Health and Human Services (HHS) has eleven operating divisions, including eight agencies in the US Public Health Service and three human services agencies. These divisions administer a wide variety of health and human services and conduct life-saving research for the nation, protecting and serving all Americans.

The office of the secretary (OS), HHS's chief policy officer and general manager, administers and oversees the organization, its programs, and its activities. The deputy secretary and a number of assistant secretaries and offices support OS.

With all of these organizations overseeing multiple areas of healthcare and business, how can a quality professional understand which of these they should focus on the most? The two most significant agencies are the Centers for Medicare and Medicaid Services (CMS) and the Centers for Disease Control and Prevention (CDC). CMS combines the oversight of the Medicare program, the federal portion of the Medicaid program and the State Children's Health Insurance Program, the Health Insurance Marketplace, and related quality-assurance activities.

The Centers for Disease Control and Prevention (CDC), part of the Public Health Service, protects the public health of the nation by providing leadership and direction in the prevention and control of diseases and other preventable conditions and responding to public health emergencies.

DOI: 10.4324/9781003358404-3

Regulation

US Department of
Health and Human
Services

HHS has 11 operating divisions, including eight agencies in the U.S. Public Health Service
and three human services agencies.

CHILDREN & FAMILIES	✳ACL	*AHRQ*	ATSDR	CDC	CMS	FDA	HRSA
Administration for Children and Families	Administration for Community Living	Agency for Healthcare Research and Quality	Agency for Toxic Substances and Disease Registry	Centers for Disease Control and Prevention	Centers for Medicare & Medicaid Services	Food and Drug Administration	Health Resources and Services Administration

	Indian Health Service	NIH National Institutes of Health	✗SAMHSA Substance Abuse and Mental Health Services Administration	

Figure 2.1   HHS organization.

CMS sets rules based on the conditions of participation (CoPs) and conditions for coverage (CfCs). Health care organizations must meet these rules in order to begin and continue participating in the Medicare and Medicaid programs. The health and safety standards are the foundation for improving quality and protecting the health and safety of beneficiaries. CMS also ensures that the standards of accrediting organizations recognized by CMS (through a process called "deeming") meet or exceed the Medicare standards set forth in the CoPs/CfCs.

CMS certification is achieved through a survey conducted by a state agency on behalf of the Centers for Medicare and Medicaid Services (CMS). However, most healthcare organizations opt to partner with a **national accrediting organization** such as the Joint Commission or DNV that develop and enforce standards that meet the federal CoPs. CMS grants deemed status to these organizations to allow them to survey and deem that a healthcare organization meets the Medicare and Medicaid certification requirements through its accreditation process.

2.2 Centers for Medicare and Medicaid Services (CMS)

So, one may ask, why is CMS so important to us as a healthcare facility? After all, our customers are not all represented by Medicaid or Medicare. Can't we choose to provide services only to customers who do not have Medicaid or Medicare? The answer is yes, and some organizations and healthcare providers choose this; however, 38% of healthcare in the country is funded by Medicaid and Medicare. Adding "other government," which usually falls under the same rules and regulations of Medicare and Medicaid, results in 50% of all healthcare payors falling in the government sector.[1] If a hospital chose to remain free of governmental control through CMS rules and regulations, they would need to give up 50% of their customer base and the revenue that comes with those customers.

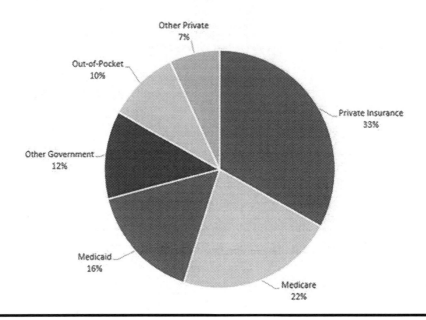

Distribution Of Healthcare Expenditure 2021

Other Private 7%
Out-of-Pocket 10%
Other Government 12%
Medicaid 16%
Medicare 22%
Private Insurance 33%

Figure 2.2 Distribution of healthcare expenditure.

Currently, physicians and other healthcare providers may register with traditional Medicare under three options: 1) participating provider, 2) non-participating provider, or 3) opt-out provider.

- **Participating providers**: Under this option, participating providers agree to accept assignment on all Medicare claims for *all* their Medicare patients, which means that they have signed a participation agreement with Medicare, agreeing to accept Medicare's fee schedule amounts as payment in full for all Medicare-covered services.
- **Non-participating providers**: Providers in this category accept Medicare patients but can choose whether to take assignment (i.e., Medicare's approved amount) on a claim-by-claim basis. Unlike participating providers, who are paid the full Medicare-allowed amount, non-participating physicians who take assignment are limited to 95% of the Medicare-approved amount.
- **Opt-out providers**: Physicians and practitioners under this option have signed an affidavit to opt out of the Medicare program entirely. Instead, these providers enter into private contracts with their Medicare patients, allowing them to bill their Medicare patients any amount they determine is appropriate.

A list of CMS-approved accreditation agencies is located on their website.[2] At the time of writing this book, there were 11 CMS-approved agencies.

Many look at their accreditation agencies as the "police," working for CMS to find their problems and expose them. The reality is that your accreditation agency is an organization designed to help you achieve accreditation with CMS and is motivated to help you succeed. For example, the mission of the joint commission "is to continuously improve health care for the public, in collaboration with other stakeholders, by evaluating healthcare organizations and inspiring them to excel in providing safe and effective care of the highest quality value."[3]

These accreditation agencies provide many services and supports to hospitals. CMS publishes their conditions of participation in thousands of pages of regulations and requirements. Although these are available for anyone to read and consume,[4] the accreditation agency translates these documents into organized and categorized documents, making the information meaningful and relevant to you. Accreditation agency documentation typically provides well-organized inspection categories with rationales to explain the intent of each requirement as well as a reference back to the original CMS conditions of participation. These, referred to as "standards," are then used to inspect and review your organization's accreditation status. CMS requires that organizations are inspected and accredited through one of these agencies at least every three years. During that time, your accreditation agency will come to your organization and perform the survey. They, in turn, will share those results with CMS, which will provide your deemed accreditation status. If you use an accreditation agency, CMS can still come in and perform an inspection on their own. This enables them to validate the results found by the accreditation agencies and hold them accountable for managing to the standards that they set.

Accreditation

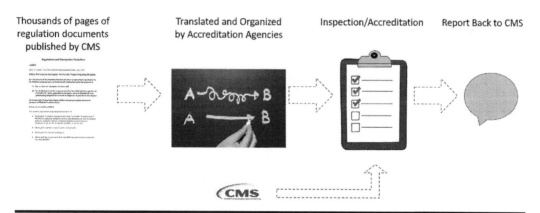

| Thousands of pages of regulation documents published by CMS | Translated and Organized by Accreditation Agencies | Inspection/Accreditation | Report Back to CMS |

Figure 2.3 Accreditation process.

The Joint Commission categorizes their accreditation standards into the following classifications:

1. APR   Accreditation participation requirements
2. EC   Environment of care
3. EM   Emergency management
4. HR   Human resources
5. IC   Infection control
6. IM   Information management
7. LD   Leadership
8. LS   Life safety

9. MM   Medication management
10. MS   Medical staff
11. NSPG National patient safety goals
12. NR   Nursing
13. PC   Provision of care, treatment, and services
14. PI   Performance improvement
15. RC   Record of care, treatment, and services
16. RI   Rights and responsibilities
17. TS   Transplant safety
18. WT   Waived testing

Similarly, but not the same, DNV categorizes these same standards into the following classifications:

1. QM   Quality management
2. GB   Governing body
3. CE   Chief executive officer
4. MS   Medical staff
5. NS   Nursing services
6. SM   Staffing management
7. MM   Medication management
8. SS   Surgical services
9. AS   Anesthesia services
10. LS   Laboratory services
11. RC   Respiratory care services
12. MI   Medical imaging
13. NM   Nuclear medicine services
14. RS   Rehabilitation services
15. ED   Emergency department
16. OS   Outpatient services
17. DS   Dietary services
18. PR   Patient rights
19. IC   Infection prevention and control program
20. MR   Medical record service
21. DC   Discharge planning
22. UR   Utilization review
23. PE   Physical environment
24. TO   Organ, tissue, and eye procurement
25. SB   Swing beds
26. TD   Admission, transfer, and discharge
27. PC   Plan of care
28. RR   Residents rights
29. FS   Facility services
30. RN   Resident nutrition

Regardless of the accreditation agency you use, ensure that you have a copy of their most recent published standards. Changes are usually seen annually and need to be obtained through your accreditation vendor.

2.3 CMS Five-Star Rankings

CMS adopted a five-star approach to measuring hospitals, which is updated annually. For Medicare patients, this ranking is a public-facing view of quality results aggregated to deem a specific star rating for individual hospitals. Every Medicare-participating hospital is available for comparison and quality measure transparency.[5]

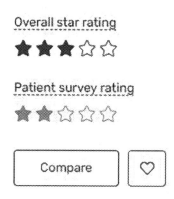

Figure 2.4   CMS five-star rating.

The data for calculating the results of the five-star quality rating comes from multiple sources. The Medicare Provider Analysis and Review (MEDPAR)[6] data is the billing data used by hospitals to obtain payment for their services. This data consists of the basic demographics of the patient but also includes the diagnoses and procedures performed during that hospital stay. Data also provided in these billing systems include the source of admission, the discharge disposition, and diagnostic-related group (DRG). Quality data that can be gleaned from this include things like mortality (e.g., discharge disposition "expired"), diagnosis (e.g., primary diagnosis code CHF), patient age, gender, and geographic location.

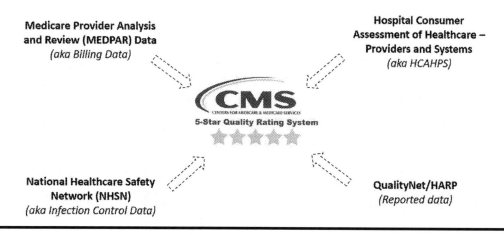

Figure 2.5   Five-star: where the data comes from.

CMS uses MEDPAR data to determine the following measures for the five-star rating:

1. Readmission rates
   a. Acute myocardial infarction (AMI)
   b. Chronic obstructive pulmonary disease (COPD)
   c. Heart failure (HF)
   d. Pneumonia
   e. Coronary artery bypass graft (CABG)
   f. Stroke
   g. Total hip replacement (THA)
   h. Total knee replacement (TKA)
   i. Hospital-wide readmissions
2. Mortality rates
   a. Acute myocardial infarction (AMI)
   b. Chronic obstructive pulmonary disease (COPD)
   c. Heart failure (HF)
   d. Pneumonia
   e. Coronary artery bypass graft (CABG)
   f. Stroke
3. Patient safety indicators (PSI)
   a. Pressure ulcer
   b. Iatrogenic pneumothorax
   c. In-hospital fall with hip fracture
   d. Perioperative hemorrhage or hematoma
   e. Postoperative acute kidney injury requiring dialysis
   f. Postoperative respiratory failure
   g. Perioperative pulmonary embolism or deep vein thrombosis
   h. Postoperative sepsis
   i. Postoperative wound dehiscence
   j. Unrecognized abdominopelvic accidental puncture or laceration
4. Medicare spending per beneficiary (MSPB)

The information utilized through MEDPAR data must be understood at a basic level. This data is often referred to as "billing data" or "claims data." Understanding what this information comprises is important, but equally important is understanding what is *not* represented in this data. Claims data contain all the diagnoses and procedure codes related to the patient's hospitalization. It also contains patient demographics such as age, location, and gender. Information regarding the visit is available through the admission date, discharge date, and provider(s) who cared for the patient. For purposes of this discussion, I will outline some of the information that is *not* in the claims data. This includes data and information such as vital signs, physician notes, nursing notes, lab results, pictures of wounds, and diagnostic images.

As clinicians, we always look at the information in the medical record and draw conclusions about that patient based on the many information sources we have. When reviewing claims data, however, many of these sources are missing. This is why, when looking at results analyzed through claims data by CMS or other reporting structures, we may be confused by their conclusions. A patient who arrived in the emergency department with lab results and physical presentation documentation of pneumonia, for example, may not be defined as a pneumonia patient if that documentation was not specific enough to generate the diagnosis code for pneumonia. The analysis of the claims data will only reveal the diagnoses code for the specific condition the measure is looking for and does not take into consideration all the other documentation that may be available to you. The issue here lies not in the analysis of the data, but in the appropriate documentation and/or coding practices that enable the appropriate diagnoses codes to be recorded.

The point of this illustration is to help you understand how the information is used so you can apply the appropriate quality management improvement initiatives to the measure. If all your clinicians are managing pneumonia patients well with evidenced-based practice, but the measurement through claims data shows poor performance, working with your clinicians to achieve better clinical results will yield nothing but frustration. If the issue is how it is documented and coded, you must first tackle that area in order to get a better sense of reality and determine if a clinical improvement initiative is warranted. This will be discussed more in Chapter 4 Quality Measurement and Analytics and Chapter 13 Managing Hospital-Acquired Conditions and Harms.

The Hospital Consumer Assessment of Healthcare – Provider and Systems (HCAHPS) data contains the results of customer satisfaction surveys sent to patients that have utilized a healthcare system. The questions used in this survey are standardized and mandated through the CMS conditions of participation. Most organizations utilize a vendor to manage their customer satisfaction surveys, results, and submission to CMS. At the time of this writing there were 25 approved survey vendors.[7]

Standardized questions utilized for the HCAHPS results published for the five-star criteria are:

1. Patients who reported that their nurses "always" communicated well.
2. Patients who reported that their doctors "always" communicated well.
3. Patients who reported that they "always" received help as soon as they wanted.
4. Patients who reported that the staff "always" explained about medicine before giving it to them.
5. Patients who reported that their room and bathroom were "always" clean.
6. Patients who reported that the area around their room was "always" quiet at night.
7. Patients who reported that they were given information about what to do during their recovery at home.
8. Patients who "strongly agree" that they understood their care when they left the hospital.
9. Patients who give their hospital a rating of 9 or 10 on a scale from 0 (lowest) to 10 (highest).
10. Patients who reported that they would definitely recommend the hospital.

QualityNet/HARP is data that is submitted by the hospitals to a central database called QualityNet for CMS. Information submitted in this format includes data under the category of timely and effective care, psychiatric services, and payment and value of care. At the time of this writing, the measures utilized for these categories were as follows:[8]

1. Timely and effective care:
   a. Sepsis care: Percentage of patients who received appropriate care for severe sepsis and septic shock
   b. Cataract surgery outcome: Percentage of patients who had cataract surgery and had improvement in visual function within 90 days following the surgery
   c. Colonoscopy follow-up: Percentage of patients receiving appropriate recommendation for follow-up screening colonoscopy

d. Heart attack care: Average (median) number of minutes before outpatients with chest pain or possible heart attack who needed specialized care were transferred to another hospital

e. Heart attack care: Percentage of outpatients with chest pain or possible heart attack who got drugs to break up blood clots within 30 minutes of arrival

f. Emergency department care: Percentage of patients who left the emergency department before being seen

g. Emergency department care: Percentage of patients who came to the emergency department with stroke symptoms who received brain scan results within 45 minutes of arrival

h. Emergency department care: Average (median) time patients spent in the emergency department before leaving from the visit

i. Preventive care: Percentage of healthcare workers given influenza vaccinations

j. Cancer care: Percentage of patients receiving appropriate radiation therapy for cancer that has spread to the bone

k. Pregnancy and delivery care: Percentage of mothers whose deliveries were scheduled too early (one or two weeks early), when a scheduled delivery wasn't medically necessary

l. Use of medical imaging: Percentage of outpatients with low-back pain who had an MRI without trying recommended treatments (like physical therapy) first

m. Use of medical imaging: Percentage of outpatient CT scans of the abdomen that were "combination" (double) scans

n. Use of medical imaging: Percentage of outpatients who got cardiac imaging stress tests before low-risk outpatient surgery.

2. Psychiatric unit services:
    a. Preventive care and screening
        i. Patients discharged on antipsychotic medications who had body mass index, blood pressure, blood sugar, and cholesterol level screenings in the past year
        ii. Patients assessed and given influenza vaccinations
    b. Substance use treatment
        i. Patients with alcohol abuse who received or refused a brief intervention during their inpatient stay
        ii. Patients with alcohol abuse who received a brief intervention during their inpatient stay
        iii. Patients who screened positive for an alcohol or drug use disorder during their inpatient stay who, at discharge, either 1) received or refused a prescription for medications to treat their alcohol or drug use disorder *or* 2) received or refused a referral for addiction treatment
        iv. Patients who screened positive for an alcohol or drug use disorder during their inpatient stay who, at discharge, either 1) received a prescription for medications to treat their alcohol or drug use disorder *or* 2) received a referral for addiction treatment
        v. Patients who use tobacco who received or refused counseling to quit *and* received or refused medications to help them quit tobacco or had a reason for not receiving medication during their hospital stay
        vi. Patients who use tobacco who received counseling to quit *and* received medications to help them quit tobacco or had a reason for not receiving medication during their hospital stay
        vii. Patients who use tobacco and at discharge 1) received or refused a referral for outpatient counseling *and* 2) received or refused a prescription for medications to help them quit or had a reason for not receiving medication

   c. Patient safety
     i. Hours that patients spent in physical restraints for every 1,000 hours of patient care
     ii. Hours that patients spent in seclusion for every 1,000 hours of patient care
   d. Follow-up care
     i. Patients discharged from an inpatient psychiatric facility who received (or whose caregiver received) a complete record of inpatient psychiatric care and plans for follow-up
     ii. Patients whose follow-up care provider received a complete record of their inpatient psychiatric care and plans for follow-up within 24 hours of discharge
     iii. Patients discharged from an inpatient psychiatric facility on two or more antipsychotic medications (medications to prevent individuals from experiencing hallucinations, delusions, extreme mood swings, or other issues) and whose multiple prescriptions were clinically appropriate
     iv. Patients hospitalized for mental illness who received follow-up care from an outpatient mental healthcare provider within 30 days of discharge
     v. Patients hospitalized for mental illness who received follow-up care from an outpatient mental healthcare provider within seven days of discharge
     vi. Patients admitted to an inpatient psychiatric facility for major depressive disorder (MDD), schizophrenia, or bipolar disorder who filled at least one prescription between 2 days before they were discharged and 30 days after they were discharged from the facility.
   e. Unplanned readmission
     i. Patients readmitted to any hospital within 30 days of discharge from the inpatient psychiatric facility
     ii. Patients who use tobacco and at discharge 1) received a referral for outpatient counseling *and* 2) received a prescription for medications to help them quit or had a reason for not receiving medication

The National Healthcare Safety Network[9] (NHSN) is yet another database that collects information from a facility on infection rates and surgical site infections. This data is usually entered by the infection control department through mandatory reporting of conditions such as hospital-acquired C-Diff, MRSA, or colon surgical site infections. Measures obtained from NHSN for the five-star ratings include:

1. Hospital-acquired catheter-associated urinary tract infection (CAUTI)
2. Hospital-acquired central line–associated bloodstream infection (CLABSI)
3. Hospital-acquired clostridioides difficile (C-Diff)
4. Hospital-acquired methicillin-resistant staphylococcus aureus (MRSA)
5. Surgical site infection abdominal hysterectomy
6. Surgical site infection colon

Many hospital systems partner with vendors for some or all of these reporting requirements. It is important for the quality professional to understand where the sources of data lie, how the data reaches CMS, and whether you have vendors that do all or part of this reporting. As a special note, while a vendor may be very willing to submit all your measures for you, some measures cannot be submitted on behalf of the hospital. In this case, you must be very clear on which measures you are specifically accountable for.

2.4 QualityNet/HARP

A good practice to get into is looking at the measures that will be required for submission to the QualityNet site annually and map those out on a calendar that can be monitored throughout the year. This helps you prepare for the updates that come quarterly and stay ahead of reporting so there is not a "firefight" at the last minute to update the measures.

There is usually only one person in an organization responsible for updating the measures in the QualityNet site, and that person is usually in the quality department. The leaders of the organization (e.g., CEO, CNO, COO) often get notifications from CMS when updates need to be made to the QualityNet site. It is good practice to share your calendar for reporting (covered in Chapter 14 Managing the Quality Team) with them at the beginning of the year, notify them of the data you plan to report before reporting it, and let them know each time you update the site. Executive leaders do not like to get emails and letters from CMS, especially when they are unfamiliar with CMS mandate requests and requirements. Getting ahead of this through organization, planning, and communication will alleviate much drama in the future.

2.5 Other Benchmarking Agencies

The Leapfrog Group:[10] A voluntary reporting group to compare data on safety and quality in healthcare. Publishes the safety grade (i.e., A, B, C, D) report card.

Agency for Healthcare Research and Quality (AHRQ):[11] Encourages voluntary reporting of information that could be used for national learning to improve patient safety and prevent harm.

Magnet American Nurses Credentialing Center:[12] A magnet-designated hospital is a medical facility considered to be the gold standard for nursing practice and innovation. Magnet hospitals are certified by the American Nurses' Credentialing Center (ANCC) as institutions where nurses are empowered not only to take the lead on patient care but also to be the drivers of institutional healthcare change and innovation.

2.6 Other Regulations Important to Quality Departments

Emergency Medical Treatment and Active Labor Act (EMTALA)[13]

In 1986, Congress enacted the Emergency Medical Treatment and Active Labor Act (EMTALA) to ensure public access to emergency services regardless of ability to pay.

Section 1867 of the Social Security Act imposes specific obligations on Medicare-participating hospitals that offer emergency services to provide a medical screening examination (MSE) when a request is made for examination or treatment for an emergency medical condition (EMC), including active labor, regardless of an individual's ability to pay.

Hospitals are then required to provide stabilizing treatment for patients with EMCs. If a hospital is unable to stabilize a patient within its capability or if the patient requests, an appropriate transfer should be implemented.

You should understand and become familiar with your hospital's policy for EMTALA. Obtain it, read it, and abide by it.

Every EMTALA violation triggers a federal investigation that can result in hospitals losing their Medicare reimbursements. With this equating to a large portion of the payor base revenue, this can create significant havoc on your organization if not done well.

Well-meaning physicians can violate EMTALA by making decisions that seem perfectly reasonable, such as sending sick patients away to bigger and better-equipped facilities, redirecting healthy young patients to urgent care, delegating the medical screening exam (MSE) to residents or a physician assistant, or simply honoring patient requests.

Key EMTALA things to look for as a quality professional:

1. Make sure all ED patients are <u>registered</u> – Understand your emergency department processes for registration and ensure patient registration is hard-wired into that process.
2. Make sure a qualified medical person performs a <u>medical screening exam (MSE)</u> – Medical screening exams must be done by a qualified medical person. This means a licensed physician or an individual who is licensed or certified and who has demonstrated current competence in the performance of MSEs. For example:
   • Registered nurse in perinatal services, depending on state law
   • Psychiatric social worker, depending on state law
   • Registered nurse in psychiatric services, depending on state law
   • Psychologist
   • Physician assistant
   • Advanced registered nurse practitioner
   • Certified registered nurse midwife
3. Make sure the MSE is performed on <u>hospital grounds</u>. EMTALA is triggered whenever a patient presents to the hospital campus, not just the physical space of the ED: that is, within 250 yards of the hospital. Patients who present to a hospital parking lot, sidewalks, and adjacent medical buildings are mandated to undergo EMTALA screening and stabilization.
4. Before initiating any patient transfer, make sure you have made a reasonable attempt to <u>stabilize</u> the patient. "Stabilized" means that, with reasonable medical certainty, "no material deterioration" should occur from or during the transfer.[14]
   • If the patient has not been stabilized, the hospital may not transfer them unless:
      a. "The individual . . . requests transfer to another medical facility" after being informed by the hospital of the risks of transfer and of the hospital's obligation to stabilize or
      b. "A physician . . . has signed a certification based upon the information available at the time of transfer [that] the medical benefits reasonably expected from the provision of appropriate medical treatment at another medical facility outweigh the increased risks to the individual and, in the case of labor, to the unborn child."
      c. The transfer, as defined by the statute, is "appropriate."
5. Ensure <u>documentation</u> for transfers are complete following the EMTALA criteria. The majority of EMTALA violations result from poor documentation. Although clinicians attempt to do the right thing by transferring a patient to the appropriate level of care, without hard-wired processes for documentation, the crisis of the moment can easily overshadow the need for good documentation. In review of "appropriate transfers" after the fact, the only way to determine this is through the documentation of that encounter. Once the decision is made to transfer the patient, there are more EMTALA requirements: <u>First</u>, the physician must obtain the patient's consent for the transfer, explaining the reasons, risks, and benefits. This must be documented on a patient transfer form. If the patient refuses the transfer, this also must be documented. <u>Second</u>, a receiving hospital must be found, be contacted by the physician, and accept the transfer.
6. All transfers should have the appropriate <u>EMTALA form</u> completed based on your hospital's policies. Ensure you have a transfer form, EMTALA form, or some type of paper or electronic form that guides your clinicians through the appropriate documentation to meet the EMTALA regulations. Figure 2.6 represents an example of an EMTALA transfer form. This form should be designed to support standard operating procedures (SOP) necessary to keep your documentation up to date and relevant regarding the rules of EMTALA.

EMTALA Transfer Record

Emergency Medical Condition (EMC) Identified: (Mark appropriate box; have physician certify if 1c or 1d selected and then go to Section 2.)

1. MEDICAL CONDITION: Diagnosis:_____ Date: ___/___/___ Time: _____ am/pm

Screening Physician's Signature (if not physician certifying transfer): _____

a. ☐ **No Emergency Medical Condition (EMC) Identified following patient examination.**
b. ☐ **Unstable Patient, Patient Requests Transfer:** The patient has been examined and an EMC has been identified and the patient is not stable. The hospital has the capability and capacity to provide the care needed but the patient has specifically requested to be transferred to another facility after being notified that the hospital can and is willing to provide the care needed to stabilize and treat the EMC.
c. ☐ **Patient Stable For Transfer:** The patient has been examined and any medical condition stabilized such that, within reasonable clinical confidence, no material deterioration of this patient's condition is likely to result from or occur during transfer.

d. ☐ **Patient Unstable:** The patient has been examined, an EMC has been identified and patient is not stable, but the transfer is medically indicated and in the best interest of the patient.

1c and 1d Physician Certification: *I have examined this patient and based upon the reasonable risks and benefits described below and upon the information available to me, I certify that the medical benefits reasonably expected from the provision of appropriate medical treatment at another facility outweigh the increased risk to this patient's medical condition that may result from effecting this transfer.*

Certifying Physician Signature: _____ Date: ___/___/___ Time: _____ am / pm

The physician is not physically present at the time of transfer and after consultation with Dr. _____, and review of the risks and benefits the patient is to be transferred.

Qualified Medical Provider: _____ Date: ___/___/___ Time: _____ am/pm

Authorizing Physician Signature: _____ Date: ___/___/___ Time: _____ am/pm

2. REASON FOR TRANSFER:
☐ Higher level of care required ☐ Patient Requested (see patient request documentation: Section 7) ☐ Specialty Services not available ☐ Physician Request ☐ On-call physician refused or failed to respond within a reasonable period of time
On-Call Physician's Name: _____ Address _____

3. RISKS AND BENEFITS FOR TRANSFER:

Medical Benefits:	Medical Risks :
☐ Obtain level of care/ service unavailable at this facility. Service: _____	☐ Deterioration of condition in route
☐ Medical Benefits outweigh the risks.	☐ Worsening of condition or death if you stay here.
☐ Other : _____	☐ Risk of traffic delay/accident resulting in condition deterioration or death.
	☐ Other: _____

4. PHYSICIAN ORDERS: (mark appropriate boxes)
Mode of transportation for transfer: ☐ BLS ☐ ALS ☐ Helicopter ☐ Neonatal Unit ☐ Other_____
Agency: _____
Name/Title of accompanying hospital employee if required: _____
Support/Treatment during transfer: ☐ Cardiac Monitor ☐ Oxygen @ _____ ☐ IV Pump ☐ Pulse Oximeter
☐ IV Fluid: _____ Rate: _____ ☐ Restraints – Type: _____
☐ other: _____ ☐ none ☐ see additional order sheets attached

_____ Date: ___/___/___ Time: _____ am/pm
Ordering Physician Signature

If physician immediately unavailable,
QMP Signature: _____ Date: ___/___/___ Time: _____ am/pm
Authorizing Physician's Signature _____ Date: ___/___/___ Time: _____ am/pm

EMTALA Transfer Record – English
Page 1 of 2

Figure 2.6 EMTALA transfer record example.

EMTALA Transfer Record

Nursing

5. **RECEIVING FACILITY AND INDIVIDUAL:** The receiving facility has the capability for the treatment of this patient (including adequate equipment and medical personnel) and has agreed to accept the transfer and provide appropriate medical treatment.

Receiving Facility: _____

Person accepting Transfer: _____ Date: ___/___/___ Time: _____ am/pm

Name Receiving MD: _____ Date: ___/___/___ Time: _____ am/pm

Questions regarding Medication Reconciliation Information may be directed to Transferring Physician.

6. **ACCOMPANYING DOCUMENTATION** sent via: ☐ Patient/Responsible Party ☐ Fax ☐ Transporter
Documentation includes: ☐ All available Medical Records ☐ Copy of Transfer Form

☐ Advanced Directive ☐ Other _____

Report given to: (Person/title): _____

Date of transfer: ___/___/___ Time: _____ am / pm Nurse Signature: _____

Transferring Unit: ☐ Emergency Department ☐ Other: _____

Vital Signs Prior to Transfer on Date: ___/___/___ Time: _____ am/pm Temp: _____ BP: _____

Respirations: _____ Pulse: _____ O2 Saturation: _____ ETCO2: _____ Fetal HT: _____

2nd Nurse Signature: _____

Patient

7. **PATIENT CONSENT TO MEDICALLY INDICATED TRANSFER or PATIENT REQUEST FOR TRANSFER:**

☐ I hereby **CONSENT TO TRANSFER** to another facility. I understand that it is the opinion of the physician responsible for my care that the benefits of transfer outweigh the risks of transfer. I have been informed of the risks and benefits of this transfer.

☐ I hereby **REQUEST TRANSFER** to _____ Hospital. I understand and have considered the hospital's EMTALA responsibilities that have been explained to me, the medical risks and benefits of transfer and the physician's recommendation. I make this request upon my own suggestion and not that of the hospital, physician or anyone associated with the hospital. I agree to accept the risks associated with my decision. The reason I request transfer is: _____

_____

Signature of: ☐ Patient ☐ Responsible Person_____

Relationship to patient_____

Signature of Witness_____ Title _____ Date: ___/___/___ Time: _____ am/pm

EMTALA Transfer Record -- English
Page 2 of 2

Figure 2.6 (Continued)

2.7 Health Insurance Portability and Accountability Act (HIPAA)

The Health Insurance Portability and Accountability Act of 1996 (HIPAA) is a <u>federal law</u> that required the creation of national standards to protect sensitive patient health information from being disclosed without the patient's consent or knowledge.

The US Department of Health and Human Services (HHS) issued the HIPAA privacy rule to implement the requirements of HIPAA.[15]

The role of the quality professional regarding HIPAA involves the following:

- Ensure you have policies and procedures in place that contain the following elements:
  - Identification of people with **access** to information
  - Delineation of specific information to **which people have access**
  - **Requirements** for people with access to information to keep it **confidential**
  - **Requirements** for **release** of health information
  - **Requirements** for **removal** of medical records
  - Protection of protected health information (PHI)
  - Mechanisms for **securing** information against unauthorized intrusion, corruption, and damage
- <u>Review policies and procedures in your organization</u> and ensure these elements are implemented.

2.8 Clinical Laboratory Improvement Amendments (CLIA)

The Clinical Laboratory Improvement Amendments of 1988[16] require any facility performing examinations of human specimens (e.g., tissue, blood, urine, etc.) for diagnosis, prevention, or treatment purposes to be certified by the secretary of the Department of Health and Human Services (HHS).

The role of the quality professional in CLIA is to ensure the laboratory directors are well versed in and capable of managing these regulations. They should be able to explain and demonstrate the following activities:

- Ongoing monitoring of each testing process used in the laboratory in order to identify errors or potential problems that could result in errors
- Taking corrective action
- Evaluating the corrective actions taken to make sure that they were effective and will prevent reoccurrence

Laboratory quality initiatives, progress, and measurement should be reported at least annually to the quality committee. This committee should oversee the activities of the laboratory.

2.9 Summary

There are many organizations under the US Department of Health and Human Services (HHS). Confusion easily sets in when you are faced with working with yet another organization. As you work with each, take the time to understand the relationships between them and why they are important. This will help with understanding in the long run.

Your accreditation vendor is a resource to you. Many mistakenly look at the accreditation vendor as a policing organization, but the fact is they want you to be successful and want to support you in your accreditation requirements.

You can spend a lifetime mastering all the complexities of every regulatory agency, regulation, and benchmarking method, or you can create alliances with those who specialize in those areas. Utilize those resources often and learn from them.

2.9.1 Key Concepts

- Conditions of participation (CoPs) are the regulations hospitals must meet to participate in the Medicare and Medicaid programs.
- Organizations opt to partner with a national accrediting organization that develops and enforces the federal CoPs.
- There are many more voluntary accreditation and benchmark agencies, such as the Leapfrog Group, Agency for Healthcare Research and Quality, and Magnet American Nurses Credentialing Center. Find out which voluntary agencies your organization chooses to participate in.

2.9.2 Areas You Can Geek Out On

- CMS's conditions of participation. Review the regulations and compare them to your accreditation agency's (e.g., JC) translated regulations: www.ecfr.gov/current/title-42/chapter-IV/subchapter-G/part-482#part-482.
- CMS approved accreditation agencies. Understand the numerous accreditation agencies available for hospitals: www.cms.gov/Medicare/Provider-Enrollment-and-Certification/SurveyCertificationGenInfo/Downloads/Accrediting-Organization-Contacts-for-Prospective-Clients-.pdf.
- CMS five-star criteria and benchmarks. Review your hospital's rankings and compare them to those of other hospitals in your area: www.medicare.gov/care-compare/.
- Map all measures reported to CMS and external agencies and identify the source of the data, how it is reported, and who (e.g., which vendors) report the data for your organization.

Notes

1 Distribution of US healthcare expenditure: www.statista.com/statistics/237043/us-health-care-spending-distribution/.
2 CMS-approved accreditation organizations: www.cms.gov/Medicare/Provider-Enrollment-and-Certification/SurveyCertificationGenInfo/Downloads/Accrediting-Organization-Contacts-for-Prospective-Clients-.pdf.
3 Joint Commission: www.jointcommission.org/about-us/.
4 Conditions of participation: www.ecfr.gov/current/title-42/chapter-IV/subchapter-G/part-482#part-482.
5 CMS five star: www.medicare.gov/care-compare/.
6 www.cms.gov/Research-Statistics-Data-and-Systems/Files-for-Order/LimitedDataSets/MEDPARLDSHospitalNational.
7 Approved HCAHPS vendors: https://hcahpsonline.org/en/approved-vendor-list/.
8 https://qualitynet.cms.gov/.
9 www.cdc.gov/nhsn/index.html.
10 www.leapfroggroup.org/.
11 www.ahrq.gov/.
12 www.nursingworld.org/organizational-programs/magnet/.
13 www.cms.gov/regulations-and-guidance/legislation/emtala.
14 EMTALA: www.ncbi.nlm.nih.gov/pmc/articles/PMC1305897/.
15 HIPAA privacy rule: www.hhs.gov/hipaa/for-professionals/privacy/index.html.
16 CLIA: www.cms.gov/regulations-and-guidance/legislation/clia.

Chapter 3

Managing Quality

Before you start to manage quality, the first thing you need to understand is that you do not have a monopoly on the definition of quality. I started this discussion in Chapter 1, but we need to look a little further into this topic. What does *quality* mean to you? If you ask 100 people their definition of *quality*, you will get 100 different responses. This is not necessarily a bad thing. The reason everyone has a different definition is that they perceive the world differently through their lenses. They each have their own experiences (good or bad) and expectations built on their education and backgrounds. I always love it when I ask this question of a highly educated process expert or c-suite executive–level leader. They immediately overthink the question and start searching their brain for a textbook definition of *quality*. The result is a series of words or phrases that the person answering does not completely understand themselves. The fact is that quality is personal for everyone, and it isn't difficult to ask yourself what you think quality means.

Where the random definitions of quality cause problems, however, is in a business or group. If an organization has a vision and mission to "improve the quality of the organization," there needs to be some commonality on the definition so everyone is on the same page working to achieve the same results. The goal to define quality is not for us to do as employees. We cannot simply meet in a conference room and come up with our definition solely based on our experiences, education, and background. Improved quality is for the customer. Since the customer is the recipient of this quality and will judge you by your level of quality as they define it, you must get feedback from those customers to define that quality. This is achieved through customer focus groups, surveys, and even asking them as you serve them.

A red flag that always puts me in alert mode is when I sit in a conference room with employees in leadership positions, and one begins to share their personal experience with healthcare in an effort to help us define quality or the vision and mission for the customer. This implies that the healthcare worker experiences healthcare in the same exact manner as those who have never worked in or don't understand the business of healthcare. Customer quality, experience, and perceptions of care should never be solely defined by those providing the service. Watch out for these red flags, and don't be afraid to add to the discussion as to how this is flawed.

3.1 The Original Mission

To reconnect with the work you do every day, it can be helpful to go back to your roots. Why did you go into healthcare? Many consistent responses are "to help people," "to improve people's well-being," "for a stable job," "for the steady income," "to travel around the world," and "to be part of cutting-edge

 DOI: 10.4324/9781003358404-4

technology, innovations, and learnings." What are some of the reasons I never hear? "To hurt people," "to get back at society," "to create chaos and disorder while I make people's lives miserable," or "to welcome federal and state agencies into our facility and participate in grueling accreditation inspections."

Go back to the basics of why you entered the space of healthcare. You are in a position to start thinking of the things you can do to fulfill this mission. The reason you went into healthcare may be very different from the reason you stayed. Take me, for example. I started in healthcare because it was an available job that I learned about from a friend of a friend. I started out as a patient transport and was able to see the truly amazing things that happened every day. I learned from people of all different backgrounds, education levels, and experiences. I literally had a front row seat to observe hundreds of career fields. Personally, I chose nursing because it seemed to be the most versatile of the careers at the time and would enable me to use those skills in a multitude of jobs. Fast-forward 30 years and many roles in healthcare and I tend to look at the question of mission differently. Healthcare has been around since the beginning of time; however, the problems we face in healthcare today are different from the problems of healthcare 50 years ago. There is always an opportunity to provide innovative approaches to managing healthcare that can help sustain for many generations to come.

3.2 The "Quality Director" as Defined by Job Descriptions

In an independent research initiative, I analyzed 20 healthcare quality director job descriptions across the United States. I looked for key themes relating to qualifications and job requirements. The results of these searches are shown in the word cluster in Figure 3.1. The words in larger and bolder font are the themes that were most frequently mentioned in the job descriptions.

1. Data collection and management
2. Analytics and reporting
3. Manage improvement projects
4. Monitor/oversee quality
5. Regulatory and accreditation
6. Manage staff
7. Participate and present committees (quality, MEC, board, etc.)
8. Strategy for quality

Healthcare Quality Director Job Descriptions – Key Themes

Figure 3.1 The top themes identified are:

Most would assume that a quality director should be well versed in clinical care, clinical practice, and quality experience. Although many met the requirement of being an RN or something similar, few specified the clinical experience of a quality director. Interestingly, these job descriptions tend to focus on the specific "pain points" of the hospital. Although most hospitals are very data rich, they are painfully information poor. Not surprisingly, then, the key themes of a quality director rely heavily on taking that data and making meaningful information from it. Data collection, data management, analytics, and reporting lead the list of qualifications in almost every job description for quality analyzed.

Following close behind information and data analytics in our top job descriptions are process improvement and project management. These are unique skills when applied in a healthcare setting and, when done well, can lead to significant improvements. The same skills, used in isolation, can also lead to significant problems. Let me explain. An understanding of process improvement methodology (e.g., Lean, Six Sigma, PDSA) must be used in conjunction with project management to not only improve clinical processes but also to successfully manage them through the multitude of clinical disciplines necessary to make them a reality.

Regulation and accreditation are topics in themselves. Experience with regulatory and accreditation requirements, processes, procedures, and expectations will certainly provide great value to your organization. If you are a good project manager and can organize the many complexities and variations, the variety, and the scope of accreditation requirements, you will be best suited to spend your efforts on project management for accreditation. Instead of focusing on knowing all areas related to accreditation for each area of the business, rely on subject matter experts for the area in which the accreditation requirements apply. For example, if you spend all your time trying to understand the components of accreditation for managing your hospital's facilities (water treatment, boilers, electrical, sprinkler systems, etc.), you will only understand a portion of the actual work. Working with your facilities experts to provide the appropriate regulations and helping them implement, manage, document, record, and improve them will provide much better value to the overall mission of accreditation. You don't need to be an expert in facilities. Let them do their job by helping them understand how they fit into the big picture.

Managing staff is a boilerplate requirement for any director role in healthcare. You can always expect this requirement to be present where you manage a quality team. Although the expectation may be standardized across all director roles, the way in which you manage a quality team should be unique. Chapter 14 will expand on some tools and techniques to manage the employees in your quality department.

Participating in and presenting at committees are specifically addressed in many of the job descriptions studied. Just like the qualification to manage employees fits across all director-level positions, participating in and presenting at committees and meetings would also seem standard for this type of position. Few director job descriptions, however, specifically call out this competency in the way the director of quality job descriptions do. It seems that a key role of the quality director is to be capable of leading and participating in committees required for accreditation, governance, and leadership. This criteria calls out the pain point felt by healthcare organizations. They are required to have these committees and meetings, yet it is difficult to find people capable of successfully leading them.

Developing a strategy for the organizational quality agenda is yet another qualification outlined in these job descriptions. This implies the qualified individual can look broadly at the organizational vision, mission, and values while developing a plan that is specific to achieving organizational success as it relates to their quality goals. Chapter 10 outlines an approach to creating a quality plan. The quality director must feel comfortable working with all levels of employees in the organization to achieve this requirement. They must be able and allowed to work with executive-level leadership and be empowered to engage employees down to the front lines to develop this strategy.

3.3 The Paradigm of Managing Healthcare Quality

There are some basic principles that need to be understood regarding healthcare quality before you begin to manage it. Start this section with three key questions:

1. Where does quality originate?
2. How do we improve quality?
3. Who has the capability to improve that quality?

These basic questions about quality can lead to some very important answers and revelations. Quality professionals, healthcare leaders, and clinicians have spent a lot of their careers thinking about key concepts such as quality. This knowledge and experience can sometimes lead us into thinking we are the engine that makes quality happen. After all, we created the systems, structures, and tools that enable a high-quality environment. We, therefore, created quality. Organizations that have invested heavily in quality tools, processes, procedures, structures, and hiring practices have still found themselves out of business because of poor quality outcomes. How can that be? They miss a very key point about quality – **quality originates at the point the employee comes in contact with the customer they are serving** (or the product they are producing). If those employees do not understand, follow, or have the motivation to provide quality care, the care will not exist, regardless of the investment and expectations set by the leadership.

To understand quality in healthcare, you must understand what creates it. Quality happens at the point where the service is applied. In this high-level process (Figure 3.2), it starts with a patient arriving at the hospital and being treated by clinicians until they get better and leave. After the patient leaves, we spend a lot of time looking at the results of this encounter, analyzing the data (the quality director's number-one role in job description), and reporting out our findings. From there, we stand at the podium and state, "The quality is good," or "The quality is poor." It is impossible to improve that quality when looking the review mirror and analyzing the data. We must first go to where the quality is produced and work on those areas. Quality professionals seldom, if ever, provide direct patient care. So what should quality professionals do? Quality professionals must focus on the areas upstream in the aforementioned process by supporting the areas that provide that care. Support may include providing transparent information on outcomes related to the care they provided, removing barriers to providing that care, providing evidenced-based practice, and providing training where needed.

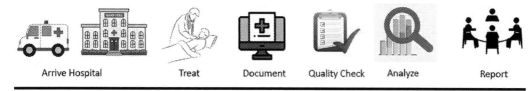

| Arrive Hospital | | Treat | Document | Quality Check | Analyze | Report |

Figure 3.2 High-level patient care process.

Now let's look back at the key qualifications found in quality director job descriptions. Where in the process of providing patient care do these qualifications most apply to the high-level process outlined here?

Figure 3.3 outlines the process once again, along with the top priorities for quality directors. The arrows represent the place in this process where those priorities and qualifications are predominately utilized. Position qualifications are seldom aimed at direct patient care. The question that must be asked at this point is "If quality happens in the first four steps of the process (where patient care exists), why do quality directors spend so much of their time in the back of the process?"

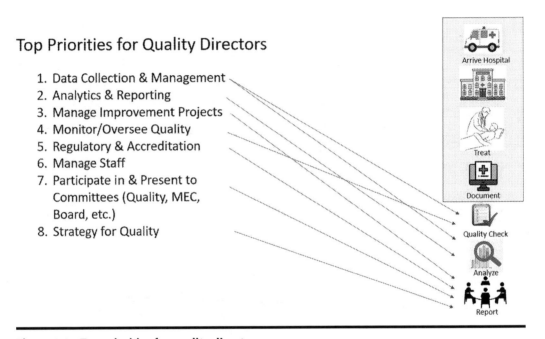

Top Priorities for Quality Directors

1. Data Collection & Management
2. Analytics & Reporting
3. Manage Improvement Projects
4. Monitor/Oversee Quality
5. Regulatory & Accreditation
6. Manage Staff
7. Participate in & Present to Committees (Quality, MEC, Board, etc.)
8. Strategy for Quality

Figure 3.3 Top priorities for quality directors.

Although the top priorities for quality director jobs are important, quality of an organization will only change if those qualifications are used to support direct patient care. Every quality director must look closely at how they will impact the way in which patient care is provided at the time it is provided. Here is an example. Imagine that you are doing chart audits on severe sepsis cases to determine if all the components of evidenced-based practice are done as part of the sepsis bundle. In this analysis, you see that only 20% of your patients received the expected 30 mL/kg of intravenous crystalloid fluid. The others all received 20 mL/kg of intravenous crystalloid fluid. Further analysis reveals that, for those receiving 20 mL/kg, the orders came from three physicians. There could be a multitude of reasons why they are ordering less than the standard. It is possible that the standard order set in the electronic medical record (EMR) contains the 20 rather than the 30 mL/kg dose. The physicians who get it right may have identified this on their own and chosen to change the order set manually every time. Perhaps there is no order set for sepsis in your EMR, or possibly, these physicians think they are following the evidence-based practice, but the standard changed, and they were not aware of it. In this example, the work that the quality director does on the backend of the processes can have a significant impact on future care of sepsis patients. This happens only if they take it to the next level of understanding with those who are actually providing the care. Is this telling clinicians how to do their work? No, it should be to support them with knowledge and information that they can utilize in their already very busy practice of providing patient care or removing barriers (e.g., EMR configuration).

The role of the quality director is not to own organizational quality. This does not sound like the logical conclusion, but it is absolutely a critical element that separates organizations that provide quality patient care from those that do not. Understanding that quality patient care results only from those who provide it enables organizations to create a systemic culture around the role of every healthcare worker and the responsibility they each hold in achieving that goal. Although this seems rather basic and potentially condescending to caregivers, it is much less about setting accountabilities with caregivers and more about giving them the autonomy and credit for doing it. Every caregiver wants to provide good quality care. The systems, processes, and environment they work in often create situations in which they cannot provide the level of quality care they want to. In this respect, a good quality director will get out of their way; provide support, resources, and knowledge; and remove barriers so they can accomplish this. Most importantly, when the quality of care is improved and awards and recognitions are given, it is not the quality director, CEO, CNO, etc. who stand on the stage to receive the award – it is the clinicians who enabled your organization to achieve it.

3.4 Quality Governance Structure

CMS:

§ 482.21 Condition of participation: Quality assessment and performance improvement program.

The hospital must develop, implement, and maintain an effective, <u>ongoing, hospital-wide, data-driven quality assessment and performance improvement program</u>. The hospital's governing body must ensure that the program reflects the complexity of the hospital's organization and services; involves all hospital departments and services (including those services furnished under contract or arrangement); and focuses on indicators related to improved health outcomes and the prevention and reduction of medical errors. The hospital must maintain and demonstrate evidence of its QAPI program for review by CMS.

JOINT COMMISSION:

Leadership 03.03.01 EP21 for hospitals that use Joint Commission accreditation for deemed status purposes: The governing body is responsible for making sure that performance improvement activities reflect the complexity of the hospital's organization and services, involve all departments and services, and include services provided under contract. (For more information on contracted services, see Standard LD.04.03.09.)

Note for hospitals that use Joint Commission accreditation for deemed status purposes: The hospital is not required to participate in a quality improvement organization (QIO) cooperative project, but its own projects are required to be of comparable effort.

> **DNV:**
>
> QM.6 SYSTEM REQUIREMENTS
>
> In establishing the QMS, the organization shall be required to have the following as a part of this system:
>
> SR.1. Interdisciplinary group to oversee the QMS with representation from/for Senior leadership, Medical Staff, Nursing, Quality/Risk Management (Management Representative), Physical Environment/Safety, Pharmacy Services, and Ancillary Services. This interdisciplinary group shall conduct Quality Management Oversight regarding the effectiveness of the QMS. The QAPI program shall be incorporated in the QMS.

The CMS regulations for healthcare management require an organized and ongoing governance structure. This CMS condition of participation states that hospitals must have a quality assessment and performance improvement program, and they must develop, implement, and maintain an effective, ongoing, hospital-wide, data-driven quality assessment and performance improvement program. That seems very logical. Basically, any company in business needs to continually improve in quality, or they will soon find themselves out of business. Here, however, CMS also continues to require the governing body to participate by ensuring the program's effectiveness and essentially lead that charge. The Joint Commission goes on to state that the quality program involves all departments and services for in-house as well as contracted services. DNV describes this as an interdisciplinary group that oversees the quality management system from senior leadership, medical staff, nursing, quality, physical environment, pharmacy, and ancillary services.

This regulation creates a tall order of requirements to fulfill. When looking at it in context, however, it seems fairly reasonable that accreditation agencies would expect quality oversight. Who wouldn't expect the leaders of the hospital organization to oversee the quality of care they provide to those who are hospitalized or undergoing surgery? This seemingly insurmountable task of overseeing all quality operations of every department and contracted services can only be done through intentionally designed systems, structures, and procedures. If you break the work down to the details and rebuild it through a set of standardized approaches, the task becomes much less daunting.

The proposed governance structure is represented in Figure 3.4. First, there are many committees operating at all levels of the organization. Although these committees do not exist for the sole purpose of quality management, a portion of their work should be related to it. What are the outcomes, barriers to success, policies and procedures, evidenced-based practices, etc.? All these things are managed by the subject matter experts who actually perform the work and are invaluable to quality management. When these committees meet, their discussions, work, and progress should be shared with the quality management committee (a.k.a. quality assurance and performance improvement, or QAPI). This is often done through sharing the minutes of those meetings or presenting a summary to the quality committee. The quality management committee then serves as a conduit for information that can be passed up to the medical executive committee (MEC) and the governing board. The MEC then receives synthesized information from the quality committee, allowing them to contribute their input, suggestions, and understanding. From the MEC, information flows up to the governing board.

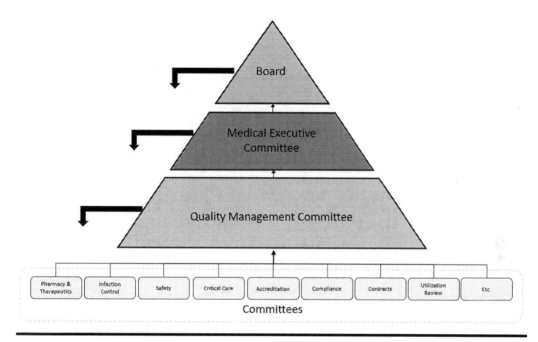

Figure 3.4   Governance structure.

This represents how information flows up, but it also allows for information to flow down. The governing board should set the strategies and goals for the entire organization. These high-level strategies and goals can only be accomplished through the work of those providing the actual patient care. If they were to challenge the organization to achieve a five-star level of performance for CMS Medicare, they understand the goal and the reason for trying to achieve it, but they have no idea how to actually make it happen. This feedback down through the ranks (so to speak) enables this message to be delivered down while the activities and plans on how to actually achieve it can be passed back up.

Any governance structure is only as good as the way it is managed. In managing a governance structure, the specific roles and responsibilities must be clearly outlined to enable each level of the structure to work with the others. You have probably heard the saying "To turn a large ship requires a team." This team approach applies here. If everyone is working on different objectives and goals, achieving those goals in isolation is futile.

ALIGNMENT REQUIRES CONVERGENCE

Have you ever experienced a rush hour nightmare? Even if you have, chances are it paled in comparison to the traffic jam on the G4 Beijing-Hong Kong-Macau Expressway in China.

This picture shows 50 lanes of traffic coming to a narrow passageway where approximately 12 cars are able to pass together. There are no lines in the road, no road signs or traffic lights – everyone simply gives and takes a little to converge in the narrow passage.

If you have been part of an organizational strategy exercise to develop key components of vision, mission, and goals, you may be familiar with the give and take concept illustrated here. The Baldridge Excellent Framework outlines strategy as its number-two category, stressing that an organization's long-term organizational success and competitive environment are key strategic issues that need to be integral parts of its overall planning. The Shingo model demonstrates strategic alignment as one of the four categories of a successful organization. And, from a personal development standpoint, Stephen Covey tells us in habit number 2 "to begin with the end in mind."

These world-class operational excellence/performance management references demonstrate the importance of organizational alignment, strategy, and getting our workforce to give and take a little to achieve a desired result or goal. If you were to assess your employees alignment to a goal, what might it look like? Would there be a clear direction? Or would a visual representation look something like multiple arrows heading in random directions?

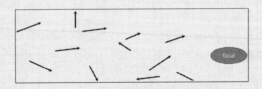

Effective leaders recognize the variation in employee alignment to goals, seek a solution, and diligently work to get everyone aligned. Much like having 50 lanes of traffic, it's necessary to get everyone heading in the same direction. Although the workforce is now "aligned," the difficulty becomes managing convergence on the same goal. It's fine when employees have their own personal goals to achieve, and they come up with individual action plans to get there, but how effective is it if every employee develops their own strategy? Is it possible to achieve a unified goal for the company under those circumstances?

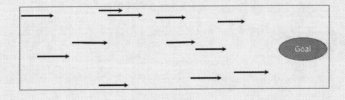

Convergence implies going in the same direction to meet at a certain point. It requires give and take by all participants to come together; adding knowledge and input; giving a little; and, in some cases, not getting your way for the benefit of the whole. If we always expect to get what we want, convergence becomes an impossibility, and the result will be a fraction of what it could have been.

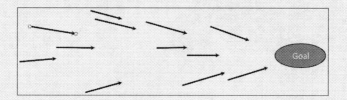

As you assess your organizational alignment, think of the behavioral principles that are necessary to allow for convergence. Allow your employees to have input into your strategies to achieve a goal, but be clear about the expectation that they come together and agree on a single method to achieve that goal – one that they all are willing to support. Not only will you be on your way to achieving alignment and convergence, but you'll also likely experience improved employee morale because they will feel more involved, valued and, engaged.

The roles and responsibilities of the committees must be to create and maintain standardized meetings and provide those results to the quality committee. This seems simple, but if these committees meet only when it is convenient, don't meet at all, or have an unstructured discussion when they do meet, then they will not be effective. The entire year's committee schedule should be set at the beginning of the year with a standard agenda template for specific committee needs as well as a section for quality oversight and process improvement initiatives.

The quality management committee should develop and manage to an annual quality improvement plan (see chapter 10). They should describe and outline specifically what they plan to achieve and stick to that plan throughout the year. A quality oversight scorecard is utilized to align all services and contracted services of the organization. Directors and/or representatives of those service areas should present their areas as they relate to quality and performance improvement to this committee at least annually.

The role and responsibility of the medical executive committee is to oversee and approve the quality plan presented to them by the quality committee. They should receive status updates throughout the year regarding the progress of the quality plan. The quality oversight scorecard (see Chapter 10) should also be available to the MEC to oversee and participate in managing quality outcomes.

The governing board is the body that is ultimately responsible to the quality program and oversight of the organization. There is an art to ensuring they have enough oversight to understand the quality management program without inundating them with all the information through the committees below them. A good start to achieving this is to build the reporting structure to the governing board in alignment with the strategies and goals they previously set. If the board reserves an agenda item at every meeting to briefly discuss quality progress, this can be achieved and allow for additional quality items that may be relevant at the time. If your organization is truly focused on quality from the board level, the board may elect to have a quality board committee dedicated to just managing quality initiatives.

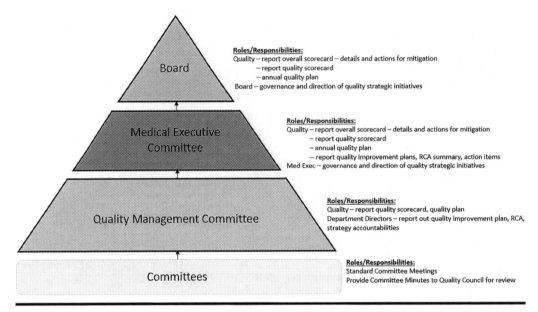

Roles/Responsibilities:
Quality – report overall scorecard – details and actions for mitigation
            – report quality scorecard
            – annual quality plan
Board – governance and direction of quality strategic initiatives

Roles/Responsibilities:
Quality – report overall scorecard – details and actions for mitigation
            – report quality scorecard
            – annual quality plan
            – report quality improvement plans, RCA summary, action items
Med Exec – governance and direction of quality strategic initiatives

Roles/Responsibilities:
Quality – report quality scorecard, quality plan
Department Directors – report out quality improvement plan, RCA, strategy accountabilities

Roles/Responsibilities:
Standard Committee Meetings
Provide Committee Minutes to Quality Council for review

Figure 3.5 Governance structure responsibilities.

3.5 The Quality Committee

The most important meeting for the quality department is the quality committee, also known as the quality assurance and performance improvement (QAPI) committee, the quality management system (QMS) committee, or the quality and patient safety (QPS) committee. The names are less important than the function, but accreditation agencies (depending on who they are) will use terminology that you may not understand when they arrive. If you call your committee the quality committee and when they show up, they ask you for all of your QAPI minutes, your first response may be "What is that?" For the purposes of this instruction, we will just call it the quality committee.

The quality committee brings all the governance structure components together and creates demonstrable evidence that the hospital "involves all hospital departments and services" and demonstrates "the hospital maintains and demonstrates evidence of its QAPI program for review by CMS" (CoP 481.21).

The quality leader should welcome the opportunity to manage and facilitate a quality committee. This enables them to get consensus and develop and manage the organization's quality improvement plan, communicate the effectiveness of this plan, and create collaboration between all disciplines throughout the organization and with the leadership. It also provides a venue to seek direction, support, funding, and guidance on the organizational quality plan while teaching and engaging all levels of the organization on the quality improvement agenda.

3.5.1 The Quality Committee Structure

The American actor Will Rogers provides a good quote that should be applied when managing your quality committee. He said, "You never get a second chance to make a first impression." Since the quality committee is, in most organizations, the "face" of the quality department, a first and long-lasting impression should be of primary importance. After all, the organization looks to this department as the model for quality. If the quality department's primary committee is disorganized and meaningless and has no perceived value, what impression will you leave with employees in your organizational?

The structure of your quality committee is critical to the success of its initiatives. The following roles should be represented on your quality committee:

- Senior leadership – CEO, CNO, CFO, COO
- Medical staff
- Nursing (if not the CNO)
- Quality/risk management
- Physical environment/safety
- Pharmacy services
- Ancillary services

Optionally, if your organization is interested in achieving Leapfrog status, you should include a community representative. Leapfrog specifically awards those who "include patients and their families in safety and quality committees."

The activities of the quality committee are extensive. Because of this, a well-organized approach to managing a standard structure will allow you to keep things on track and reduce confusion for those attending.

Here are the steps to creating your quality committee:

1. Develop the committee attendance structure – Meet with each individual and explain his or her role, the importance of the quality committee, and the goals you want to achieve.
2. Initiate a standard meeting time and set up meetings for the entire year.
3. Create a standard meeting agenda template.
4. Create a presentation schedule for all department directors throughout the year, and schedule them well in advance to the meeting.
5. Create a committee minutes review schedule.
6. Create a standard template for department director report-outs.
7. Create a standard template for quality committee minutes.

Regardless of your experience as a quality leader and your feeling of competence when it comes to quality management, one thing you have in your control is your preparation and attention to detail; facilitate a professional, well-organized, and efficient meeting. Just doing this will help ensure your organizational customers that they can feel secure in knowing the quality department can service their organization and departments well.

Some tips for running a meeting:

- Always state the purpose of the meeting.
- Start and end the meeting on time.
- Use a "parking lot" process to keep the meeting on track. The parking lot method can be a white board or a poster board. If an attendee wants to discuss a topic that is off track with the agenda, you show respect to them by hearing their concern and recording it on the parking lot for later discussion. This keeps you from ignoring the topic but enables you to keep the meeting on track and organized.
- Always keep notes and record action items – Always revisit the action items at the end of the meeting.
- Send a meeting recap or follow-up to attendees after the meeting.

1. Develop the committee attendance structure.

A well-organized and efficient meeting is one in which all members understand their role and the purpose for being there. One-on-one interactions with these team members enable the quality leader to clearly articulate the goals and meeting purpose while making those things relevant to the specific needs of the attendee. For example, if the ED director is in attendance and they already had an ED committee meeting, they may wonder why they were asked to attend yet another meeting. Providing them with details regarding their participation and their influence on quality planning throughout the year applicable to the work they are trying to accomplish in the ED will help solidify the purpose for them and give them the encouragement to show up and actively participate.

2. Initiate a standard meeting time and set up meetings.

    Set a standard meeting time for the attendees for the entire year (e.g., second Thursday of every month @10 a.m.). This creates consistency and organization that all team members can rely on.

3. Create a standard meeting agenda template.

    Create a standard agenda template for your quality committee. This not only allows for efficiency in managing your committee, but it also provides a consistent, professional appearance for your members. This standard template should include all things that should be reviewed by the committee, regardless of whether they are reviewed at every meeting. Having this standardized approach enables the quality leader to manage and keep track of things that randomly impact the organization. For example, if you were required to implement an action plan around a specific accreditation finding, it will more than likely involve communication through your governance structure and quality committee. You can simply add that standard agenda item to all future quality committee agendas for as long as deemed necessary.

    An agenda may include:

    — Review and approval of last quality committee minutes
    — Review and approval of committee minutes
    — Quality council business
        • Improvement projects status
        • RCA summary and open action items
        • Infection control report-out
        • Accreditation/internal audit status
        • Awards/recognitions
        • Quality plan status
    — Department report-outs (see Figure 3.7)

Quality Committee Agenda			
Hospital Name			
Date: MM/DD/YYYY		**Time:** 1500 - 1700	
Members: John Doe, CEO, Mary Sue, CNO, etc.		**Guests:** ICU Director, Med Surg Director, Dialysis Director	
Purpose: The purpose of the Quality Committee is to support, communicate and oversee the quality initiatives throughout the organization and drive our organization to provide the best quality care for our patients.			
Topic	**Facilitator**	**Materials?**	**Time**
Previous Meeting Minutes Review/Approval	Quality Director	Yes – Minutes	5 min
Committee Meeting Minutes Review: - P&T Committee 1/10/2021 - Infection Control Committee 1/20/2021	Quality Director	Yes - P&T Minutes - IC Minutes	5 min
Quality Department Business - Improvement Project Status - RCA Summary - Open Action Items - Infection Control Scorecard/Days since last	Quality Director	Yes - Improvement project summary - RCAs - Action Items	20 min
Accreditation Updates	Quality Manager	No	10 min
Quality Plan Status	Quality Director	Yes – QA Plan	10 min
Department Report-Outs - ICU - Med Surg - Dialysis	ICU Director Med Surg Director Dialysis Director	No	15 min 15 min 15 min
Awards & Recognitions	CEO	No	10 min
Closing and Action Item Review	Quality Director	No	5 min

Figure 3.6 Quality committee agenda example.

Quality Committee Schedule		Monthly Quality Council Meetings															
Department	Person	9/22	10/27	11/24	12/29	1/26	2/23	3/23	4/27	5/25	6/22	7/27	8/24	9/28	10/26	11/23	12/28
Adm/Business			X														X
Ancillary Services (Radiology, Respiratory)				X		X											
Anesthesia							X										
Biomed																	
Dialysis			X	X	X	X		X	X			X			X		X
Dietary Services																	
ED/ICU				X		X				X			X			X	
Employee Health																	
Environmental Services								X									
Facilities		X			X												
HIM			X														
Hospitalists								X									
Infusion						X							X				
IT				X													
Lab/Pathology			X		X			X			X			X			X
Materials		X	X								X			X		X	
Med/Surg/OB		X			X			X	X		X			X			X
Medical Staff					X							X					
Pharmacy		X			X												
Practice Management			X														
Quality/Infection Control		X	X	X	X	X	X	X	X	X	X	X	X	X	X	X	X
Risk							X					X					
Safety/Security																	
Skilled Therapies				X													
Sleep Lab							X										
Staff Management (HR)									X								
Surgical Services		X	X	X	X	X						X	X				
Trauma															X		
Utilization Review/Discharge					X	X	X						X				

Figure 3.7   Quality committee schedule for presentation.

4. Create a presentation schedule for all department directors throughout the year and schedule them well in advance to the meeting (Figure 3.7)

As part of quality oversight across the organization, the quality leader's role is to allow collaboration among the departments and the leadership through a lens of quality patient care. List every department and its director, determine the reporting frequency (monthly, quarterly, annually), and create a schedule for them to present to the quality committee. Provide each director with their role and responsibility and the expectation of the committee (e.g., complete report-out template quarterly, present to committee, 15 minutes or less). Create a report-out template for the directors to utilize and set up their scheduled meeting time on their calendars.

In Figure 3.7, each department is listed with an *X* for the meeting they are scheduled to present at throughout the year.

5. Create a committee minutes review schedule.

It is important that all committees communicate their work and initiatives to the quality committee members. Identify a list of all committees that report their minutes to the quality committee. Complete a schedule of committee meetings so you are aware of when they meet and know when to expect their minutes and set the expectations of committee leaders to send minutes to quality when approved. Create standard procedures for the distribution of the committee minutes to quality committee members at least 24 hours in advance of the meeting, and document which committee minutes were distributed on the standard quality committee agenda.

A sample template used for managing committee minutes is shown in Figure 3.8. This spreadsheet lists each committee, when they meet, and whether those minutes were reviewed by the quality committee.

Committee Schedule
for Quality Committee Review

Committee	Committee Owner	Frequency	Jan-21	Feb-21	Mar-21	Apr-21	May-21	Jun-21	Jul-21	Aug-21	Sep-21	Oct-21	Nov-21	Dec-21
Pharmacy and Therapeutics	John Doe	Monthly	MRQ	MRQ	MRQ	MRQ								
Infection Control	Jane Doe	Quarterly			MRQ									
Safety	Mary Sue	Monthly	MRQ	MRQ	MRQ									
Critical Care	Fred Smith	Quarterly		MRQ										
Accreditation	Jose Martinez	Monthly	MRQ	MRQ	MRQ	MRQ								
Compliance	John Johnson	Monthly		MRQ	MRQ									
Contracts	Sue Smith	Quarterly			MRQ									
Utilization Review	Ann Jo	Monthly	MRQ	MRQ	MRQ	MRQ								

MQR = Minutes received and reviewed at Quality Committee

Figure 3.8 Committee schedule review.

6. Create a standard template for department director report-outs.

It is important that each department and discipline report the quality activities of their areas to the quality committee. You will find that, without structure, these report-outs will be verbose, derail your committee agenda, and go much further into the weeds than they need to. Create a standard template for presenters to use in the committee, and set time limit expectations. Explain to each presenter the role of the quality committee and what they should expect from presenting to the group.

An example of a template (Figure 3.9) for presenting at the quality committee involves four main areas:

1. Quality scorecard review
2. Process improvement and RCA events
3. Accreditation readiness activities
4. Needs from the quality committee

Regardless of the categories used by your organization, the benefit of having a template is to maintain consistency and organization for all meeting presenters.

Quality Committee

Department Report-Out

Department:	
Date:	
Quality Scorecard Review	
Process Improvement and RCA Events	
Accreditation Readiness Activities	
Needs from Quality Committee	

Figure 3.9   Quality committee department report-out.

In this template example, the quality oversight scorecard is reviewed for the specific department presenting. Here they add discussion points regarding scorecard measures and opportunities for improvement. Under the section "Process Improvement and RCA Events," they would describe areas in which process improvements are taking place with the department and provide the status, progress, and goals of those events. "Accreditation Readiness Activities" are specifically called out so each presenter can outline the accreditation readiness activities taking place. Lastly, "Needs from the Quality Committee" provides an opportunity for the presenter to specifically outline the needs they have related to organizational quality in their area from quality committee leadership.

7. Create a standard template for quality committee minutes.

Every accreditation agency will ask for the minutes from your quality committee. It is important to have a standard template so items required in those minutes are not overlooked. If action items are managed through your minutes, ensure there is a process for follow-up and follow-through on those action items. Minimally required content for your minutes includes:

– Date/time of meeting
– Attendees and role

   – Minute approvals
   – Discussion topics and details
   – Action items
   – Follow-up on previous action items

A simple template for meeting minutes is demonstrated in Figure 3.10. Note: If action items are updated and managed in another process, you must state that here. Otherwise, accreditation agencies will look for follow-up of action items in your minutes. These minutes imply that the organization utilizes another process called the <u>action item tracker</u>, which will be described in Chapter 7.

Quality Committee Meeting Minutes
MM/DD/YYYY

Standing Members								

Presenter/Guests								

This document is confidential and generated for and as a result of Quality Assurance activities.

Topic	Findings/Conclusions	Recommendations/Follow-up Actions *Note: Action items managed on the action item tracker*
Call to order		
Approval of Minutes		
Committee Minutes for Review		
Quality Council Business		
Accreditation Updates		
Quality Plan Status		
Department Report-Outs		
Awards and Recognitions		
Closing and Action Item Review		
Adjournment		

Figure 3.10   Quality committee meeting minute example.

3.6 The Medical Executive Committee (MEC)

The best way to report to the medical executive committee is to be organized and consistent. After your first meeting with the MEC team to inquire about their expectations for a quality report-out, create a standard report-out template containing topics that cover their expectations as well as topics you want to engage them in for your quality plan and agenda. Monthly updates to this template should take less than 30 minutes once you have a standard in place. After a couple of meetings, everything will flow smoothly, the committee members will know what to expect, and participation will be geared towards the quality items that are important. An example of an MEC template is shown in Figure 3.11.

Medical Executive Monthly Quality Report-Out					
Hospital Name					
Date:			MM/DD/YYYY		
Quality Strategic Scorecard					
Measure	**Description**	**Goal**	**Jan-20**	**Feb-20**	**Total/YTD**
HAC CLABSI	Central Line Associated Blood Stream Infection	0.468	0.000	0.000	0.000
HAC CAUTI	Catheter-Associated Urinary Tract Infection	0.554	0.000	0.000	0.000
SSI - Colon	Surgical Site Infection for Colon Procedures	0.538	0.000	0.000	0.000
SSI - Hyst	Surgical Site Infections for Hysterectomies	0.364	0.000	0.000	0.000
HAC MRSA	Methicillin-resistant Staphylococcus Aureus	0.569	0.000	0.000	0.000
HAC C. Difficile	Clostridium difficile	0.526	0.433	0.433	1.1%
SEP-1 Early Mgt Sepsis	Early Mgt bundle, severe sepsis/septic shock	64.5%	71.9%	66.6%	72.0%
SEP-1a Sepsis 3 Hour	Severe sepsis 3 hour bundle compliance	84.5%	81.3%	78.1%	73.7%
SRE	Serious Reportable Event	0	4	3	7
Quality Committee					
Last Quality Committee Date:			MM/DD/YYYY		
Minutes:			Attached		
Quality Committee Action Items					
Action Item			**Status**		
Follow-up on dialysis metrics for scorecard			Open		
Committee changes for Quality Plan			Complete		
Days Since Last					
Measure			**Days**		
C-Diff			10		
MRSA			335		
CAUTI			28		
CLABSI			80		
Fall w/Injury			102		
PU Stage 3			14		
Quality Project Status					
Project			**Status**		
PDSAs Completed YTD:			9		
Inpatient Flow			Initiate Spread Charter - closing initial project		
BPAM Project			Measure phase		
Case Management-LOS			Measure phase		
Hand Hygiene			Implementation - Currently 73%		
Regulatory					
CMS Survey			Window for survey between 1/2022 – 3/2022		
DOH Action Items			Completed from Visit on 2/1/2021		
Needs from MEC					
Review the proposed Quality Plan for 2022 and provide feedback at the next Board Meeting.					

Figure 3.11   MEC report-out example.

3.7 The Governing Board

Likewise, the best way to report to the board is to be organized and consistent. After meeting with the board to inquire about their expectations for a quality report-out, create a standard report-out template containing topics that cover their expectations as well as topics you want to engage them in for your quality plan and agenda. Monthly updates to this template should take less than 30 minutes once you have a standard in place. After a couple of meetings, everything will flow smoothly, the committee members will know what to expect, and participation will be geared towards the quality items that are important. An example of a governing board template is shown in Figure 3.12.

Governing Board Monthly Quality Report-Out
Hospital Name

Date:			MM/DD/YYYY		
Quality Strategic Scorecard					
Measure	Description	Goal	Jan-20	Feb-20	Total/YTD
HAC CLABSI	Central Line Associated Blood Stream Infection	0.468	0.000	0.000	0.000
HAC CAUTI	Catheter-Associated Urinary Tract Infection	0.554	0.000	0.000	0.000
SSI - Colon	Surgical Site Infection for Colon Procedures	0.538	0.000	0.000	0.000
SSI - Hyst	Surgical Site Infections for Hysterectomies	0.364	0.000	0.000	0.000
HAC MRSA	Methicillin-resistant Staphylococcus Aureus	0.569	0.000	0.000	0.000
HAC C. Difficile	Clostridium difficile	0.526	0.433	0.433	2.108
SEP-1 Early Mgt Sepsis	Early Mgt bundle, severe sepsis/septic shock	64.5%	71.9%	66.6%	72.0%
SEP-1a Sepsis 3 Hour	Severe sepsis 3 hour bundle compliance	84.5%	81.3%	78.1%	79.7%
SRE	Serious Reportable Event	0	4	3	7
Quality Committee					
Last Quality Committee Date:			MM/DD/YYYY		
Minutes:			Attached		
Quality Committee Action Items					
Action Item			Status		
Follow-up on dialysis metrics for scorecard			Open		
Committee changes for Quality Plan			Complete		
Days Since Last					
Measure			Days		
C-Diff			10		
MRSA			335		
CAUTI			28		
CLABSI			80		
Fall w/Injury			102		
PU Stage 3			14		
Quality Project Status					
Project			Status		
PDSAs Completed YTD:			9		
Inpatient Flow			Initiate Spread Charter - closing initial project		
BPAM Project			Measure phase		
Case Management-LOS			Measure phase		
Hand Hygiene			Implementation - Currently 73%		
Regulatory					
CMS Survey			Window for survey between 1/2022 – 3/2022		
DOH Action Items			Completed from Visit on 2/1/2021		
Needs from Governing Board					
Review the proposed Quality Plan for 2022 and provide feedback at the next Board Meeting.					

Figure 3.12   Governing board report-out example.

3.8 Summary

Managing quality and filling in the gaps for organizational pain points are not the same thing. Many organizations struggle with getting the appropriate information and meeting accreditation requirements, but focusing on those pain points alone will not lead to a quality organization. A quality professional must engage those who are providing direct patient care and support them in providing quality care.

Have a clear plan for your quality governance structure. This chapter outlined a plan that you can use for governance. It enables communication and coordination of quality initiatives at all levels in the organization. Designing a structure like this and managing it effectively will make it clear to everyone (including accreditation agencies) how your organization oversees and manages quality.

The most important committee for the quality professional is the quality committee. You should put significant effort into organization, planning, and managing your quality committee. Consistency, organization, reliability, and professionalism are just a few terms that others should use when describing your quality committee. Set the bar high when it comes to managing your own quality initiatives, and others will begin to model that example. Anything less will result in a lack of credibility, which will hurt your ability to drive quality for those you serve.

3.8.1 Key Concepts

- The quality governance structure for your organization should be intentionally designed.
- Organization and consistency are critical to role modeling quality.
- A small amount of planning for quality meetings at the beginning of the year will save you a lot of time throughout the year.
- Standard report-out templates are an efficient way to standardize and organize your governance structure activities.

3.8.2 Areas You Can Geek Out On

- Read the leadership chapter for Joint Commission standards. Even if your organization does not use the Joint Commission as your accreditation agency, much of the material in this chapter will help you understand how you can support the leaders in your organization with a quality agenda and plan.

Chapter 4

Quality Measurement and Analytics

4.1 Basics of Quality Measurement

In order to discuss quality measurement, you must first understand some concepts around the elements that you measure. Measurement and analytics are critical to the success of a quality oversight program. Without them, it is impossible to see where you have been, where you are today, and where you plan to go.

In this section, we will start with the concepts of the data-information-knowledge-wisdom (DIKW) hierarchy. Your role in quality is to utilize data and move your organization up the DIKW pyramid to make this data transparent in a meaningful way to the entire organization.

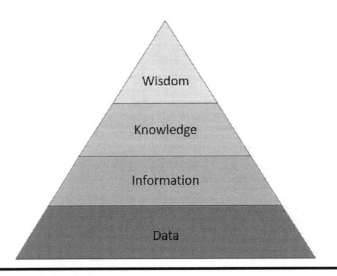

Figure 4.1   DIKW triangle.

 DOI: 10.4324/9781003358404-5

Data is equivalent to raw symbols. It has no significance beyond its existence, and it does not have meaning by itself. Organizations are full of data in this sense of the word. An example of data can be seen in Figure 4.2. Here we see only numbers in rows and columns. It is unknown what those numbers represent or what they mean.

| Data | Information | Knowledge | Wisdom |

29	29	25	5	2	0	3	1	0
18	18	11	7	0	0	22	15	2
22	22	22	11	0	0	7	1	1
14	14	11	1	0	0	5	0	0
78	78	78	54	10	10	9	2	11
30	30	30	21	6	6	4	0	2
63	63	55	52	16	13	16	10	1
282	282	245	172	44	29	45	42	29
62	62	62	30	0	0	0	0	1
173	173	173	113	8	8	14	4	24
88	88	44	31	8	6	9	0	6
34	34	31	21	2	2	16	0	2
42	42	21	14	2	2	18	3	6

Figure 4.2   DIKW – data example.

Information is data that has meaning by way of relational connection. It is data in context. In the example in Figure 4.3, we now have information, with each row and column identified. We are able to see that the raw data (the number) is associated with a data type (e.g., all hospital beds) for a particular hospital on a specific date.

Data   Information   Knowledge   Wisdom

Reporting Date	Hospital Name	All Hospital Beds	All Adult Hospital Beds	All Hospital Inpatient Beds	All Hospital Beds Occupied	Total Staffed ICU Beds	Staffed ICU Bed Occupancy	Mechanical Ventilators	Mechanical Ventilators In Use	Hospital Patients Confirmed COVID
12-Jan	Hospital 1	29	29	25	5	2	0	3	1	0
12-Jan	Hospital 2	18	18	11	7	0	0	22	15	2
12-Jan	Hospital 3	22	22	22	11	0	0	7	1	1
12-Jan	Hospital 4	14	14	11	1	0	0	5	0	0
12-Jan	Hospital 5	78	78	78	54	10	10	9	2	11
12-Jan	Hospital 6	30	30	30	21	6	6	4	0	2
12-Jan	Hospital 7	63	63	55	52	16	13	16	10	1
12-Jan	Hospital 8	282	282	245	172	44	29	45	42	29
12-Jan	Hospital 9	62	62	62	30	0	0	0	0	1
12-Jan	Hospital 10	173	173	173	113	8	8	14	4	24
12-Jan	Hospital 11	88	88	44	31	8	6	9	0	6
12-Jan	Hospital 12	34	34	31	21	2	2	16	0	2
12-Jan	Hospital 13	42	42	21	14	2	2	18	3	6

Figure 4.3   DIKW – information example.

Knowledge is an appropriate collection of information, such that its intent is to be useful. Knowledge means understanding the significance of the information. In this example (Figure 4.4), the information makes known the number of ventilators in a hospital and the number of <u>ventilators that are currently in use</u>. Those numbers provide each hospital's percentage of ventilators in use and the cumulative hospitals ventilators in use: the knowledge we need to make the information actionable.

Data   Information   Knowledge   Wisdom

Reporting Date	Hospital Name	All Hospital Beds	All Adult Hospital Beds	All Hospital Inpatient Beds	All Hospital Beds Occupied	Total Staffed ICU Beds	Staffed ICU Bed Occupancy	Mechanical Ventilators	Mechanical Ventilators In Use	% Ventilators In Use	Hospital Patients Confirmed COVID
12-Jan	Hospital 1	29	29	25	5	2	0	3	1	33%	0
12-Jan	Hospital 2	18	18	11	7	0	0	22	15	68%	2
12-Jan	Hospital 3	22	22	22	11	0	0	7	1	14%	1
12-Jan	Hospital 4	14	14	11	1	0	0	5	0	0%	0
12-Jan	Hospital 5	78	78	78	54	10	10	9	2	22%	11
12-Jan	Hospital 6	30	30	30	21	6	6	4	0	0%	2
12-Jan	Hospital 7	63	63	55	52	16	13	16	10	63%	1
12-Jan	Hospital 8	282	282	245	172	44	29	45	42	93%	29
12-Jan	Hospital 9	62	62	62	30	0	0	0	0	0%	1
12-Jan	Hospital 10	173	173	173	113	8	8	14	4	29%	24
12-Jan	Hospital 11	88	88	44	31	8	6	9	0	0%	6
12-Jan	Hospital 12	34	34	31	21	2	2	16	0	0%	2
12-Jan	Hospital 13	42	42	21	14	2	2	18	3	17%	6

Figure 4.4 DIKW – knowledge example.

Wisdom is applied knowledge. This involves the process by which we discern between right and wrong, good and bad. At this point in the DIKW model, computers lose much of their ability. Technology like artificial intelligence is challenging this space, but the reality is that those capabilities are seldom readily available to the masses. An example of wisdom arising from the information displayed in Figure 4.5 could lead someone to make the decision to move ventilators from one hospital (with few in use) to another hospital that is in short supply.

Data   Information   Knowledge   Wisdom

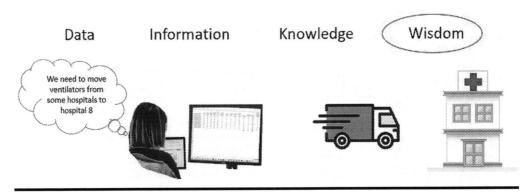

We need to move ventilators from some hospitals to hospital 8

Figure 4.5 DIKW – wisdom example.

4.2 Quality Measurement and Analytics

Under the accreditation requirements for hospitals, it is stated that the quality assessment and performance improvement program incorporate quality indicator data. This includes patient care information and other relevant information such as data submitted to or received from Medicare, quality reporting, and quality performance programs. In fact, there is language throughout the accreditation criteria under the Joint Commission that specifically relates to measurement and analytics. These include:

- Techniques to Analyze and Display Data (PI.02.01.01)
- Uses the Results of Data Analysis (PI.02.01.01)
- Collects Data to Monitor Its Performance (PI.01.01.01)
- Provides Incidence Data (PI.02.01.01)
- Evaluate the Effectiveness (LD.03.05.01)
- Hospital Analyzes and Uses Information (LD.03.09.01)
- Quality Indicator Data (LD.03.02.01)
- Hospital Collects Data . . . (PI.01.01.01)
- Analyzes Data Collected (PI.02.01.01)
- Planning . . . Information Sources (LD.03.03.01)
- Evaluate Culture of Safety and Quality (LD.03.01.01)
- Data and Information Used throughout the Hospital (LD.03.02.01)
- Reviews and Analyzes (PI.02.01.01)
- Analyzes and Compares Internal Data over Time (PI.02.01.01)
- Identify the Frequency of Data Collection (PI.01.01.01)
- Patterns, Trends, or Variations in Its Performance (PI.02.01.01)

As we enter into the section of quality measurement and analytics, it is critically important to realize the role this has in improving quality. Without an understanding of where you currently are through measurement, it is impossible to understand if where you are going is actually an improvement.

> "If you cannot measure it, you cannot improve it."
> William Thompson (a.k.a. Lord Kalvin)
>
> "Measurement is the first step that leads to control and eventual improvement. If you can't measure something, you can't understand it. If you can't understand it, you can't control it. If you can't control it, you can't improve it."
> H. James Harrington

For example, suppose you gave a patient Tylenol for the purpose of reducing their temperature. You didn't take the patient's temperature prior to administering the medication, did not look at the patient for obvious signs of fever, or touch them to determine if they felt warm. How would you know if providing Tylenol actual produced a clinically acceptable result? The fact is you wouldn't know, and your intervention would be meaningless if not potentially harmful.

The same is true at a macro organizational level. Many will express their opinions of the current state of the organization: "The process is never followed," or "It happens all the time." Subjective statements should always be listened to because they show how people feel, <u>but</u> they should always be backed up with data.

An exercise I use frequently involves converting these felt impressions into actual data statements. For example, in one scenario, we were discussing follow-up care for patients discharged with congestive heart failure (CHF). One of the emergency room nurses spoke up and stated, "These patients always come back to the hospital within a week of being discharged." This is certainly a perception worthy of attention; however, I asked "How many patients each week are discharged with congestive heart failure?" The answer was not specifically known, but another member of the team said it was about 20 patients. Knowing the emergency department had a weekly visit number of about 50 patients, I asked a clarifying question: "So about 40% of your emergency room visits are returning CHF patients?" The emergency room nurse quickly responded with, "Well, no, but it seemed like a lot." This dialogue allowed the team to move forward with the understanding that current state measurement was vitally important to initiate an improvement. Although her perception was important, it is equally important to understand the problem we are addressing. If the readmission rate for CHF was 10%, the nurse in the emergency department could accurately state they had approximately two patients a week returning with CHF. By acknowledging the nurse's concern, we were able to correct a misperception with true and accurate data. This allowed the team to focus on the specific problem at hand, apply specific interventions to improve the process when appropriate, and remeasure to see if their intervention resulted in an improvement.

4.2.1 Exercise

To demonstrate and practice the principles of quality measurement, this next section provides another experienced example of a scenario to address acute myocardial infarction (AMI) hospital mortalities. A sample dataset is provided at www.Innovate2Accelerate.com if you would like to try the analysis for yourself.

Situation: Your organization is striving to achieve five-star CMS status. When you look at the measures that contribute to five-star, you identify that your mortality measure for AMI is greater than expected (Figure 4.6).

Measure	Benchmark Goal	Jan	Feb	Mar	Apr	May	Jun	Jul	Aug	Sep	Oct	Nov	Dec	Year
Acute Myocardial Infarction (AMI) Mortality	5.0%	9.1%	9.0%	9.3%	15.3%	11.0%	10.0%	8.2%	9.8%	10.2%	10.3%	11.5%	12.8%	9.2%

Figure 4.6 AMI mortality dashboard.

This image reflects the portion of the organizational scorecard representing the AMI hospital mortality percentage by month for one year. The organizational goal is less than or equal to 5%, yet each month, the percentage is significantly above that target.

Solution: There are multiple ways to start working on this problem. The first important step has already been done. That is to make sure the information is transparent. Through this dashboard, the current measurements are displayed with meaning. The months are separated to enable the consumers of the information to see the trend, and a comparison to goal or benchmark is clearly identified.

Now that we know we have a problem, and people are made aware of it, the next step is to engage clinicians and stakeholders. Quite often, key people have no idea there even is a problem. Asking simple questions of your clinicians and stakeholders can be educational and provide you with the information you need to move forward in your analysis. I suggest the following two questions:

1. What do you see as contributing reasons for these outcomes?
2. What areas would you investigate to find the causes of these outcomes?

After your educational sessions with the clinicians and stakeholders, go out and find all the relevant data you can.

Dig deeper: You should obtain the data from your electronic medical record showing all AMI patients who died while hospitalized for the time period represented in the dashboard in Figure 4.6. What would you do with this data? What can you discover from its content?

Go to www.Innovate2Accelerate.com to download the complete data sample spreadsheet.

From the groupings of data, you can determine how your analysis can be organized. For example, each case is identified with the gender of either male or female. Group all your data based on gender. What percentage of the mortalities are male versus female? Are females more likely to arrive by private vehicle than males? And so on.

Looking at your data, determine the questions you could answer with the information available. Some examples from this dataset include:

1. What ages comprise the most mortalities for AMI?
2. Are there differences in mortality based on gender?
3. Do some months have greater mortality than others? Days of the week?
4. Is there a correlation between the procedure(s) performed and mortality?
5. Does the arrival method have any significance?
6. Do transfers to the facility from another facility have any significance?

Assessing your data and the data available to you is only a starting point. In many cases, if not most, you will need to do some additional research to answer questions that cannot be obtained from the data you have. In this example, clinicians may ask additional questions about lab results, providers, time of day, and medications, just to name a few. None of these categories of data are in our current dataset, so they would need to be obtained through other means.

The key point to understand is that data found in electronic systems does *not* provide all the information for finding the root cause or opportunities for improvement. What the data *does* do, if analyzed correctly, is eliminate subjective inferences about what people think the causes may be. **The key is learning how to ask good questions so you can use that information in your analysis**.

Now that the clinicians and stakeholders have been interviewed and the data has been reviewed, you will want to combine your lessons learned from each. In this exercise, some of the actual responses from clinicians and stakeholders were:

- "It is because of delays in transfers to our facilities from other hospitals, so there is nothing we can do about it."
- "Most are train wrecks, and they arrest outside our facility."

MRN	Age	Sex	Encounter Start	Encounter End	Proc Completed	Date of death	Present to ED	POYME MS	Out of Hospital arrest	Inpt-Op mortality	Transfer in?	Transferring facility	Transfer hospital procedure	Intubated Before/After Arrival	Code called	DNR activated during hospitalization	Hospice Ordered	Death within 48 hours	Cause of Death
1000001	83	Male	1/12/2018	1/14/2018	PCI	1/14/2018	Yes	EMS	No	No	No	X	X	N/A	Bradycardiac	No	No	Yes	cardiac arrest secondary to PEA
1000002	83	Female	1/24/2018	1/27/2018	CABGx3	1/27/2018	No	EMS	No	No	Yes	Hospital A	coronary angiograph	After	Bradycardiac	No	No	No	CAD
1000003	56	Male	1/15/2018	1/20/2018	LHC	1/19/2018	Yes	EMS	Yes	No	No	X	X	Before	No	Yes	No	No	cardiac arrest
1000004	73	Male	2/7/2018	2/7/2018	PCI	2/7/2018	Yes	EMS	No	No	No	X	X	Before	No	Yes	No	Yes	Cardiac arrest due to Vfib
1000005	74	Female	2/17/2018	2/17/2018	PCI	2/17/2018	Yes	EMS	No	No	No	X	X	After	Ventricular fibrillation	Yes	No	Yes	cardiac arrest/STEMI
1000006	76	Male	1/30/2018	2/1/2018	Swan insertion	2/1/2018	No	EMS	No	No	Yes	Hospital A	Aortobifemoral angiography Coronary artery angiography Placement of Impella	Before	Asystolic	Yes	No	No	Cardiac arrest
1000007	61	Female	3/13/2018	3/14/2018	LHC, Stent DES coronary, IABP insertion	3/14/2018	Yes	air lifted	Yes	No	Yes	Hospital B	thrombolytics	After	N/A	Yes	No	Yes	Cardiogenic shock
1000008	85	Male	3/23/2018	3/23/2018	N/A	3/27/2018	Yes	EMS	No	No	No	N/A	N/A	Yes	Bradycardiac	No	Yes	Yes	PEA, Metastatic cancer
1000009	68	Male	4/11/2018	4/13/2018	LHC, PCI, Stent DES, IABP	4/13/2018	Yes	EMS	Yes	No	Yes	Hospital C	thrombolytics	Before	No	Yes	No	Yes	Cardiogenic shock; multiorgan failure
1000010	78	male	4/7/2018	4/14/2018	EGD Diagnostic; Afib cardioversion	4/14/2018	ED	ED	No	No	No	N/A	N/A	Yes	Yes	Yes	No	No	Ischemic Cardiomyopathy
1000011	74	Female	5/14/2018	5/17/2018	LHC, PCI, Stent DES; Impella	5/17/2018	No	air lifted	No	No	Yes	Hospital D	N/A	After	Yes	Yes	No	No	Cardiogenic Shock
1000012	71	Male	4/30/2018	5/5/2018	LHC, Stent DES, IABP	5/5/2018	No	EMS	Yes	No	Yes	Hospital E	cath	After	Yes	Yes	No	No	AMI, cardiogenic shock
1000013	64	female	5/3/2018	5/4/2018	LHC, emergency sternotomy and chest exploration	5/4/2018	Yes	EMS	yes	Yes	No	N/A	N/A	Yes	Yes	No	No	Yes	cardiac tamponade
1000014	46	Male	6/19/2018	6/23/2018	LHC	6/23/2018	No	air lifted	No	No	Yes	Hospital F	labs, echo, started on nitro and heparin	After	Yes	No	No	No	Ventricular tachycardia
1000015		Male	6/22/2018	7/3/2018	Coronary Angiography; ventricular septal defect repair	7/3/2018	Yes	EMS	Yes	No	Yes	Hospital G	N/A	After	No	No	No	No	Acute MI; multiorgan failure
1000016	64	male	7/25/2018	7/26/2018	coronary angiography; PCI; Stent DES	7/26/2018	Yes	EMS	No	NO	No	N/A	N/A	After	No	Yes	No	Yes	post procedural hemorrhage; cardiogenic shock, STEMI

Figure 4.7 AMI raw data.

- "If patients would call EMS instead of driving themselves in, we would have better success."
- "Our patients are the sickest of the sick, so we can't be compared to other facility AMI rates."

Addressing and/or answering some of these questions before going into a process improvement event with clinicians and stakeholders can significantly increase your chances of moving toward real solutions.

After reviewing the statements and/or questions from clinicians and stakeholders, review your data and try to find a correlation metric to either answer the question or support or disprove subjective assumptions.

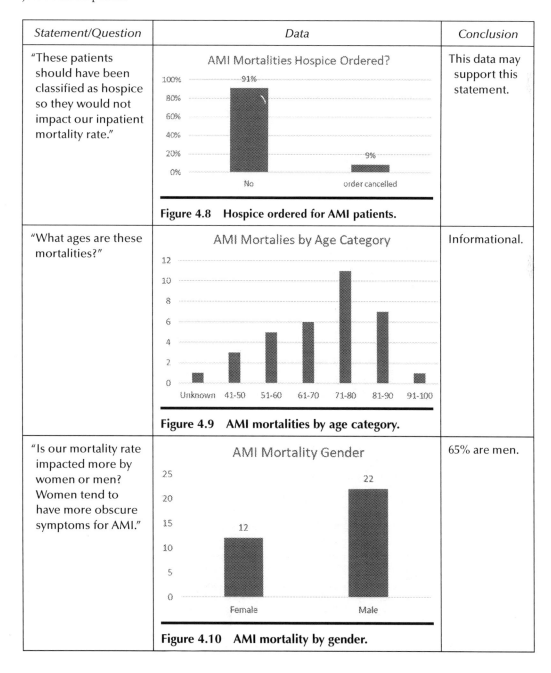

Statement/Question	Data	Conclusion
"These patients should have been classified as hospice so they would not impact our inpatient mortality rate."	**Figure 4.8 Hospice ordered for AMI patients.**	This data may support this statement.
"What ages are these mortalities?"	**Figure 4.9 AMI mortalities by age category.**	Informational.
"Is our mortality rate impacted more by women or men? Women tend to have more obscure symptoms for AMI."	**Figure 4.10 AMI mortality by gender.**	65% are men.

Statement/Question	Data	Conclusion
"In what time frame did these occur? Were they worse in May when we had part of the cath lab down for remodel?"	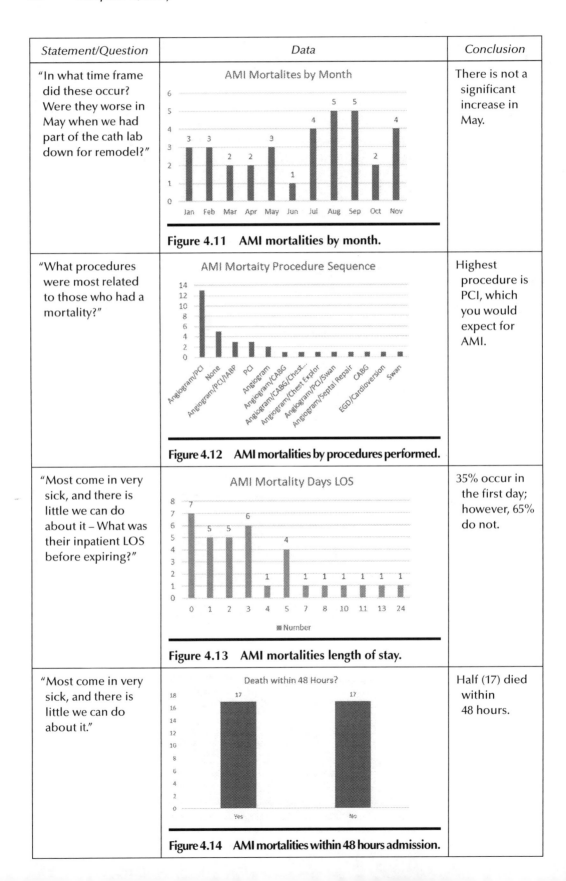AMI Mortalites by Month Figure 4.11 AMI mortalities by month.	There is not a significant increase in May.
"What procedures were most related to those who had a mortality?"	AMI Mortaity Procedure Sequence Figure 4.12 AMI mortalities by procedures performed.	Highest procedure is PCI, which you would expect for AMI.
"Most come in very sick, and there is little we can do about it – What was their inpatient LOS before expiring?"	AMI Mortality Days LOS Figure 4.13 AMI mortalities length of stay.	35% occur in the first day; however, 65% do not.
"Most come in very sick, and there is little we can do about it."	Death within 48 Hours? Figure 4.14 AMI mortalities within 48 hours admission.	Half (17) died within 48 hours.

Statement/Question	Data	Conclusion
"They are all probably DNR."	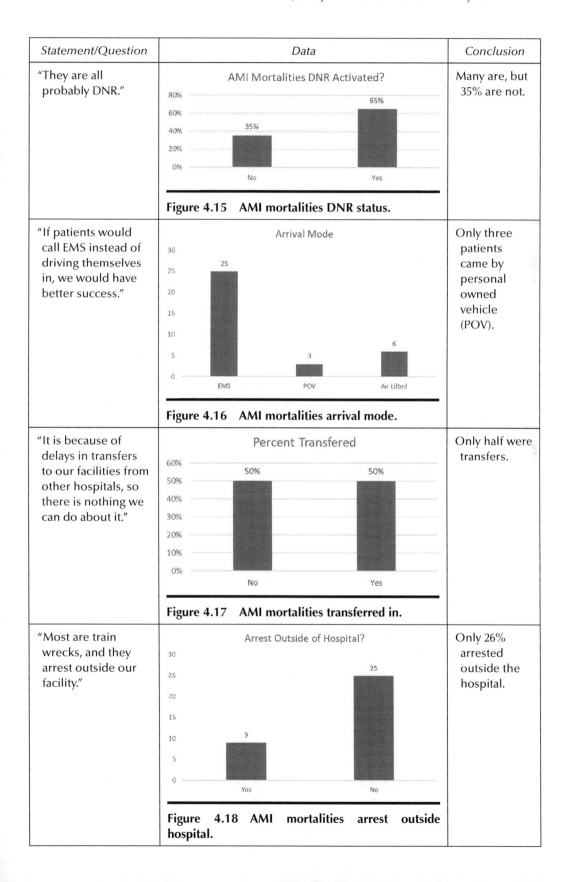Figure 4.15 AMI mortalities DNR status.	Many are, but 35% are not.
"If patients would call EMS instead of driving themselves in, we would have better success."	Figure 4.16 AMI mortalities arrival mode.	Only three patients came by personal owned vehicle (POV).
"It is because of delays in transfers to our facilities from other hospitals, so there is nothing we can do about it."	Figure 4.17 AMI mortalities transferred in.	Only half were transfers.
"Most are train wrecks, and they arrest outside our facility."	Figure 4.18 AMI mortalities arrest outside hospital.	Only 26% arrested outside the hospital.

The intent of this exercise was to demonstrate an actual scenario that you can apply to many other examples in healthcare. Any quality initiative worth improving in healthcare should start with a current state measurement compared to your goal or benchmark. In this moment of transparency, you and your team will be able to determine if further action needs to take place to improve it. Improving the metric involves making those measures transparent to the clinicians and stakeholders and engaging them to get their opinions and experiences to help you determine the reasons why. It is always best to engage your clinicians and stakeholders *before* doing your analysis so you can determine the analysis focus and attempt to anticipate the assumptions and/or questions they will have in the future.

Utilize all your available data sources. Some of those may be the electronic medical record, data registries, risk management systems, and quality management systems.

The methods for using this analysis will be utilized in Chapter 5 with the introduction of plan-do-study-act (PDSA).

4.3 SMART Goals

Before moving forward with utilizing measures for process improvement, one basic principle needs to be clearly understood: the use of specific, measurable, attainable, relevant, time-based (SMART) goals. Very few quality programs address this specifically, but most imply they are doing it.

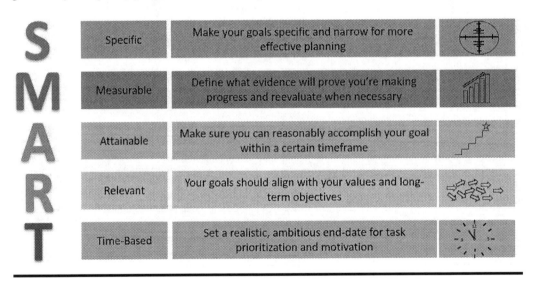

Figure 4.19 SMART goal.

When creating a goal or outlining a problem statement, the term *SMART* can guide you to ensure you have all the necessary components to move forward for improvement. It has five key elements:

1. Specific – Make your goals specific and narrow for more effective planning.
2. Measurable – Define what evidence will prove you're making progress and reevaluate when necessary.
3. Attainable – Make sure you can reasonably accomplish your goal within a certain time frame.
4. Relevant – Your goals should be aligned with your values and long-term objectives.
5. Time-Based – Set a realistic, ambitious end-date for task prioritization and motivation.

I must admit that so many have heard of SMART goals that when I introduce the topic, they often roll their eyes with an expression of "Oh, here we go again on this topic." The one thing I have found, however, is even though the term is very familiar to them, very few remember what each letter stands for, and even fewer actually practice it in their daily work. Let's look at some examples.

In one strategic planning session, an organization was looking at their CMS rating. They were currently rated two stars. The leadership looked at their local competition and outlined how most of their competitors were four-star hospitals. Knowing they wanted to be better than their competitors, they initiated their strategic goal as "attaining five-star status." Admittedly, strategic goals and five-year plans are usually lofty and ill-defined at the tactical level. They eventually need to be outlined in a way that employees can perform activities that actually help achieve them. Let's break down this strategic goal as it relates to the SMART goal model:

	Attain Five-Star Status
Specific	The measure itself is specific relating to five-star status, but it also implies the reader understands that this relates to Medicare's star program. A more appropriate statement would be **Attain the National Medicare Star Rating of Five.**
Measurable	The measurable component of this goal is "five." The hospital is currently a "two," but the strategic goal in itself does not provide that information. A more appropriate statement would be **Improve the National Medicare Star Rating from Two to Five.**
Attainable	This criterion forces you to look at what can be "reasonably accomplished" within a time frame. Currently, only 14% of all hospitals in the nation have a five-star rating. This hospital, currently ranked at two stars, would need to surpass 58% of the hospitals in the country ranked at three or four stars to attain a five-star rating. A more appropriate statement would be **Improve the National Medicare Star Rating from Two to Three.**
Relevant	Relevant applies to the direction the company wants to take. In this case, we are using a strategic goal that is typically an overarching goal of the company. Had it been a departmental goal or something lower, you would check its relevance by aligning it to one of your strategic goals. For example, if your only strategic goal was to improve the national Medicare star rating, a goal to move your labor and delivery operations to a new building may not align.
Time-Based	This is the most often missed criterion of the SMART goal. Most goals are initiated with good intent, but the one thing they lack is the analysis of the time needed to accomplish that goal with a definitive end date. A more appropriate statement would be **Improve the National Medicare Star Rating from Two to Three by 12/31/2024.**

This example is related to a high-level strategic goal. In reality, as a quality professional, you will be faced with writing goals almost daily. These are initiated through process improvements, root-cause analyses, and team goal setting.

4.3.1 Exercise

Suppose you review your critical quality indicator outcomes and determine your PSI 03 pressure injury rate is higher than expected. After meeting with the executive team, they agree you should implement a process improvement for your pressure injury rate. If you leave others to set this goal for you, it is not unlikely that you will get objectives like "Fix it," "Improve pressure injuries," or "Make the process more efficient." Our job as quality professionals is to make these requests more tangible.

What information would you need to create a SMART goal for this project?

Utilizing the concepts of the SMART goal criteria, write a goal statement for the pressure injury issue.

A SMART goal for this particular issue may look something like this:

> Improve the pressure injury rate for the general medical unit from the current rate of 1.65 per 1,000 bed days to 1.0 by January 1, 2024.

In this example, the goal is:

- Specific – "pressure injury rate for the general medical unit"
- Measurable – "current rate of 1.65 per 1,000 bed days to 1.0"
- Attainable – eliminate fewer than 1 (0.65) additional pressure injuries per 1,000 bed days
- Relevant – given the organizational strategies to improve its star ranking, PSI03 pressure injuries are among the measures contributing to that ranking.
- Time-Based – specifically stated as "by January 1, 2024."

This example clearly states where you are and where you need to be by a specific date.

Other Examples of Converting Goals to SMART Goals	
Stated goal	Convert to a SMART goal
Improve our falls	Reduce our fall rate for inpatient units from 1.12 patients per 1,000 bed days to 0.7 patients per 1,000 by January 2024
Transition the psych unit to the new building	Move the psychiatric unit and its operations from hospital A to hospital B by 12/31/2025
Improve hand hygiene	Improve hand hygiene compliance for inpatient units from 67% to greater than 80% by May 2024

In his book *The Speed of Trust*, Stephen Covey states, "Results matter! They matter to credibility." SMART goals provide a wealth of information for the quality professional and for everyone involved. If you are having a difficult time aligning your organization to goals, this simple concept can help you address these and many other issues. SMART goals:

- Create focus and eliminate confusion
- Get everyone on the same page
- Define what you are going to do and what you are *not* going to do
- Define the credibility of the quality professionals
- Eliminate the concept of "We will work on that when we have time"
- Provide the right information for communicating process improvement status reports
- Create a measurable data point for scorecards and metrics

4.3.2 SMART Goals for Individual Tasks

The SMART goal is the initiating premise for setting goals for the organization as a whole. In the example of the pressure injuries, it enables the leadership of the organization to effectively communicate what they are trying to accomplish to everyone in the organization. When we start to look for individual actions or tasks to improve the goal, we need one additional key element – **accountability!** A strategic initiative implies that the accountability applies to all who are working for the organization, but when you get to the level of individual goals or tasks, a specific accountable person needs to be identified. Accountability as it relates to tasks is covered extensively in Chapter 7 Project Management.

4.4 In-Process versus Outcome Measures

In this section, we address the concept of in-process versus outcome measures. Some refer to these concepts as leading versus lagging indicators, but for the purpose of discussion, I will use in-process and outcome measures.

Outcome measures are the high-level clinical or financial outcomes that concern healthcare organizations. They are the quality and cost targets you are aiming to improve. These measures are often reported to government and commercial payors. Some examples of outcome measures are:

- Mortality rates
- Readmission rates
- Hospital-acquired conditions
- Surgical site infections
- Patient safety indicators
- Length of stay

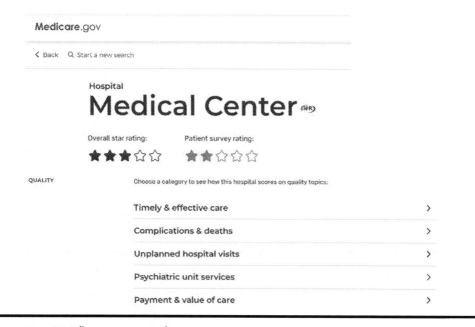

Figure 4.20 CMS five-star categories.

<u>In-process measures</u> are specific to the steps in a process that lead – either positively or negatively – to a particular outcome measure. In-process measures are predictive – that is, they help predict what the outcome will be.

A simple example to explain this concept can be driving to work. If the goal is to get to work by the quickest means necessary, you may set off to seek the most efficient path. Your experiment has you recording the time it takes to get to work each day. This measure is your outcome measure. Through the process, you learn that the first ten miles of your commute is shortened by three minutes if you take Highway 125 rather than Interstate 40, even though the rest of your commute is the same for the side streets leading to your place of employment. Your <u>in-process measure</u> is the change in process using Highway 125 rather than Interstate 40. In this example, you changed your process to achieve a different outcome.

The key to changing an outcome measure is to understand the process. You cannot improve an outcome if you are unfamiliar with the process that created the result. W. Edwards Deming is quoted as saying, "Every system is perfectly designed to get the results it gets." If you wonder why your outcomes are bad, it is because your process is designed to produce them.

To demonstrate this concept, look at a high-level process related to acute myocardial infarction (AMI) mortality.

Figure 4.21 High-level AMI process.

In this process, the patient comes to the emergency department with the primary complaint of chest pain. They are triaged, and an electrocardiogram (EKG) is performed. Based on those results, they are sent to the cardiovascular laboratory, and a percutaneous coronary intervention (PCI) is performed. They recover in an inpatient unit and are then discharged from the hospital.

The outcomes of this process are measured in terms of length of stay, mortality, readmission, patient safety indicators, and complications.

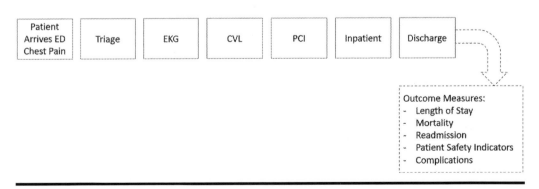

Figure 4.22 High-level AMI process with outcome measures.

If these outcomes were unfavorable (e.g., rate of AMI in hospital mortality greater than expected), the only way to improve that outcome is to review and analyze the process.

If you are unfamiliar with the process and the evidence-based practices utilized for patients with chest pain, you should interview clinicians and review the literature for caring for patients with these conditions. You will find in this example that a significant predictor of inpatient mortality for patients with heart attacks is the time it takes to diagnose and open the blocked heart artery. This will lead you to review the time associated with those interventions.

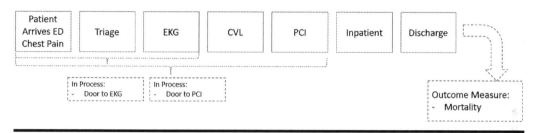

Figure 4.23   High-level AMI process with in-process measures.

The associated in-process measures outlined are the time between the patient entering the hospital and the first EKG performed (time to diagnoses) and the time it takes between the patient entering the hospital and the point at which the percutaneous coronary intervention (PCI) is performed (time to intervention). Although there are other contributing factors to inpatient mortality, in this particular example, improving the processes outlined in the evidence-based practice guidelines should be your target for improvement if you want to achieve an overall improvement in the outcome-based mortality measure.

Other examples of outcome measures with associated in-process measures include the following:

Outcome Measure	Related In-Process Measures
Average length of stay	Discharge order to discharge time ED admit to inpatient arrival time Daily patient rounds
Pressure injury rate	Daily skin assessments High-risk skin care management plans Dietary consults for high-risk patients
Sepsis mortality rate	Blood culture time Lactate lab order time Time to administer antibiotics Time to administer fluids
Patient fall rate	Admission fall risk assessment Daily fall risk assessment High-risk interventions in place
Central line–associated blood stream infection (CLABSI)	Central line days Dressing changes

4.5 Trending Data

Trending data (a.k.a. run charts) allow you to provide a visual representation of your measures over a period of time. The important factor is that time is assumed to have an impact on the results of your measure. We know that many things change over time: patient populations, staffing, process improvements, and leadership, just to name a few. Trending data over time gives you a high-level perspective of how some of those changes may impact your outcomes.

You can evaluate the logic of trending data over time if you wonder, "How has the measure performed over the last X period of time?" In some cases, this may be by month or year (e.g., readmission rates), by day of week (e.g., emergency department visits), or by the hour (e.g., lab result times).

Depending on the circumstances, the data you trend may be something completely new and unique. An example of this is ventilators in use. Before the COVID pandemic, I had never researched the number of ventilators available in an organization. Prior to that, the respiratory department did a good job of understanding the demand for ventilators, and as programs expanded, they requested capital for additional ventilators. With the rapid change from the COVID pandemic, everyone in the country started monitoring the number of available ventilators. This example demonstrates the need for additional ventilators based on the impact of the COVID pandemic. It creates a visual representation for leadership to monitor the increased demand over time and proactively develop strategies to mitigate impending crises (Figure 4.24).

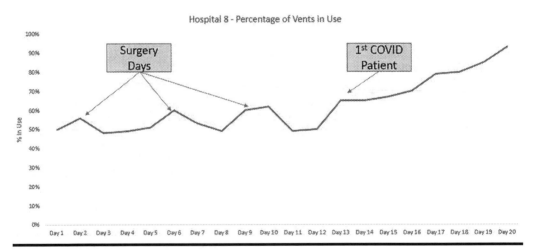

Figure 4.24   Percentage of vents in use trending.

Another reason to trend data over time is to tell your story. If you have an improvement project and you apply interventions to improve a measure over time, you will want to track the progression of that improvement. Figure 4.25 represents an improvement project for pressure injuries.

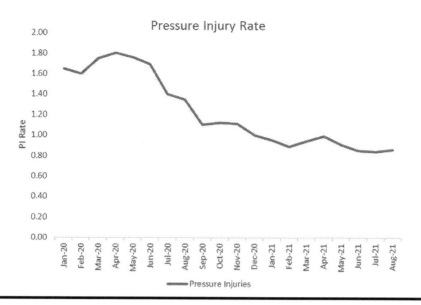

Figure 4.25   Pressure injury rate trending.

This trending graph (Figure 4.25) shows the picture of the pressure injury improvement, but it lacks the ability to tell the whole story. When using trending data to tell a story, remember you want the person reviewing the graph to know exactly what is going on. To do this, you can turn the graph into something much more informative, as shown in Figure 4.26.

First, you should never assume that the person receiving the information is aware of whether a good measure is low or high. This can be easily identified on the graph by placing an arrow in the direction of good.

Second, if you followed the criteria to create a SMART goal, there should always be a goal or target for the measured improvement. Put that goal or target on the graph with the trended data.

Third, tell the story by adding notes relevant to the process improvement over time. Sometimes, this is as simple as adding a note about the time frame when you initiated your improvement, but it can also include all the steps along the way if they're relevant.

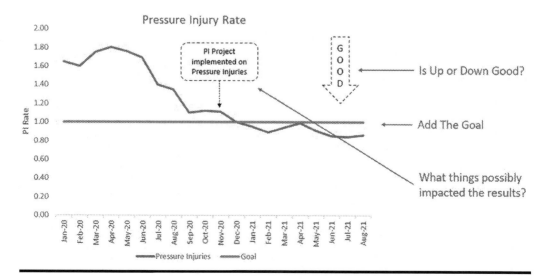

Figure 4.26   Pressure injury rate trending with explanations.

Trending data can help you look for anomalies in the data over time and start looking at other variables that may impact what you see. Other variables, such as number of COVID patients, day of the week, staffing levels, total patient census, and process improvement initiatives are examples of some of the many items you can compare to the data to look for similarities. In statistics, we call these comparisons correlations and try to determine from the data whether we can predict the impact of one measure on another. For example, when staffing levels go down, length of stay goes up. Although there are many factors that may impact a certain metric, these correlations can help you identify the root cause and guide you to the right measure to try and improve. If it was clear that the only measure that impacted length of stay was staffing levels, interventions to improve length of stay would be meaningless if they did not work to improve staffing levels.

4.6 Control Charts

Control charts are trending data (or run charts) with some statistical interpretation. Although this book does not go into statistical methodology in depth, a control chart is the one statistical method that will be helpful to your work as a healthcare quality professional.

To understand a control chart, you first need to understand normal distribution, also known as the bell curve.

The normal distribution is a distribution that occurs naturally in many situations. A good analogy is observed with grades in a class. The bulk of students will score the mean (or the average) of a C, while fewer students will score a B or a D. An even smaller percentage will score an F or an A (Figure 4.27). In a bell curve, half the data will fall to the left of the mean, and half will fall to the right of the mean. The bell curve utilizes the data from the dataset being analyzed to determine the standard deviation. The formula for standard deviation is represented in Figure 4.28. For those who have never seen this formula or haven't the slightest idea how to calculate it, don't worry. Tools like Microsoft Excel can calculate the square root of any dataset in a matter of seconds. See the appendix for instructions on how to use MS Excel to obtain your standard deviation.

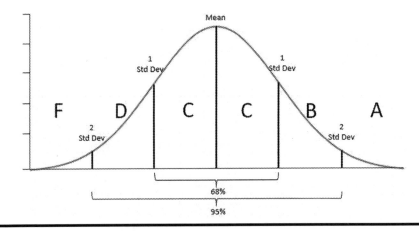

Figure 4.27 Class grades normal distribution.

$$\sigma = \sqrt{\frac{\sum(x_i - \mu)^2}{N}}$$

Figure 4.28 Standard deviation formula.

The principle of normal distribution states that 68% of your data will fall within one standard deviation of the mean – that is, to the left and right of the mean by one standard deviation. Ninety-five percent of your data will fall within two standard deviations of the mean – to the left or right. When you introduce a new element into your dataset, you can evaluate where that result lies as it relates to the normal distribution.

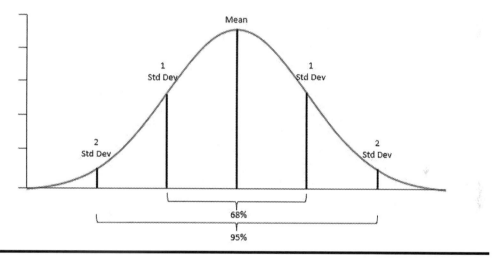

Figure 4.29 Normal distribution/bell curve.

Let's use a practical example. Suppose you have data for the number of emergency department visits per day for the last 12 days. You are using this data to ensure you have enough staffing for the volume of patients that will be needing services. For the last 12 days, the volumes are 50, 51, 59, 52, 49, 47, 60, 61, 48, 53, 55, and 54. If you were to obtain the mean (or average) number of visits per day from this dataset, you would get 53 patients per day. If you calculate the standard deviation for this group of numbers, the result would be 5. This means that 1 standard deviation from the mean is 5 patients – either to the right or left of the mean. Two standard deviations from the mean would be 10 (5*2) patients. For the purpose of illustrating this, Figure 4.30 represents a bell curve with the associated number of emergency department patient visits by day (the star) and the range for each standard deviation.

The stars in the bell curve represent the actual day and the number of ED visits for that day. Suppose you wanted to manage and keep track of the number of emergency department visits each day and determine where they fall on this distribution. You know that anything between 45 and 63 patients a day represents what is considered "normal"; however, on one particular day, there were 85 patients. That would certainly create alarm in the staff, and you probably didn't need to look at data to

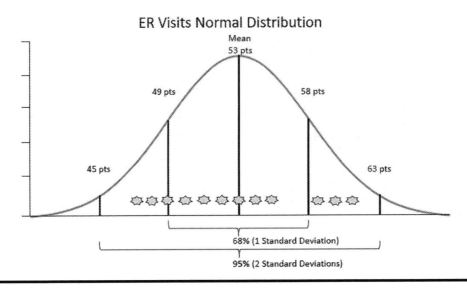

Figure 4.30 Normal distribution ER visits.

know about it. In purely statistical terms, that would be considered an "outlier." Statisticians warn us not to react to one specific outlier in your data, but you can certainly start watching the data to determine if there are any trends moving forward or do some research to determine if it is a simple anomaly or something more permanent. A simple example could be that the free-standing emergency department down the street was closed for the day because of a maintenance issue, so those patients came to your site instead. On the other hand, the free-standing emergency department down the street may have closed indefinitely. With that knowledge, you would need to rapidly intervene.

Getting one step closer to a control chart, let's illustrate by turning the normal distribution graph on its side and including time on the X-axis (Figure 4.31).

This graph is a mess, but it is a great way to demonstrate a key point. The same normal distribution curve has been turned sideways in an effort to start developing our trend chart. Each day's volume is represented along the X-axis on the graph, with a star representing the number of patients for that day.

With an understanding of the normal distribution, we can now put together our control chart (Figure 4.32).

This graph represents a control chart for the same data. The average number of visits is represented by the straight line through the center. The two dashed lines represent the upper and lower control limits (UCL, LCL). These control limits can be set to be within one, two, or three standard deviations from the mean. Typically, most control charts (including this one) are set at two standard deviations. With two standard deviations, we can expect that 95% of our results will stay within that range.

Now suppose we did have one data point that represented 85 patients in one day. The control chart in Figure 4.33 displays how this anomaly would look.

Day six is clearly above the upper control limit. It was probably a topic of discussion for many days: "Remember that day six! Wow, I don't ever want to do that again!" In this example, however, it was a single data point, and the volumes went right back to normal after that. Had you increased staffing for the days to follow after receiving this one data point, you would have introduced more problems than solutions, given staffing and productivity sensitivities.

Templates for statistical control charts are available at www.Innovate2Accelerate.com. These contain all the formulas you need to create a control chart in Excel.

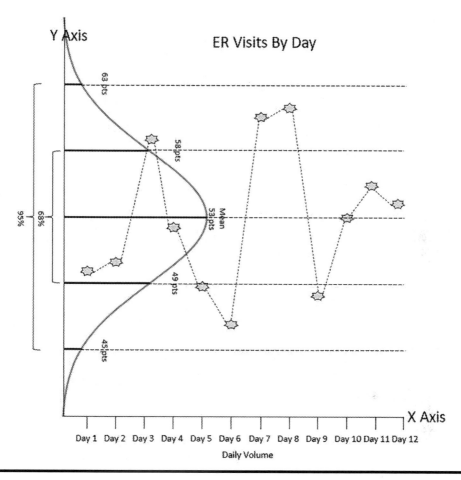

Figure 4.31 **Normal distribution ER visits sideways.**

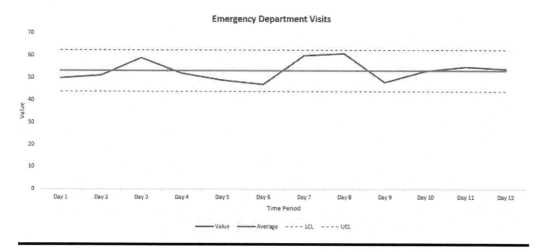

Figure 4.32 **Control chart ER visits.**

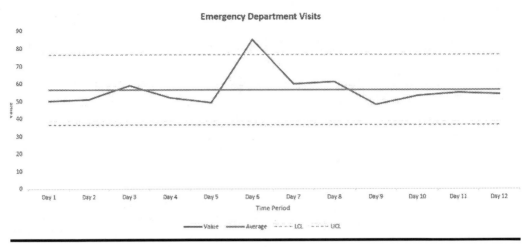

Figure 4.33 Control chart ER visits outlier.

There are some key points you must remember when using trending data:

1. **Reacting** to a single data point in a control chart may lead you to **undesirable** results.
2. The control chart defines the **predictability** of a process and allows you to see if it's **stable**.
3. Your process is specifically **designed** to get the kind of results you are receiving.
4. The only way to get different results is to change the **process** that created them.

4.7 Pareto Chart

The Pareto principle states that for many outcomes, roughly 80% of consequences come from 20% of causes. Pareto's observation was in the connection between population and wealth.[1] Pareto noticed that approximately 80% of Italy's land was owned by 20% of the population.

There may be many reasons why a patient leaves the emergency department before being seen (waited too long, registration person rude, noisy, felt better, phone call needing attention, forgot something, etc.), but if you were to sum up all the reasons from those who left using this principle, 20% of those reasons would contribute to 80% of the patients responses.

A Pareto chart can be very useful in your quality initiatives for grouping and prioritizing your data. There are many statistical software tools that can automatically create a Pareto chart for you, but it can be easily done in MS Excel.

The steps to creating a Pareto chart:

1. Organize your data as seen in Figure 4.34. This example shows the number of responses by customers who left the emergency department for each category.
2. Highlight all the columns of data in Excel, go to the Insert tab, and select the arrow at the bottom of the Charts section (Figure 4.35).
3. Select All Charts > Histogram > Pareto and click OK (Figure 4.36).

The result is a Pareto chart created by Excel (Figure 4.37). You can format this standard chart any way you wish. In this example, two of the nine categories (Waited too long and Noisy) (22%)

	A	B
1	Category	Number
2	Waited too long	30
3	Noisy	20
4	Uncomfortable	5
5	Irritated by people	2
6	Registration Rude	2
7	Forgot Something	1
8	Phone call needing attention	1
9	Ride was leaving	1
10	Changed mind	1

Figure 4.34   Customer response categories.

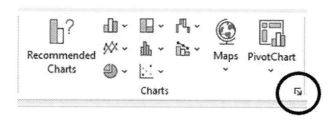

Figure 4.35   Pareto chart step 1.

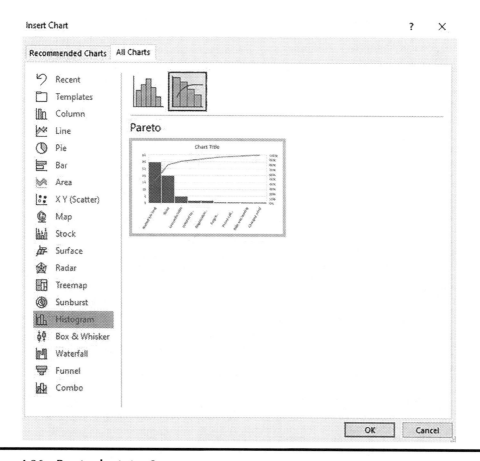

Figure 4.36   Pareto chart step 2.

contribute to almost 80% of the responses. The line delineated by the Y-2 axis represents the cumulative percentage of responses until it reaches 100%.

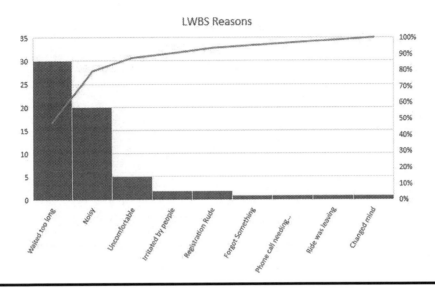

Figure 4.37 Pareto chart outcome example.

Pareto charts are very useful:

■ When analyzing data about the frequency or causes of problems in a process
■ When there are many problems or causes, and you want to focus on the most significant
■ When analyzing broad causes by looking at their specific components
■ When communicating with others about your data

4.8 Cascading Measures

The next area of discussion involves cascading measures. High-level strategies within an organization are important, but how important are those measures on the front line where the work happens day in and day out? It can be motivational to know that an organization is striving to be the best at something or that there is some large lofty goal to achieve, but those goals often leave employees wondering, "What can I do to help make this happen?"

Early in my career, I approached a nurse in the emergency department and discussed the organizational strategies. This nurse had a lot of character, and you never had to guess what was on her mind. I told her about this great goal that the organization had to reduce mortalities. Like the fool that I was, I asked her what she thought she could do to help with that strategy. She paused for a moment and looked at me as if I had just gotten off the administrative bandwagon of Kool-Aid drinkers and said, "Try not to kill them?" As shocked as I was, it created an exceptional learning opportunity for me. Unless I could facilitate the connections between what this nurse was passionate about and did every day to the greater organizational goals, we would never achieve the objective of reducing hospital mortalities, an objective that was completely dependent on caregiver participation.

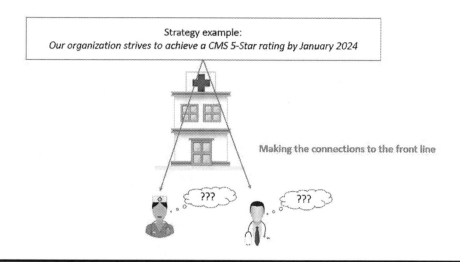

Figure 4.38 Making the connection to the front line.

A cascading measure is one that can be broken down into smaller, more meaningful measures that have an impact on the overall goal. If your organizational leadership defines a strategy to achieve CMS five star, for example, they must determine what specific criteria will enable them to achieve that goal and engage the employees and clinicians in ways that will accomplish it.

If done correctly with SMART goals, most strategic initiatives provide the criteria to achieve them. In other words, the answers to the test are in plain sight; you just need to achieve them. In the example of achieving five-star status under CMS, the criteria are clearly defined: customer satisfaction, readmission rates, mortality rates, hospital-acquired infections, and a few others set the rules for achieving your goal.

Step 1: Understand what to measure.

> Determine what criteria you will evaluate and measure to achieve your goal.

Step 2: Determine how you are currently doing with those measures.

> Obtain current-state data and determine how you rank today. "Today" is a key data point. Data utilized by CMS for the five-star criteria, for example, can be as old as 18 months. There is, unfortunately, a huge lag in the government resources showing your efforts.
>
> Figure 4.39 is an Excel spreadsheet representing all the measures important to achieving five-star status and the current state of each measure. Comparisons, goals, and benchmarks can all be represented in the same diagram. This simple exercise provides the ability to determine those quality measures that require the most attention and prioritize them higher.

Step 3: Prioritize those areas you want to improve.

> This should *not* be done in isolation. To achieve such a goal, every leader in the organization will need to be engaged and participate.

Step 4: Identify the correct workforce.

> This step involves identifying those employees who have the most impact on achieving improved results specific to the measure. You would never ask housekeeping to be the sole department responsible for improving hospital-acquired pressure injuries. A simple exercise, as depicted in Figure 4.40, can enable you to align measures with the appropriate staff. This can be done easily by soliciting feedback from employees in each of those areas.

Measure	Goal	Benchmark	Current	Color Status
Person and Community Engagement Domain (HCAHPS)				
Communication with Nurses	80.00%	87.36%	74.0%	Yellow
Communication with Doctors	80.00%	88.10%	76.2%	Yellow
Responsiveness of Hospital Staff	70.00%	81.00%	61.4%	Red
Communication about Medicines	60.00%	74.75%	57.6%	Red
Cleanliness of Hospital Environment	80.00%	79.58%	71.6%	Yellow
Quietness of Hospital Environment	70.00%	79.58%	51.9%	Red
Discharge Information	80.00%	92.17%	82.3%	Green
Care Transition	70.00%	63.32%	47.2%	Red
Overall Rating of Hospital	80.00%	85.67%	70.0%	Yellow
Safety Domain	Goal	Benchmark	Current	Color Status
HAC CAUTI	0.554	0.000	0.000	Green
HAC CLABSI	0.468	0.000	0.000	Green
HAC C-DIFF	0.526	0.067	0.433	Green
HAC MRSA	0.569	0.000	0.000	Green
SSI Abdominal Hysterectomy	0.379	0.000	0.000	Green
SSI Colon	0.590	0.000	0.000	Green
CMS Patient Safety Indicator (PSI) 90	50%tile	75%tile	Current	Color Status
PSI 03 Pressure Ulcer	0.470	0.200	1.2	Red
PSI 06 Iatrogenic Pneumothorax	0.140	0.000	0.0	Green
PSI 08 In-Hospital Fall with Hip Fracture	0.000	0.000	0.0	Green
PSI 09 PeriOp Hemorrhage or Hematoma	1.860	0.930	2.5	Red
PSI 10 PO Acute Kidney Injury Requiring Dialysis	0.450	0.000	0.0	Green
PSI 11 PO Respiratory Failure	2.970	1.550	0.0	Green
PSI 12 PeriOp PE or DVT	2.700	1.850	1.1	Green
PSI 13 PO Sepsis	3.290	1.400	1.2	Green
PSI 14 PO Wound Dehiscence	0.000	0.000	0.0	Green
PSI 15 Unrecognized Abdominopelvic Accidental Punct/L	0.850	0.000	0.0	Green
Mortality	50%tile	75%tile	Current	Color Status
Acute Myocardial Infarction (AMI) Mortality	4.0%	2.7%	1.39%	Green
Chronic Obstructive Pulmonary Disease (COPD) Mortality	2.1%	1.2%	0.00%	Green
Heart Failure (HF) Mortality	2.2%	1.5%	4.4%	Red
Pneumonia, Adult Mortality	4.0%	2.9%	4.7%	Red
Coronary Artery Bypass Graft (CABG) Mortality (Graft Only)	3.7%	0.0%	0.00%	Green
Stroke Mortality, Ischemic	2.6%	1.3%	0.00%	Green
Hospital Readmissions	50%tile	75%tile	Current	Color Status
Acute Myocardial Infarction (AMI)	8.5%	6.5%	10.9%	Red
Chronic Obstructive Pulmonary Disease (COPD)	15.6%	12.7%	10.00%	Green
Heart Failure (HF)	16.7%	14.2%	23.3%	Red
Pneumonia, Adult	12.1%	10.2%	9.21%	Green
Coronary Artery Bypass Graft (CABG)	8.2%	6.2%	5.00%	Green
Total Hip/Knee (THA/TKA)	2.3%	1.6%	1.64%	Green
Stroke	7.2%	4.2%	0.00%	Green
Hospital Wide Readmission (HWR)	10.5%	9.1%	10.7%	Red

Figure 4.39   CMS five-star scorecard example.

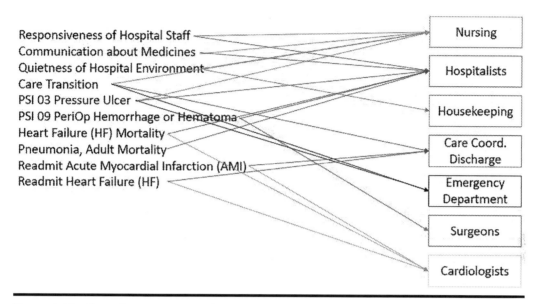

Figure 4.40   Cascade measure mapping.

Step 5: Facilitate strategy discussions.

Plan any number of strategy discussion meetings as appropriate and invite employees for each of the areas identified in the previous step. These discussions are best done as a group, but you should never underestimate the importance of one-on-one discussions you can have with employees and clinicians while walking down the hall.

Share the organizational strategy with them and the methods you used to get to the prioritized measurement outcomes. Your intent is to get information from them and ideas about improvement. Some example questions are:
- What do we do that contribute to these results?
- Is there evidenced-based practice around procedures leading to these outcomes that we can investigate?
- What things can we do to work toward an improvement?

Step 6: Develop your strategic measurement system.

After gathering all your data, aligning the correct staff, and obtaining feedback. It is time to create a high-level outline for the measures owned by each department contributing to the overall strategic goal. Figure 4.41 is a visual of a strategic goal aligned to specific employee and clinician areas. These areas contain the measures that are important to them as employees and clinicians and are prioritized as key to achieving the overall strategic goal. A high-level visual can be used to represent your cascaded metrics assigned by department and aligned to the organizational strategy.

Going back to the situation I shared earlier with the emergency department nurse and mortality improvement goals, if I had followed these steps, the conversation would undoubtedly have been more successful. Reduction in hospital mortality may have still been a strategic initiative, but after evaluating the data, I would have learned that the mortality category that needed to be improved

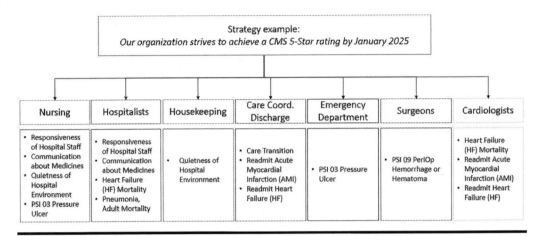

Figure 4.41   Cascade measure visual presentation.

was acute myocardial infarction (AMI). Looking at the current rates along with the evidenced-based practice related to AMI mortality may have revealed a poor result for the time it takes to provide an electrocardiogram (EKG) for patients arriving at the emergency department with chest pain. A discussion with the emergency department nurse about our mortality rates for AMI and associated results for timely EKGs would have solicited an entirely different and more meaningful conversation.

Remember, although it is important to involve everyone in the planning for your strategy, this in itself does not provide the improvements necessary to achieve the goal. Chapter 5 will cover process improvement techniques that can be applied to these goals, enabling you to begin the quality improvement journey.

4.9 The Quality Oversight Scorecard

§482.21 Condition of participation: Quality assessment and performance improvement program.

STANDARD: PROGRAM SCOPE
1. The program must include, but not be limited to, an ongoing program that shows measurable improvement in indicators for which there is evidence that it will improve health outcomes and identify and reduce medical errors.
2. The hospital must measure, analyze, and track quality indicators, including adverse patient events, and other aspects of performance that assess processes of care, hospital service, and operations.

STANDARD: PROGRAM DATA
1. The program must incorporate quality indicator data including patient care data and other relevant data such as data submitted to or received from Medicare quality

reporting and quality performance programs, including but not limited to data related to hospital readmissions and hospital-acquired conditions.
2. The hospital must use the data collected to:
    a. Monitor the effectiveness and safety of services and quality of care
    b. Identify opportunities for improvement and changes that will lead to
       improvement
3. The frequency and detail of data collection must be specified by the hospital's govern-
    ing body.

Once you understand your organizational strategies and the measures that are important them
and cascade them throughout the relevant areas of the organization, it is time to pull all this
together into a quality oversight scorecard. This scorecard consists primarily of outcome measures,
but it provides visibility into the things that matter most to the organization. Although accreditation standards do not specifically state how quality measures are overseen, they state it must be
done. Without a concise tool to manage this, how would you have this transparency? Remember,
leaders in the organization along with quality professionals need to have an understanding of current quality throughout the entire organization. The quality oversight scorecard is a great tool for
achieving this.

The level of sophistication and complexity of your scorecard is highly dependent on the
resources available to your organization. Some organizations have purchased software tools that
provide some, if not all, measures important for quality management. In my experience, few
actually have something flexible enough to consolidate their scorecard measures in a manner that
is meaningful and easy to obtain. I will include a way that allows anyone with a computer and
Microsoft Excel to create a quality oversight scorecard. This is not the only correct way to maintain a scorecard, but it is a process that will work for you.

Reality check: Many folks will argue that they have automated and/or EMR-related dash-
boards that can provide quality data for them. The reality is that few will combine those measures
into something meaningful. Each requires the user to go to the application, run a report, look at
the data, and react to it. The reality is that people don't do this. They get too busy, are not focused
on it, or forget how to access the reporting.

Process for developing your quality oversight scorecard:

1. List all the departments that need to be included in your quality oversight. These consists of
   all the key areas of your business, such as the operating department, general medical unit,
   emergency department, facilities, housekeeping, dietary, etc.
2. Identify the department owners for each of these units. Typically, this will be the department director, but it should be someone accountable for the operations in the area.
3. Identify the executive leader of each unit. This is usually the person the department director reports to. For example, the CNO typically oversees the nursing units and emergency
   department.
4. Identify any programs that require individual measurements and/or scorecards. Beyond
   departments, there are usually programs that spread across all departments (e.g., sepsis,
   STEMI, and stroke).

5. Design Tab 1 of the Excel scorecard:
   a. Tab 1 consists of all the units you listed in Step 1 combined with the programs listed in Step 4. Figure 4.42 is an example of that page.
   b. List the executive owner, quality director, and quality manager on this first tab.
   c. A special note is added to this example informing everyone not to include patient health information (PHI). The quality oversight scorecard is easily emailed and passed around, so it should not include PHI. If a patient's name or identifiable information is included, we want to respect their privacy (e.g., MRSA event, patient Jane Doe, 5/1/2022).
   d. Description of the scorecard, its specific use, and how it is utilized.
   e. All departments are listed. Notice in the example that each department has a hyperlink. When all the scorecards in each tab are created, a simple hyperlink will help you quickly navigate through the scorecard.
6. Create tabs for all departments.
   a. Create a tab for each department in Excel (Figure 4.43).
7. Create a template scorecard.
   a. Create a template scorecard in Excel like the example in Figure 4.44 containing the following elements:
      i.   Department description
      ii.   Executive owner of that department
      iii. Department owner accountable for quality metrics
      iv.   Date updated
      v.   Measure – short description of the measure
      vi.   Description – longer description of the measure
      vii. Source – description of the source the information is retrieved from. This is optional but helpful when trying to remember where to get the data
      viii. JC criteria – Joint Commission or other accreditation agency criteria related to the measure (if applicable)
      ix.   Goal – goal for the measure
      x.   Separate column for each month if measured monthly; this can be configured for yearly or quarterly as well
      xi.   Year to date – the year-to-date result for the measure
      xii. Link at the top of the page named Cover Page hyperlinked to Tab 1 of your document
8. Copy and paste the template scorecard in all department tabs to use as a starting point.
9. Update the measures and, if available, data for the departments.
   a. Working with each of the department directors, update each of the scorecards. More detail regarding this process will follow.
10. Update the goal for each measure.
    a. Update the measure goals based on organizational strategies, evidence-based practice, or department goal setting.
11. Set conditional formatting on cells in the scorecard.
    a. Conditional formatting allows you to color code the cells based on the current month's measure as it relates to the goal. For simplicity and consistency, I suggest only making measures red if they do not meet the goal. Many insist on having green, yellow, and red conditional formatting, but this creates a formatting complexity that requires a lot of time and commitment to maintain. Figure 4.45 shows an example of a scorecard with measures and conditional formatting.

2023 Quality Oversight Scorecard

Year:	2023
Executive Quality Oversight:	Executive over Quality
Quality Director:	Director over Quality
Quality Manager:	Manager over Quality
Version:	1.0

Note: This document should not contain patient identifiable information (PHI). Please do not add patient identifiable information in notes or comments.

Description

The quality oversight scorecard is used to continuously evaluate the metrics and performance for each department and program. Each scorecard is specifically tailored to monitor the metrics related to patient care in that specific area while addressing specific accreditation criteria. These measures are reviewed and monitored at the monthly Quality Committee.

Departments:

Strategic Scorecard	Medication Management
Anesthesia	Oncology
Biomed	Operating Department
Birth Center	Organ Donation
Cardiovascular Lab	Pathology
Diagnostic Imaging	Plant Operations
Dialysis	Therapy Services
Dietary Services	Quality
Emergency Department	Registration
ED Physicians	Respiratory Therapy
Employee Health	Risk
Environmental Services	Safety/Security
Health Information Management	Sepsis
Hospitalists	STEMI
Human Resources	Sterile Processing
Intensive Care Unit	Stroke
Information Technology	Supply Chain
Infection Control	Surgical Unit
Lab	Trauma
Medical Staff	Utilization Review/Discharge
Medical Unit	Version Control

Figure 4.42   Quality oversight scorecard cover page.

| Cover | Anesthesia | Biomed | BirthCenter | Cardiovascular Lab | DiagnosticImaging | Dialysis | Dietary Services | Emergency Dept | ED Physic ... ⊕ ⋮ |

Figure 4.43   Quality oversight scorecard tabs.

Cover Page

Department Description:		
Executive Owner:		
Department Owner:		
Date Updated:		

Measure	Description	Source	JC Criteria	Goal	Jan	Feb	Mar	Apr	May	Jun	Jul	Aug	Sep	Oct	Nov	Dec	Total/YTD

Notes:

Figure 4.44   Quality oversight scorecard department template.

Department Description:	Unit ABC
Executive Owner:	John Doe
Department Owner:	Mary Smith
Date Updated:	9/1/2022

Cover Page

Measure	Description	JC Criteria	Target	Jan-22	Feb-22	Mar-22	Apr-22	May-22	Jun-22	Jul-22	Aug-22	Sep-22	Oct-22	Nov-22	Dec-22	Total/YTD
Customer Experience Hospitalist Specific																
Overall Rating of Hospital	Rate the Hospital 9-10 Percent	LD.03.02.01 MS.03.01.01.05	66.3%	54.90%	61.64%	68.52%	69.23%	70.21%	64.44%	60.61%	65.96%					60.15%
MD Communication Percent	HCAHPS Communication with Doctors Perform.	LD.03.02.01 MS.03.01.01.05	90%	70.37%	80.72%	72.39%	82.60%	73.37%	79.45%	74.46%	72.79%					69.50%
Doctors treat with courtesy/respect	HCAHPS PressGaney Scores	LD.03.02.01 MS.03.01.01.05	informational	78.43%	86.30%	83.33%	88.89%	81.82%	89.13%	80.30%	85.11%					79.79%
Doctors listen carefully to you	HCAHPS PressGaney Scores	LD.03.02.01 MS.03.01.01.05	informational	66.00%	78.08%	70.37%	77.78%	70.21%	80.43%	75.38%	70.21%					65.08%
Doctors expl in way you understand	HCAHPS PressGaney Scores	LD.03.02.01 MS.03.01.01.05	informational	66.67%	77.78%	63.46%	81.13%	66.09%	68.89%	67.69%	63.04%					63.64%
HCAPS Number Respond	Number of Surveys		informational	51	73	54	54	48	46	66	47					439
Quality - Hospital Acquired Conditions (HAC) Hospitalist Specific																
HAC C-Diff	Hospital Acquired C-Diff infection	IC.02.01.01.8	0	0	1	0	0	0	0	3	1					5
HAC MRSA	Hospital Acquired MRSA infection	IC.02.01.01.8		0	0	1	0	0	0	0	0					1
HAC CAUTI	Hospital acquired CAUTI infection	IC.02.05.01.3		0	0	0	0	0	0	0	0					0
HAC CLABSI	Hospital acquired CLABSI infection	IC.02.05.01.3		0	0	0	1	2	0	0	0					3
SSI - Colon	Surgical Site Infection for Colon Procedures	IC.02.05.01.3		0	0	0	0	0	0	0	0					0
SSI Hip	Surgical site infection	IC.02.05.01.3		0	0	0	0	0	0	0	0					0
SSI Laminectomy	Surgical site infection	IC.02.05.01.3		0	0	0	0	0	0	0	0					0
Infection VAC	Ventilator associated condition	IC.02.01.01.8														0
SSI knee	Surgical site infection	IC.02.05.01.3		0	0	0	0	0	0	0	0					0
SSI - Hyst	Surgical Site infections for Hysterectomies	IC.02.05.01.3		0	0	0	0	0	0	0	0					0
Quality - Serious Reportable Events (SRE)																
Falls	Number of patient falls	PC.01.02.08.2	0	5	6	5	4	4	2	10	5					41
Fall With Injury	Fall with injury	PC.01.02.08.2		1	1	0	0	0	0	0	0					2
Stage 3, 4, Unstageable Pressure Injury	Hospital acquired stage 3, 4 or Unstageable PI	LD.03.02.01		0	0	0	0	0	0	1	0					1
Sentinel Events	Sentinel Events	LD.03.09.01.10		0	0	0	0	0	0	1	0					1
Quality - Process Indicators																
Hospital Wide Readmissions	Hospital Wide Readmission Rate (one month behind)	LD.03.02.01	TBD	5.7%	7.7%	9.9%	9.8%	7.1%	7.7%	6.2%						7.7%
Mortality	Hospital Wide Mortality Rate	LD.03.02.01	1.0	1.22	0.78	0.67	0.72	0.89	0.46	0.80						0.8

Figure 4.45   Quality oversight scorecard unit example.

Once the basic outline of your scorecard is in place, you can work with each of the department leaders to create applicable measures for their department. Ideally, this comes through the cascade process described previously to align the correct measures with the correct departments based on the strategic initiatives. For example, suppose one of your strategic initiatives is to reduce mortality rates for acute myocardial infarction (AMI) patients. You may want to align that measure with the emergency department. Which measures would be related to the work of the emergency department in preventing AMI mortality? A couple of important alignments could be door-to-EKG for chest pain, door-to-PCI, or even door-to-triage time, relating to the time it takes to diagnose chest pain. Each of these measures, among others, could provide good-quality outcome data related to the strategy in the organization. The importance is to align them and help clinicians understand why those measures were selected for quality oversight.

QUESTIONS TO GET TO QUALITY MEASURES

"What measures are important to your department?"
"At the end of the day, how do you know if you did a good job?"

Reality check: Another reality check worthy of discussing is quality measures for each department. If every measure on a department scorecard was aligned with the strategic initiatives, the reality is that you would have a lot of work to do before you could get started, or you might skip over measures that are important to that department. A good way to start out a quality scorecard for each department is simply to as ask that department, "What measures are important for your department?" Even if they don't have specifically designed or measured areas within their department, they usually know what is important. Start with what they know and have been utilizing and get something in place on your scorecard. In this case, don't let perfect be the enemy of good enough, or you will never get your scorecard off the ground. Get it started and get moving.

More is not better when it comes to scorecard measures at the department level. Two or three well-intentioned measures are better than a hundred measures that are spit out of some electronic system because the software "just does that" or because "it's what we've always done." First, learn to measure, respond to, and improve the most important measures. This exercise will allow each department to evolve into higher complexities of measures, having understood the basic approach first.

Last, don't be overly concerned about getting the measures up and running for every department right away. You can utilize the techniques discussed in Chapter 3 for quality committee reports to evolve your scorecard. When departments are scheduled to present to the quality committee for the first time, you will be given the opportunity to help them create their dashboard metrics. In this respect, it may take up to a year to have all your scorecards populated.

4.10 Updating the Quality Oversight Scorecard

Now is the time to ensure the scorecard is maintained and updated monthly. It is incredibly important to engage every department in the organization and make them accountable for updating their own scorecard. I have heard many arguments regarding this step: "This is a manual effort; we don't have time for this!"; "We don't have access to that data"; "Its quality's job to update these measures"; or "Shouldn't there be an electronic system to do this for us?"

Let's me address each one of these statements:

"This is a manual effort; we don't have time for this!" The proposed scorecard format presented here requires a manual effort to populate the data. Computer automation may be available to populate and manage a quality oversight scorecard.[2] The problem with organizations starting their journey with software, however, is that it removes the visibility and accountability to update and review measures they are accountable for. When you auto-populate measures for a department owner, they will likely show up to present their dashboard to the quality committee every six months, and, quite possibly, that will be the first time they've looked at the measures they are accountable for! It is important to automate and use technology wherever appropriate to improve the efficiency for our workforce, but when leaders are involved with their measures and operations, manually updating them creates an ongoing familiarity and intimacy with these critical points. Once leaders develop the routine of continually reviewing and responding to these measures (regardless how they are populated), automation can have a relevant place.

"We don't have access to that data." Imagine telling a patient that there is a quality measure that is really important to their outcome, but you don't have access to the information, so just ignore it. What if you didn't have access to the information systems. Would you continue treatment and care without knowing those results? If it is important to measure, put it on the scorecard. Even if the measures are not populated for a time, list it and work to develop processes to obtain the data. This may mean working with your information technology team, searching for a vendor application, or collecting the data manually. Sometimes this is as easy as putting check marks on a piece of paper or counting stick marks on a Post-It note. The point is that if the data is important to patient care, you can't ignore it because you don't have access to it or an easy means of collecting it.

"It's quality's job to update the measures." Although some measures are updated and managed by quality (serious reportable events, mortality rates, readmissions, etc.), leaving measures for those owned by department leaders up to quality to manage removes the accountability from each department. Remember, the quality department does not *do* quality. Managing and updating quality measures is the responsibility of those closest to providing the care. Our function is to provide them with the tools and support for achieving this goal.

"Shouldn't there be an electronic system to do this for us?" Although the answer to this is invariably yes, few organizations have the resources, finances, or means to implement it. You can go through the process of obtaining a software vendor, securing funds, implementing a contract, engaging information technology to set up interfaces, and train on a new system over a period of six months to a year, or you can open up Microsoft Excel and have something ready to go in a matter of days. If your organization has the means to obtain and implement electronic software for your quality scorecard, then do it, but don't let that be a barrier to having something in place.

As a quality professional, you will be faced with these along with many other scenarios. Keep your focus on what you are trying to accomplish in managing quality oversight. Barriers will be mere speed bumps in the road. Don't allow small barriers to become complete road blocks. That will render your quality program ineffective, impotent, and possibly nonexistent.

4.11 Summary

Understanding the DIKW model for data and information is an important step for analytics and reporting in quality. Many organizations have data, but if you want to become successful in quality management, you must utilize that data to get to the levels of knowledge and wisdom on the DIKW triangle.

Driving quality change in the organization involves much more than reviewing measures of outcomes. Successful quality programs outline and understand the processes that lead to process outcomes and manage to improve the in-process activities and measures that create them. Engage everyone in the organization with measures that are relevant and meaningful to them. It is this transparency and engagement that will get you down the path to improvement.

4.11.1 Key Concepts

■ Data, information, knowledge, wisdom – Understand how to classify the maturity of your measurement and analytics.
■ Measurement for quality oversight – Those things that cannot be measured cannot be improved. Create transparency for quality measures.
■ Your process is specifically **designed** to get the kind of results you are receiving.
■ The only way to get different results is to change the **process** that is creating them.

4.11.2 Areas You Can Geek Out On

■ Review the Joint Commission criteria involving data and analytics:
  • Techniques to Analyze and Display Data (PI.02.01.01)
  • Uses the Results of Data Analysis (PI.02.01.01)
  • Collects Data to Monitor its Performance (PI.01.01.01)
  • Provides Incidence Data (PI.02.01.01)
  • Evaluate the Effectiveness (LD.03.05.01)
  • Hospital Analyzes and Uses Information (LD.03.09.01)
  • Quality Indicator Data (LD.03.02.01)
  • Hospital Collects Data . . . (PI.01.01.01)
  • Analyzes Data Collected (PI.02.01.01)
  • Planning . . . Information Sources (LD.03.03.01)
  • Evaluate Culture of Safety and Quality (LD.03.01.01)
  • Data and Information Used throughout the Hospital (LD.03.02.01)
  • Reviews and Analyzes (PI.02.01.01)
  • Analyzes and Compares Internal Data over Time (PI.02.01.01)
  • Identify the Frequency of Data Collection (PI.01.01.01)
  • Patterns, Trends, or Variations in Its Performance (PI.02.01.01)
■ Create a dashboard using Microsoft Excel, Key formatting techniques are available in the appendix for this chapter.
■ Experiment and play with some control charts. Templates can be downloaded at www.Innovate2Accelerate.com.
■ Learn how to calculate the square root of a dataset in MS Excel.

- Use this reference to understand the standard deviation formula: www.mathsisfun.com/data/standard-deviation-formulas.html.
- Identify your organization's strategic goals. How can those goals be aligned with unit level measures throughout the organization?

Notes

1 Pareto, Vilfredo; Page, Alfred N., *Manual of Political Economy*, A. M. Kelley (1971).
2 Software for quality management dashboard: www.Innovate2Accelerate.com.

Chapter 5

Quality Improvement

Have you ever worked for an organization that initiated a process improvement project? This usually begins when someone convinces the executive-level leadership that they needed to perform process improvement in their organization. They drill into their minds that they are trailing their competitors, do not have good quality outcomes, and are required to initiate process improvement programs because of the CMS accreditation standards. Since the publication of *To Err is Human*[1] and many publications like it, they make the case that we must make healthcare safer. We should learn and improve by adopting techniques from companies such as ThedaCare, Virginia Mason, Mayo, Toyota, and Apple. With that message sold, leadership begins to work a strategy around process improvement. They secure a budget and assign someone to research and obtain the skills of a consultant to bring process improvement into their organization. The level of your process improvement initiative depends in large part on the amount of money, resources, and time your leadership is willing to give. Some give a lot and start system-wide programs that involve everyone in the organization, whereas some give little, hire one process improvement expert, and ask them to make it happen.

One thing that is consistent is this: The organization started with process improvement. They brought in the "experts" and went to the front lines to describe to everyone in the organization that they were there to help and were going to solve their problems. If you're picking up the tone of my writing here, you are probably catching my distain for such an approach. It seems, after all, that this is the correct approach. Most of us have seen it over and over again by very successful companies. But are they successful in process improvement? The number-one complaint that I hear about process improvement is sustainability. Yes, it was great, we had a great time, learned a lot, and even saved some very tangible money, yet it never seems to go beyond a year of sustained improvement.

There are many reasons things don't sustain, and I don't propose to tell you I have the single solution to the problem. However, I do realize sustainability involves people, and those people are the ones who are doing the work every day. It they don't have the passion and involvement in process improvement that the experts do, the improvements will soon disappear after they are gone. The key reason I believe this approach to be in error is this: Process improvement starts with the fact that something needs to be improved, and you have a problem. The problem is the *problem*. For our efforts to work, we must find a problem to solve. We see problems everywhere we go! We walk into a restaurant and see a long line at the counter = problem. We look at the supply room and

 DOI: 10.4324/9781003358404-6

see excess stock = problem. We see customers waiting for a service = problem. Through the lens of a process improvement person, problems are seen everywhere. However, the people you need to have believe in your process improvement are not looking through your lens. Their lens involves the day-to-day operations, the experience they have surviving throughout their career, and the pride they take in the successful job they have done and are currently doing. When you walk into their life and explain they need process improvement, you must first point a big finger at them and tell them they have a problem! How did you react the last time someone told you that you were wrong, or you had a problem?

Figure 5.1 Selling process improvement.

In this respect, we should never lead with looking for the problem. Since process improvement needs a problem to solve, the exercise of improving something must come last.

Although there are scores of books that discuss how businesses should be run, there is a very simple approach that can and will lead an organization to a better place. This three-step approach consists of:

1. Transparency
2. Accountability and ownership
3. Process improvement

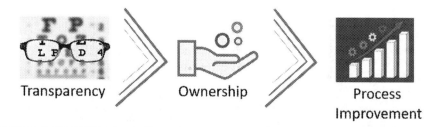

Figure 5.2 Transparency-ownership-process improvement.

First, we make those things that are important to managing patient care *transparent*. It is impossible to improve the things we cannot see. Transparency enables all caregivers to see and understand their current state. Through transparency, we must first identify how the business or process is run, define the measures within that process that are meaningful to the customers and those doing the work, and make these measures transparent for everyone.

Second, *accountability* and *ownership* take place when meaningful and transparent measures are provided to those who have a direct influence on them. I have never met an employee who came to work and said, "I want to do a bad job today!" Although the word *accountability* often has a negative connotation in business, it is anything but negative. When people feel accountable, they know what they need to do, understand how their work contributes to the overall mission, and personally take pride in how they deliver service. As they look back on their day accompanied by transparency in how they performed, they can confidently state, "I did that!" And so begins the positive culture of accountability.

The last step on this pathway is *process improvement*. Although most organizations start with process improvement and look for a problem to solve, I suggest putting process improvement and all its schoolbook techniques, Japanese terminology, and certification acronyms last. Here is where the process improvement expert gets to share their tools. Those doing the work now have transparent measures to define the outcomes of their work, are taking ownership of those outcomes, and seek help and support to achieve their goals. When process improvement experts are approached to help solve a problem, those leading process improvement have significant accountability to support employees in solving the problems they identified.

In this way, employees are aware of the important measures and outcomes (transparency), take ownership of those measures they contribute to (accountability), and request the support of process improvement techniques to improve them (process improvement).

Last but not least, although this was described in three seemingly simple steps, they are anything but that. Once process improvement experts are given a process improvement model or steps to follow, most are inclined to organize them into timelines and instructions while mapping out a project plan to get it done. This is *not* one of those models. Each step must become mature in at least a portion of your business before you move on to another. Accountability and ownership are a culture derived completely by individuals and can only come from within by those doing the work. This could take days, or it could take years, **but until it is achieved, no amount of process improvement will succeed or sustain**.

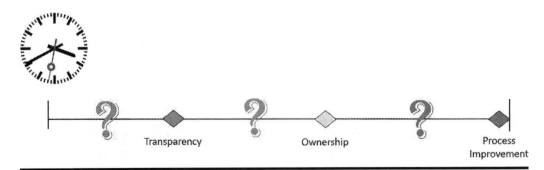

Figure 5.3 Transparency-ownership-process improvement timeline.

5.1 Process Improvement Techniques

After attaining some level of transparency and accountability, you can now apply some process improvement techniques. There are many ways to perform process improvement. The important point is that your organization has an organization-wide model for quality improvement that includes assessment, planning, implementation, and evaluation of continuous improvement. This will be a brief discussion of each process improvement methodology but will drill down in detail on plan-do-study-act (PDSA). Although there are multiple ways to do process improvement, starting with a simple approach like PDSA will <u>get you going in the right direction</u>. Additional sources of information and in-depth training are available for each methodology but require much longer training sessions and didactic learning.

5.1.1 Lean

Lean methodology is a business approach that promotes the flow of value to customers by embracing a mindset of continuous improvement and respect for people. Unfortunately, it isn't always understood. Many folks make statements like "Lean out staff," "Make our work leaner," or "Lean out our workforce." They use the term *Lean* in their statements but corrupt its meaning. Let's see if we can set the record straight.

Lean Misunderstood	*Lean – A Positive Action*
"Lean out staff" = staff cuts	Eliminate double work
"Make work leaner" = shortcut processes	Remove waste and improve efficiency
"Lean out workforce" = downsize	Get people working on the correct things

There are hundreds of books on Lean, but for our purpose of instruction, I am going to distill the concepts into a few paragraphs. Let's start with some. Lean follows five basic principles:

1. Value
2. The value stream
3. Flow
4. Pull
5. Perfection

The goal and outcomes of Lean, if properly done, are:

1. Minimize waste
2. Reduce inventory
3. Increase productivity
4. Improve quality
5. Increase customer satisfaction
6. Reduce costs
7. Increase profits

Lean is a toolset, a management system, and a philosophy that can change the way hospitals and other businesses are organized and managed.

Mark Graben, in his book *Lean Hospitals*, states

> Lean is different in that the methodology shows people how to look at the details of processes, fixing things where the work is actually done, by the people who do the work, rather than relying on experts to tell them exactly what to do.[2]

My Lean instructor, Michael Hogan,[3] continuously told me that Lean was a way of thinking. Until I applied the concepts and had some significant experience with Lean, I didn't fully understand his statement. Learning and applying the concepts of Lean will change your way of thinking in many ways. You will constantly look at processes and work using an analytical mind and see waste in inventory, rework, labor, etc. and start asking questions to gain more knowledge of how the work is done. Here's an example that happened yesterday. I was working with a nurse in the emergency department, who is passionate about improving the efficiency of her department. She performed a small test of change using Lean techniques for two days by changing the way patients were triaged and entered into their system. She described the improvement as "very successful" but had little data to prove that. I started asking questions, looking at the data, and comparing the volumes and left without seeing numbers. I compared the outcomes for the two days of improvement to the rest of the year's trends to determine if there was a difference. Although two days is hardly a large enough sample to change standard operations, we still wanted to get an idea of the impact. The outcome data showed they saw an additional 22 patients per day on those days compared to the mean. Twenty-two patients a day equated to 8,030 patients a year and over $5 million in revenue. We questioned if this just happened to be two days that had a significant increase in patients or if there was an external influence. We discovered the volumes coming in the door were the same as any other day. It was the number of patients who left without being seen that was significantly lower, thereby increasing the number of patients treated. In essence, their inefficiencies were enormous. A change in operations that resulted in more happy patients being treated with an increase in revenue (win/win).

In this example and many like it, Lean enables organizations to improve efficiency, generate revenue, and improve customer satisfaction. Statements like "Lean out staff" are framed with a negative connotation and do not represent the reality of what Lean can potentially do for an organization.

5.1.2 Six Sigma

Six Sigma (6σ) is a set of techniques and tools for process improvement. It is a collection of managerial and statistical concepts and techniques that focus on reducing variation in processes and preventing deficiencies in product.

Variation in a process is denoted by sigma (σ), which is the standard deviation of measurements around the process mean. Six Sigma relies heavily on statistical methodologies to analyze and measure results.

A Six Sigma process is one in which 99.99966% of all opportunities are statistically free of defects.

Six Sigma uses a process model called DMAIC. Each letter represents a stage of the process improvement initiative, and the stages are followed in this order: define, measure, analyze, improve, and control. These stages and the steps utilized under each form a well-organized set of tools that allows you to have a clearly defined project plan approach to process improvement. It also enables learning because it reminds you of the work that needs to be done as you follow each stage of the improvement.

1. Define

   The first phase of any process improvement is to define it. This involves understanding where you are and where you want to be. The define stage called out in Six Sigma reminds you of the steps required to plan your improvement before jumping in and making changes.

   The key steps of the define phase are:
   1. Charter
   2. Problem statement
   3. Cost of poor quality (COPQ)
   4. Team identification
   5. Suppliers-inputs-process-outputs-customers (SIPOC)
   6. Critical to quality
   7. Project plan

2. Measure

   The measure phase of a Six Sigma project relies heavily on data and statistical analysis. If you are not a statistician or find little excitement in understanding statistics, do not fear. There are a multitude of educational tools that can help you through this work.

   The key steps of the measure phase are:
   1. Measure
   2. Process map(s)
   3. Data collection
   4. Measurement system analysis (MSA)
   5. Baseline performance
   6. Process capability
   7. Pareto
   8. Cause/effect
   9. Failure modes effects analysis (FMEA)

3. Analyze

   The analyze phase of Six Sigma enables you to start developing theories related to the cause of your problem. This is a phase that generally excites the team because of the time that was invested in defining and measuring the problems and processes before they could move ahead. Most people want to jump in and start creating solutions to problems on day one, but the Six Sigma model keeps you from doing that to prevent going down the wrong path.

   The key steps of the analyze phase are:
   1. Theories listed
   2. Data collection plan
   3. Theories tested
   4. List proven causes

4. Improve

   A team generally gets very excited at the improve phase. This is where everyone rolls up their sleeves to start making changes. The clear distinction with Six Sigma is that, as you create an improvement, you should know exactly what data you are expecting to impact by each change. This enables you to carefully monitor the impact the change has (either negative or positive) on the outcomes you predicted. Never assume your improvement plans will work out exactly how you planned them. There are always anomalies that must be addressed in this phase of the project that will lead you to additional learnings. A good process improvement expert is able to roll with the punches and readily adopt new or different techniques.

The key steps of the improve phase are:

1. List remedies for each root cause
2. Pugh matrix
3. Design of experiments
4. Revised process map
5. Updated FMEA
6. Implementation plan
7. Statistical analysis – results

5. Control

The control phase of Six Sigma is where you step back and watch the new processes that have been implemented. This is the most criticized phase of Six Sigma. This is because of the relationship between control and actually sustaining the changes that were implemented. Sustainment is a problem across all process improvement techniques. There are many valid theories as to why, but Six Sigma specifically calls out the control phase to help you mitigate those issues.

The key steps of the control phase are:

1. Control plan
2. Communication and training plans
3. Control charts
4. Statistical analysis
5. Results – Metrics and cost of poor quality (COPQ)
6. Project plan
7. Lessons learned

Fun Facilitation Idea: When working on large project using Six Sigma, participants are sometimes frustrated because they are not allowed to jump ahead into the improve phase with solutions. Everyone has a tendency to "jump to a conclusion." A way to lighten this anxiety and make it fun is to put a jar in the improvement room called the "out of order" jar (or something like that). When someone on the team wants to jump to solutions for implementation they are required to put a dollar in the jar along with the solution they wanted to implement. When your team does get to the improvement phase, start off this phase with a celebration and use the money that is in the jar to fund lunch for the team. During that celebration, open all of the solutions previously submitted and see how relevant they are to the team's finalized improvement plan. You may be surprised to witness the fun dialogue and camaraderie that energizes the team forward into the implementation phase.

Six Sigma tends to get a lot of bad publicity mainly due to the strict project plan and time frame. Hospital leadership may lack the patience to follow all the steps in Six Sigma for the period of time it normally takes to complete. This is generally not a problem just because it is Six Sigma. The problem arises when a process improvement expert has little or no flexibility in the way process improvement is done, without considering the operational need to achieve an outcome. If, for example, the business requires a solution in one month and the Six Sigma approach is only set up to do an improvement over six months, the Six Sigma approach will fail. Most timelines for Six Sigma programs are defined by their process improvement methodology rather than the actual business need. Just because its approach is typically more complex than other improvement methodologies does not mean the DMAIC steps cannot be expedited. A one-month DMAIC process improvement is certainly achievable.

5.1.3 ISO 9001

ISO 9001 is the international standard that specifies the requirements for a quality management system (QMS). Organizations use the standard to demonstrate their ability to consistently provide products and services that meet customer and regulatory requirements. It is the most popular standard in the ISO 9000 series and the only standard in the series to which organizations can certify.

ISO 9000 is not specific to healthcare. These standards were first published in 1987 by the International Organization for Standardization (ISO). The 9001 version was released in 2015.

ISO follows seven quality management principles:

1. QMP 1 – Customer focus
2. QMP 2 – Leadership
3. QMP 3 – Engagement of people
4. QMP 4 – Process approach
5. QMP 5 – Improvement
6. QMP 6 – Evidence-based decision making
7. QMP 7 – Relationship management

If your organization utilizes DNV as their accreditation agency for CMS, ISO 9001 standards[4] are required within three years.

5.1.4 Plan-Do-Study-Act (PDSA)

> If I had one hour to save the world, I would spend 55 minutes defining the problem and only five minutes finding the solution.
>
> Albert Einstein

Lean, Six Sigma, and the standards of ISO 9001 are all very in-depth process improvement methodologies not described in detail here. More time is spent on this next section of process improvement known as plan-do-study-act (PDSA). This book is intended to be an overview of the necessary steps to create a quality management system in healthcare. Process improvement is one of those necessary steps, and PDSA has versatile and implementable techniques that can be easily understood by most people in the organization. The other tools and techniques are invaluable and highly recommended but they are more complicated, and it will require more time to grasp all that is packed in them. As we know, quality improvement involves everyone in the organization. Because of this, it's reasonable to have a process improvement methodology that everyone can understand and participate in.

The PDSA cycle is designed to be used as a dynamic continuous improvement model – allowing the energy (e.g., the ideas and possible solutions) from one phase to continue to the next. The cycle will ensure that the root cause is identified and subsequently create the correct plan to put proper measures in place to eliminate it. However, if the problem persists (e.g., the root cause was not identified correctly or no controls were implemented), then the cycle will repeat itself.

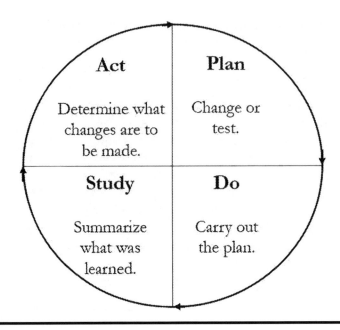

Figure 5.4   PDSA cycle.

5.1.4.1 PDSA's Three Magical Questions

PDSA has three main questions at its foundation. The simplicity of asking these three questions leads to tremendous insight. Have you ever asked someone in the middle of doing something, "What are you trying to accomplish?" It trains the brain to think about the outcome before you start. Someone driving their car for example, may just think they are driving, but if you ask them what are they trying to accomplish (rather than what they are doing), they may explain they are "going to the grocery store." If others are in the car, they may think they are going to get ice cream.

What are we trying to accomplish?

How will we know that a change is an improvement

What change can we make that will result in improvement?

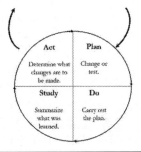

Figure 5.5   PDSA cycle questions.

In this case, both know *what* they are doing – driving – but each one has a different goal in mind. Stating the exact goal you are trying to accomplish gets everyone on the same page and working towards the same goal.

How will we know that a change is an improvement? This question addresses the need to define what an improvement looks like. Since everyone's perspectives are different, the team needs to define what will be a success: 10% improvement, 40%?

What change can we make that will result in improvement? This is *what* you are going to do to try to make the improvement.

PDSA is an iterative process. There are no failures. If the first process improvement does not result in the improvement you were looking for, you have still succeeded. How? You succeed by learning from each PDSA and improving the next one. Suppose you initiated a process to improve the wait time for patients in your clinic. In implementing the change, you found a significant reduction in wait time, but you also saw a reduction in customer satisfaction. The PDSA was successful in determining ways to reduce wait times but equally successful in showing you how that change impacted customer satisfaction. Your next improvement can work to address both those needs. In a process that did not return the expected result, you learned that the intervention that you tried will not lead you to the desired result. The next PDSA will start with that learning in mind.

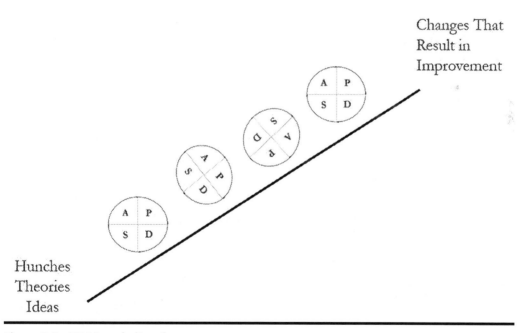

Figure 5.6 PDSA cycle iterations.

5.1.4.2 The Steps

Plan – The first step of the PDSA cycle is to choose an area that offers the most return for the effort and provides the biggest bang for your buck – the low-hanging fruit.

- Identify the problem – not the symptom.
- Write a SMART (specific, measurable, attainable, realistic, time-sensitive) improvement goal.
- Determine what you need to do to achieve the goal.

Do – Implement the change you chose in the plan phase. Communicate what is happening to everyone affected by the change. Perform the interventions in a way that isolates any external customers from any and all potential problems that may have a negative impact.

- Complete necessary training
- Prepare
- Implement change

Study – What was learned and/or what went wrong? This is a crucial step in the PDSA cycle. Once you have implemented the change for a short time, you must determine how well it is working. Is it really the improvement that you had hoped for? Decide on several measures with which you can monitor to gauge the level of improvement.

- Assess the effectiveness of the improvement strategy
- Evaluate data
- Study results

Act – After planning, implementing, and monitoring the change (improvement initiative), you must decide whether it is worth continuing the change that was done. If it consumed too much of your time, was difficult to adhere to, too expensive in resource allocations or costs, or even led to no improvement, you may consider abandoning the change and planning a new one. However, if the change led to a desirable improvement or outcome, you would expand the changes to a system- or enterprise-wide implementation.

- Take steps to make improvements permanent.
- Determine changes for the next cycle.

There are a multitude of process improvement tools (Figure 5.7) that can be used at each level of the PDSA cycle. This book is not about teaching each of those tools independently, but as you do process improvement, you can add tools as you need them and expand your knowledge in the areas of Lean, Six Sigma, total quality management (TQM), and others.

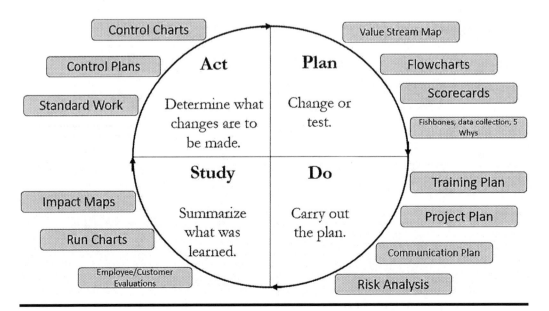

Figure 5.7   PDSA tools.

To simplify the PDSA cycle and documentation for iterations of improvement, I created this four-block form (Figure 5.8). These can be carried around with you and filled out by hand at every opportunity for improvement. The key to successful employee engagement, however, is not to *own* the project plan and activities. You can complete this form while coaching and mentoring others but ensure that everyone is accountable for the action plan in Step 4.

Step 1 is outlining the issue (or the plan phase). What is the issue, and what are we trying to accomplish? This form clearly asks, "What about this condition isn't ideal?" This forces us to think through the real issue or problem. We often attempt to mitigate or apply improvements to the symptom of a problem rather than looking deep into the actual problem. For example, "We have a high number of errors in applications." This is a symptom of many other problems, such as misunderstanding, configuration errors, the clarity of the question, etc. In Step 1, we also clearly identify the measurement criteria. How do we currently measure it? How did we know it was a problem to begin with? What is the current measurement status? Many times, we express problems in the form of anecdotal statements or feelings. These types of problems can never be improved because you are unable to determine if the intervention you applied had an impact on the outcome since it is not measured. Many PDSAs actually start with an improvement on setting up collection and measurement criteria just so you can apply an improvement. If the problem cannot be measured, ideas are generated and developed to obtain baseline measurements. For example, "I spend way too much time fixing application errors, and it is a waste of time." The question would be "How much time do you spend fixing application errors?" If that cannot be measured, the next step of the PDSA would be to do some analysis to get the specific amount of time it takes to fix an error. Interventions are then applied to that baseline measure, and it is remeasured to determine whether the interventions made an improvement.

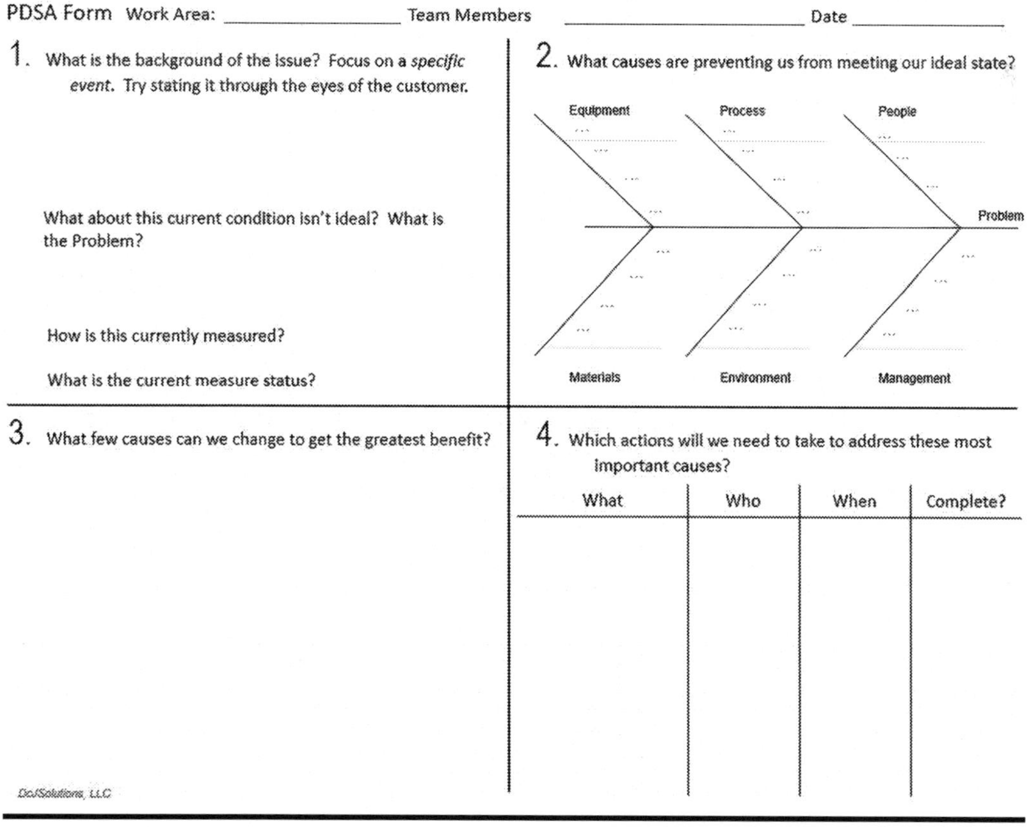
PDSA Form Work Area: ________ Team Members ________ Date ________

1. What is the background of the issue? Focus on a *specific event*. Try stating it through the eyes of the customer.

What about this current condition isn't ideal? What is the Problem?

How is this currently measured?

What is the current measure status?

2. What causes are preventing us from meeting our ideal state?

3. What few causes can we change to get the greatest benefit?

4. Which actions will we need to take to address these most important causes?

What	Who	When	Complete?

DoJSolutions, LLC

Figure 5.8 PDSA template.

Step 2 of the PDSA deals with root-cause analysis. It utilizes a Ishikawa fishbone diagram[5] for our purposes. Although this is not the only root-cause analysis tool that can be used, it is generally used for PDSAs. Here, the problem is listed to the right of the categories. Six categories are listed that contribute to the problem. These categorizes are not set in stone; rather, they are used as suggestions. It is particularly helpful to use the categories with people so they can focus their minds on root causes in multiple areas. For example, one person may have it in their mind that the root cause of the problem is the customers. They feel the customers don't follow their instructions; consequently, it leads to a problem. As you look at the problem and guide the team to look at other contributing areas, it opens up the possibility of other factors. As you progress through the fishbone categories, you may find that the customer isn't given the tools to follow the healthcare instructions as you expected.

Step 3 is when you list the ideas that you want to implement. It is not recommended to attempt to solve every problem and identify every root cause concurrently. This can cause a mess of unknown countermeasures and have a bad effect on your outcomes. For example, if you feel the customer web application is not configured correctly for a specific measure, don't waste resources changing the entire website at the same time when a simple change to the configuration of one field may give you the desired result. Try one thing and see if that change by itself has the desired effect. If not, add another improvement and measure again.

Step 4 is the plan – This is the most underutilized area of process improvement. Everyone wants to get engaged in improving things and give their ideas and input, but few want their name attached to a task – much less a task with a due date! If you skip this step, you will soon be ineffective at process improvement. Assign the specific task; give it an owner and a due date <u>right away!</u> Be cautious of ambiguous owners and multiple owners (e.g., clinical education, IT, leadership) in a task because <u>when it is more than one person's job, it is no one's job</u>. The accountability will always be deferred.

5.1.5 Root-Cause Analysis

Root-cause analysis is a popular term in healthcare quality. A root cause is defined as a factor that caused a <u>nonconformance</u> and should be <u>permanently eliminated</u> through process improvement. The root cause is the core issue – the highest-level cause – that sets in motion the entire cause-and-effect reaction that ultimately leads to the problem(s).

Using the PDSA template provided in the previous section will help you navigate the root-cause analysis method.

The key is to find the core issue. In the PDSA information in the previous section, the portion of the root-cause analysis is the Ishikawa fishbone diagram in the template (Figure 5.9).

Some things to consider when performing a root-cause-analysis:

Why do errors occur?

■ Ask "Why?" instead of "Who?"
■ The five whys method.
■ Be proactive and anticipate errors – failure modes and effects analysis (FMEA).
■ Don't settle for the statement "That's just the way we have always done it."

The way to work through issues to determine the root of the problem is with questions. When facilitating process improvement initiatives, what you say is far less important than the questions

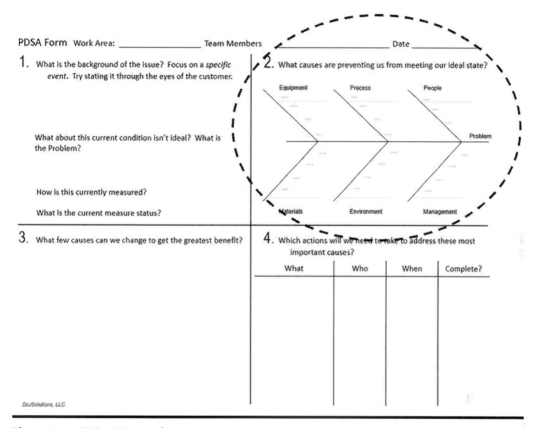

Figure 5.9 PDSA RCA section.

you ask. A methodology called the five whys is one such approach. Ask the question "Why?" up to five times to get to the root cause. Here is an example:

Problem statement – The patient had a central line–associated infection.

1. Why did the patient end up with an infection? "Because they were in the hospital a long time."
2. Why did being in the hospital a long time impact this? "Because they needed many dressing and catheter changes."
3. Why does the number of catheter or dressing changes contribute to infection? "Because it introduces much more room for contamination error."
4. Why is there risk for error? "Because not everyone manages the dressings based on policy or evidence-based practice."
5. Why doesn't everyone manage the dressings according to policy? "Because the policy is unclear and not well understood."

In this example, had the facilitator not asked *why?* multiple times, the root cause may have been determined to be the fact that the patient was in the hospital for a long time. As silly as that may seem, it is a very real scenario in which clinicians often stop digging too soon and write off the complication as something they have no control over preventing.

5.2 Change Management

Change management can be defined as the methods and manners in which a company describes and implements change within both its internal and external processes. This includes <u>preparing</u> and <u>supporting</u> employees, establishing the <u>necessary steps</u> for change, and <u>monitoring pre- and post-change</u> activities to ensure successful implementation.

Figure 5.10   Change management.

We have all experienced change in our lives. How we handle change is as unique as we are as individuals. It is important to realize that humans all react to change differently at different times. I have worked with people who adopted and thrived on change for a long time, only to find out later that a different type of change was completely disruptive and stressful to them. The point is that change involves people, and you cannot ignore the fact that change elicits varying degrees of response in each individual.

Since we already discussed the normal or bell curve in relation to data, let's use it to describe change management. Figure 5.11 represents a normal distribution in relation to introducing change. The data utilized is the number of people impacted by the change. In this example, the majority of people are fairly indifferent to the change being introduced. As you move further to the right of the curve, you will find a small number of people who are in favor of the change. Go far enough and you will see people not only in favor of but also very excited about the change. The inverse is true as well. The farther you go to the left, the more people you will find who are against the change. And so passionately against it that you might hear people state they will quit their jobs before adopting the proposed change.

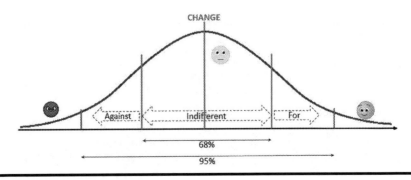

Figure 5.11   Change management curve.

Those heavily against the change may talk to those in the indifferent position and attempt to convince them the change is negative, thereby pulling more and more people to the left.

Often, failed approaches in change management are to identify people on the far left (very against) and move them to the middle of the bell curve. We think, "If only they would be indifferent and not cause a problem." There is a significant flaw in this type of thinking. It is important to realize that those people to the far right (in favor of) the change have something in common with those on the far left (very against). They both are very passionate about their beliefs and convictions. It is impossible to take a very passionate person from the left and move them over to the indifferent area. They are not indifferent people. They never have been. You must work with each of these people and strive to move them from the far left to the far right, keeping them in the only category they belong in – passionate.

It may seem impossible to move someone from the far left to the far right. After all, that requires a large journey to convert their thought process. Actually, it doesn't. If you were a physician and you truly felt that the change that was being proposed would harm patients, wouldn't you be passionately against it? The fact is that physician may have some well-founded risks about the change being introduced. Your job in change management and process improvement is to be aware of that information and those concerns. This is not an exercise in manipulation. Understanding why people are against a change will enable you to come up with more informed changes and improve your ability to get them implemented.

A simple exercise, compliments of George Eckes[6] in his book *Making Six Sigma Last*, involves a change management assessment at the employee level. In this assessment, you should first list all the people your change will impact and list them in a tool resembling Figure 5.12.

The first step in utilizing this model is to assess where each person needs to be in order for the change to be effective. In some cases, this is easy to understand, and in others, it is not. For example, if the change involves the housekeeping department because it changes their workload and schedules, the director of that department could significantly impact the success of the change, depending on their perception of it. In this case, you would need them to be strongly for the change. This assessment should not be based solely on organizational roles or levels of leadership. You should also assess employees based on their influence within the process. Every group has what can be described as informal leaders. These are the people who are usually highly respected and looked up to in their roles. They may have been at the organization for a number of years, have a lot of experience, or be consulted by peers.

Stakeholder	Strongly Against	Somewhat Against	Indifferent	Somewhat For	Strongly For
CEO					X
CNO			X		
Nursing Director				X	
Charge Nurse					X
Housekeeping Director					X

X = Need to Be

Figure 5.12 Stakeholder analysis where they are.

You should be recognizing at this point is that change is personal. There is no one-size-fits-all approach to adopting and accepting change. You need to assess each person individually for their perception of the change.

Once you identify where you believe people should be in the change management grid, it is time to meet with them and determine where they are. This does not need to be significantly complex. When you meet with them, describe the change that you are proposing and get their reactions. This comes through verbal and non-verbal communication, so meeting in person is the best way to do this. After this meeting, it should be fairly obvious to you where to place them on the change management grid. Using a different symbol, update the change management grid for each individual where you assess them to be. Figure 5.13 is an example showing where each person needs to be and where you think they are.

Stakeholder	Strongly Against	Somewhat Against	Indifferent	Somewhat For	Strongly For
CEO			O		X
CNO			X	O	
Nursing Director				⊗	
Charge Nurse					⊗
Housekeeping Director		O			X

X = Need to Be   O = Where they Are

Figure 5.13 Stakeholder analysis where they need to be.

Now that your assessment is done, you can look at the gaps on an individual level (Figure 5.14). In some cases, people are more for the change than they need to be. In others, there is a gap that is negative. You can now spend your efforts specifically on the things that prevent those with these negative gaps from being where they need to be.

Stakeholder	Strongly Against	Somewhat Against	Indifferent	Somewhat For	Strongly For
CEO			O ⟶		X
CNO			X ⟵ O		
Nursing Director				⊗ √	
Charge Nurse					⊗ √
Housekeeping Director		O ⟶			X

X = Need to Be   O = Where they Are

Figure 5.14 Stakeholder analysis gaps.

In the example, the CEO and the housekeeping director are not as supportive as you need them to be. Efforts should be made to understand why and to mitigate their concerns. All learners are different. Some may require additional data to become more comfortable. Others may need to see a process that is related to what you are proposing, and still others may need literature that supports the change. In any event, it is important that you determine each person's needs and work to alleviate their concerns through those methods. By following this approach, you will probably learn something along the way. The reasons for their lack of acceptance may be well founded, and they will introduce things that you overlooked or did not consider. Finding those things and addressing them not only makes those naysayers more in favor of the change, but it also creates a more successful improvement.

5.3 Summary

In summary, we introduced the concepts of transparency, ownership/accountability, and process improvement. These steps are critical to achieving quality patient care. We shared some high-level details about Lean, Six Sigma, ISO 9001, PDSA, and root-cause analysis. You can use each of these, as well as others, to instill process improvement capabilities into your organization when the time is appropriate. Lastly, we discussed change management and the importance of working with individuals to make it happen.

5.3.1 Key Concepts

- Transparency, ownership/accountability, and process improvement – Process improvement is last. Make sure the steps of transparency and ownership/accountability are not overlooked.
- Process improvement should address assessment, planning, improvement, and evaluation of continuous improvement. Most if not all techniques will provide this pathway, but there are many process improvement methodologies to choose from.
- PDSA is a process improvement methodology that can be easily understood, taught, and adopted by everyone in the organization. Since quality is everyone's responsibility, having a tool that they can apply will serve your organization better.
- Change management is an intentional activity. Through the culture of change, specifically addressing change management techniques will yield much better outcomes in process improvement.

5.3.2 Areas You Can Geek Out On

- Lean
  - Kim Barnas, *Beyond Heroes: A Lean Management System for Healthcare* (ThedaCare Center for Healthcare Value) 2014.
  - David Mann, *Creating a Lean Culture: Tools to Sustain Lean Conversions* (Productivity Press) 2005.
  - Charles Kenney and Donald M. Berwick, *Transforming Healthcare: Virginia Mason Medical Center's Pursuit of the Perfect Patient Experience* (CRC Press) 2010.
  - Books about the Toyota manufacturing model that later was referred to as Lean
    - Jeffrey K. Liker, *The Toyota Way: 14 Management Principles from the World's Greatest Manufacturer* (McGraw-Hill) 2004.

- Mike Rother, *Toyota Kata: Managing People for Improvement, Adaptiveness, and Superior Results* (McGraw-Hill) 2010.
- Jeffery K. Liker and David Meier, *Toyota Talent: Developing Your People the Toyota Way* (McGraw-Hill) 2007.

■ Six Sigma
- F. Gryna, R. Chua, and J. Defeo, *Juran's Quality Planning and Analysis for Enterprise Quality* (McGraw-Hill) 2007.

■ PDSA
- G. Langley, K. Nolan, T. Nolan, C. Norman, and L. Provost, *The Improvement Guide: A Practical Approach to Enhancing Organizational Performance* (Jossey-Bass) 1996.

■ Other performance improvement techniques
- Total quality management (TQM): https://asq.org/quality-resources/total-quality-management.
- Continuous quality improvement (CQI): www.ncbi.nlm.nih.gov/books/NBK559239/.
- Malcolm Baldrige National Quality: https://baldrigefoundation.org/.

■ Root-cause analysis (RCA)
- Bjorn Anderson and Tom Fagerhaug, *Root Cause Analysis: Simplified Tools and Techniques*, Second Edition (ASQ Quality Press) 2006.
- Bjorn Anderson and Tom Fagerhaug, *The ASQ Pocket Guide to Root Cause Analysis* (Quality Press) 2013.

■ Change management
- George Eckes, *Making Six Sigma Last: Managing the Balance between Cultural and Technical Change* (John Wiley & Sons, Inc.) 2001.
- Jeffrey Hiatt and Timothy Creasey, *Change Management: The People Side of Change* (Prosci) 2003.
- Stephen C. Beeson, MD, *Engaging Physicians: A Manual to Physician Partnership* (Fire Starter Publishing) 2009.

Notes

1 *To Err is Human: Building a Safer Health System*, Institute of Medicine (US) Committee on Quality of Health Care in America.
2 www.markgraban.com/.
3 Michael Hogan, Progressive Business Solutions, LLC
4 www.iso.org/.
5 Ishikawa fishbone diagram: https://asq.org/quality-resources/fishbone.
6 www.georgeeckes.com/.

Chapter 6

Quality Training

6.1 Role of the Quality Professional in Training

This chapter will address the role of the quality professional in quality training. This chapter does not utilize the same techniques as professional educators implementing lesson plans. Those specifically trained to be educators are very specialized in this area of expertise. Although it is always good to seek their counsel on methods for education, the training done by quality professionals and described here is less formalized and outlines a practical approach for everyday quality management.

If I were to ask you, "What is the role of a quality director?" what would your answer be? Allow me to share some common responses:

"Trains quality principles."
"Accountable for results!"
"Own quality for the organization."
"Support caregivers."
"Facilitate improvements."
"Oversee outcomes and make adjustments."

Was your answer within this realm? All these answers (and many not listed) contain valuable information, specifically that there is a common perception of quality professionals "owning" or "being accountable for" quality. As mentioned earlier, quality professionals *do not* own quality; those individuals who provide and do the work directly for the customer/patients are the true and proper owners of organizational quality. **We support them**.

If you are a quality professional or want to be one, before you get comfortable with the fact that you don't own quality, remember the responsibility you own is very significant. The responsibilities of communicating the quality plan and initiatives; educating all staff on quality improvement initiatives, including leaders; engaging all employees in quality initiatives; overseeing the current state, past performance, and future goals; and simplifying the complexity of accreditation, quality rules, and reporting are absolutely critical to the proper functioning of an organization.

As discussed in Chapter 3, if quality takes place at the point where care is provided, the efforts of the quality professional must be applied there as well. Your goal as a quality professional must be to engage with and influence the people providing care for your patients in the quality agenda.

DOI: 10.4324/9781003358404-7

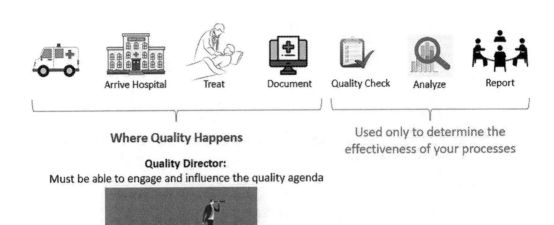

Figure 6.1 High-level patient process quality involvement.

"Every moment is a teaching moment." We have heard statements like this before as we raise children or work with others. As a quality professional, you should always keep this statement in the forefront of your thoughts. It will keep you alert to opportunities to use as teaching moments.

> Every moment is a teaching moment.
>
>   Pat Summit

What are some of the ways that you can turn each moment into a teaching moment? There is always formal training. Set up some slides on PDSA, for example, and bring a group together and train them in process improvement concepts. Go beyond the formal training approach and embrace the significance of something as simple as utilizing your daily dialogue. Utilizing questions like those found in the PDSA model and applying them in normal conversations is powerful. "What are we trying to accomplish?"; "How will we know a change is an improvement?"; "What change can we make that will result in an improvement?" Use the five whys. We all benefit from asking why more often. Asking why will elicit learning for everyone speaking and listening; it's not just for your benefit! In order to be a good educator, you must first observe, learn, and ask many relevant questions. Ken Coleman, author of the book *One Question,*[1] said **"Good questions inform, great questions transform."** It is not the statements you use that will teach the people and make your organization successful; it is the art of asking the right questions at the right place and time. The next time you are in a group discussion or facilitating a group discussion, practice asking questions instead of making statements. Intentionally work on thinking through which question you might ask while the group dialogue is taking place. Chances are there are some key things people are not thinking about, and all they need is a question to set them in the right direction.

Another skill that a good quality professional holds is the ability to simplify the message. There are many seemingly complex areas in healthcare and quality management. The CMS five-star methodologies, calculating the standardized infection ratio (SIR) rate, understanding Lean concepts, and calculating a disease-specific 30-day mortality rate appear hard. When you break concepts like these down for people, remember they are not experts in each one. First, try to understand what they need to know, and present the information that is relevant and applicable to the work they do each day. This involves the use of analogies, examples and, in some cases, didactic material. You, as the educator, are responsible for breaking this down in a way that can easily be understood.

As an exercise, I challenge you to work with your peers and each share a recent dialogue you had with a clinician. What areas of this conversation could have been used as teaching moments? How can asking the right questions direct the conversation differently?

6.2 Employee Engagement

Engagement with nurses, physicians, and employees is part of every technique delivered in quality management. Tools such as PDSA, root-cause analysis, defining the quality strategy, communicating results, and performing process improvement initiatives all help support engagement. There are certainly techniques related to employee engagement, but one thing to always keep in mind is that engagement isn't something you do to people; it is something you are. How would you feel if someone met with you and said, "I am here to engage you," versus "I'd like to discuss your ideas and thoughts so we can work together to improve quality."

Before talking specifically about engaging people, it is important to understand what engages us.

6.2.1 Motivation

Motivation comes in two forms: extrinsic and intrinsic.

Extrinsic motivation is reward-driven behavior. It involves working at activities in order to gain some type of known, external reward. Examples of extrinsic motivation are praise, awards, fame, bonuses, a pizza party, and money. This motivational technique is most commonly associated with the carrot-and-stick management style of command and control. The carrot is the reward for doing well. The stick is punitive when you don't.

Figure 6.2 Carrot and stick.

Source: Christoph Roser at AllAboutLean.com under the free CC-BY-SA 4.0 license

Knowing this about extrinsic motivation may lead you to ask, "Does it work?" It depends on the situation. Extrinsic motivational techniques can be effective for mechanical, rule-based, simple, short-term work for which there are a simple set of rules and a clear solution. Extrinsic motivational techniques can be applied to a group of employees for a short period of time. However, if you are using this type of motivation as a standard mode of ongoing operations, you will be disappointed. Allow me to share a successful, short-term example of extrinsic motivation. We were opening a brand-new hospital. All the supplies and equipment for the clinical units were delivered and ready to be deployed. In an effort to get the sizeable quantity of items distributed, we asked for volunteers from the staff (and their families) to spend a Saturday with us at the hospital, getting things in order. In return, they would get a pizza party celebration at the end of the day. This task involved simple instructions and a clear solution. The attendance was extraordinary. Over half the staff showed up with their spouses and significant others! The benefits of this exercise not only allowed us to get the task done under budget, but it also created an incredible opportunity to initiate a culture of collaboration and teamwork not just among employees but also their family members.

This example worked as a single event and one-time need. If we had decided to continue Saturday events by outlining work and providing a pizza party, the participation would have quickly dwindled.

The second technique is known as intrinsic motivation. This form of motivation comes from within. Activities motivated by intrinsic motivation are done because people enjoy the work, and they get personal satisfaction from it. An interesting point about intrinsic motivation is that if you try to use an extrinsic motivational technique on people who are intrinsically motivated, you will actually demotivate them. Imagine that you were very passionate about patient care, and you really wanted to make a difference in the outcomes for those patients. By employing self-study, you research the literature, engage other clinicians, and come up with a plan to provide more efficient quality patient care. With this information, you implement your plan, and the data shows a clear improvement in efficiency and quality patient care. Without realizing the impacts, you also notice a significant increase in patient and employee satisfaction and increased revenue for the organization. Everyone is overwhelmed and excited with the results! Then your boss shows up and hands you a fifty-dollar gift certificate for a local restaurant. Although the gift is a nice gesture and gratefully accepted, the purpose for implementing this plan had nothing to do with the reward of receiving a gift certificate.

Now imagine another scenario. Like before, you are very excited about improving patient care. You have some great ideas, and you want to implement them. Before moving forward with the resources and funding you need to implement these new ideas, you seek approval from the boss. As you explain the plan, your boss responds with statements like "We tried this before, and it didn't work," and "I don't think senior leadership will buy into this plan." You are defeated and feel powerless. Your boss later comes up with a plan much like the one you proposed and tells the staff they will receive a $100 bonus if they participate. How likely are you to jump on board for the $100 bonus?

The fact is, if you try to reward an intrinsically motivated person with extrinsic rewards, it will eventually fail. Although we all need the financial incentive to work and provide for ourselves and our families, intrinsically motivated people do not get out of bed every day because of the extrinsic rewards. They are passionate about what they do, how they do it, and the impact they make in their community.

Daniel Pink, in his book *Drive: The Surprising Truth about What Motivates Us*,[2] speaks of three components of intrinsic motivation. The first is autonomy. This is the need to direct your own life. If you want engagement, you need to create an environment for self-direction. An example is Google. They have a concept called 20% time, in which employees are encouraged to work on anything they want for 20% of their working hours. About half of Google's product innovations come from that 20% time. The second is mastery. This is the desire to improve at something that matters to you. Solving complex problems requires an inquiring mind and the willingness to experiment one's way to a fresh solution. The last is <u>purpose</u>. Purpose is to be in service of something worthy and larger than ourselves. It is important that employees have a connection to a purpose. This is not how they do the work, but why they do it.[3] Leadership's role is to bring people together to create value, realizing no single person can achieve it by themselves. Observe people working in your organization. Do they refer to the company as "they" or "we"?

How does all this motivation discussion fit into the role of a quality professional? If you remember, earlier we discussed where quality exists in caring for patients. Quality happens where the work is actually done. If you are going to be effective leading people to better quality results, you must be able to engage and motivate them to do so.

> Hire good people, and leave them alone.
>
> William McKnight
> (president and chairman of 3M)

There are three activities that the quality professional and leadership *must* address before they can turn their attention to those in the organization:

1. Define the ideal behaviors (beginning with themselves) based on their understanding of the principles they want the organization to aspire to.
2. Personally practice and model the ideal behaviors.
3. Create new kinds of conversations in their interactions with others, in particular the conversations with people on the front line. (I call them "the value creators.")

Defining ideal behaviors means specifically stating which behavioral techniques best represent your organization. Do you want people to be friendly, learners, respectful, or accountable? These are a few of the behavioral principles I have seen organizations aspire to. Once defined, these behaviors should be clearly spoken about, rewarded, and observed throughout the organization. For example, one organization wanted to be known as "friendly" to their customers and staff. They implemented a five-foot rule, meaning if you came within five feet of another human being (customer or employee), you were expected to acknowledge that person. Acknowledgement came in many forms: a simple hello, eye contact with a nod of the head, or a smile. The experience that customers had went well beyond the service they received. They felt like they were welcome, they mattered, and staff was glad to have them there. In this example, the concept of being "friendly" was specifically defined through behaviors that demonstrated it.

Personal practice in modeling these behaviors is critical. Once you identify the behaviors important to your organization, the best way to implement them is through demonstration. Watching your CEO walk through the organization utilizing the techniques expected of all employees motivates everyone to follow suit. The inverse is also true and can be very detrimental to your goals. If your CEO demands that you follow the five-foot rule yet personally ignores everyone they pass throughout the day, they show they are not interested in the behavioral principles and will push employees to act out negatively against them. Make this more personal and think of yourself as a quality professional. If you convince your staff you are passionate about quality patient care yet you continually ignore patient care incidents that should be addressed, you are doing the same thing. You will not be able to motivate others in the organization to be passionate about quality patient care.

Lastly, in order to keep your behavioral principles active and alive, you must create new conversations utilizing these principles with others in the organization. These can be formal conversations, such as having an agenda item on your daily safety huddle to speak about examples of people demonstrating these principles. They can also be informal, such as pointing out positive behavior and thanking someone in the moment or shortly after.

6.2.2 Assessing the Current State of Employee Engagement

The current state of your employees' engagement can be assessed by asking a few questions.

Q: How are you currently engaging with directors, managers, and staff?

A: This question seems simple, but I challenge you to find the answers. Typically, there are many answers to this question, depending on who you ask. A culture that has opportunity for improvement is one in which each person randomly answers the question in a way that is not consistent with others. For example, "We have a monthly all-hands meeting where the C-level team communicates to the employees," or "We do daily safety huddles where each department reports out any safety issues." These answers provide some substance, but they are scratching the surface of what could be. Engagement among staff must be designed, planned, and intentional.

A better finding for this assessment may be a standardized answer involving a known communication plan outlining the activities relevant to each method of engagement. For example, "Our communication plan outlines what we are trying to accomplish through multiple activities in the organization. Our quarterly all-hands employee meeting is a venue for our leadership to share our vision, mission, values, and strategic plans and the current status of our initiatives. We have a daily huddle with all department leaders to discuss patient safety events and daily operations. Our department leaders have daily huddles with their teams utilizing daily huddle boards. Here employees can bring up opportunities for improvement, discuss improvements, and review their specific operational metrics." Although this example is a simplified version of what it could be, by using it, you should understand the intentionality of an organization having a communication and engagement plan that is understood. Leaders should be able to easily speak to it.

	Description	Frequency	Audience	Delivery Method	Purpose
	Governing Board	Monthly	C-Suite and Board Members	In Person Meeting	Govern operations and strategic initiatives
	Newsletter	Monthly	Employees and Physicians	Email	Inform activities, changes, success stories, current strategic status
	IntraNet	Ongoing	Internal Employees	IntraNet	Current updates, events, notifications
	Leadership Meeting	Weekly	C-Suite, Director/Manager all Departments	In Person Meeting	Current Updates, HR, Quality, Marketing, Provider Services
	Safety Huddle	Daily	C-Suite, Director/Manager all Departments	Phone Conference	20 Minute call-in to report out current status and safety issues
	Unit Huddles	Daily	Director/Manager for each Department with all Employees	In Person Meeting	Daily unit status, safety, measurements, and updates

Figure 6.3 Communication plan.

Q: Do you see evidence of command-and-control management styles?

A: A command-and-control approach to leadership is authoritative in nature and uses a top-down approach, which fits well in bureaucratic organizations in which privilege and power are vested in senior management. It is founded on and emphasizes a distinction between executives and workers.

Q: Are you giving staff the ability to raise problems, present opportunities for improvement, or share ideas?

A: It is one thing to tell everyone you want their ideas and input to make the organization better, but when you give them no means to do so, it becomes lip service. As a quality professional, always have a means to obtain feedback from front-line employees. This can be through an application, email, or even a phone call. The point is, they must know how they can express their concerns and feel confident that they are being listened to. Feedback mechanisms for problems, opportunities, and ideas must be in place. Often, people claim they submitted an idea "into a black hole" as a result of never receiving feedback.

Q: When problems surface, what is the process to solve them?

A: Once problems hit the surface, a specific process must be in place to address it. The process to work through these issues should also include a prioritization mechanism, allowing you to address the top concerns addressed. You will never be able to address all concerns, but if you prioritize them in a consistent manner and share the prioritization results with everyone, people will understand why their concern is or is not being addressed.

6.3 Catch-Ball Sessions

Another effective way to engage people is through what's called a catch-ball session. Meetings where the loudest voice and most outgoing person monopolize the time and the views of everyone are very frustrating. The catch-ball session is an approach that enables everyone to be heard and reduces the ability of one person to monopolize the entire discussion.

This process allows for feedback and ideas from people at all levels of the organization, decreases barriers to cross-functional collaboration, clarifies ownership and accountability, and allows you to align goals and objectives.

The catch-ball approach is simple:

1. Identify participants (from the systems/service lines impacted).
2. Create an agenda with ground rules.
3. Share the purpose and vision of the meeting.
4. Share relevant information with the team.
5. Use the catch-ball process during the meeting.

Identifying participants for your catch-ball session first involves understanding the process you are studying. Within that process, who are the key people involved? For example, if you are looking at pressure ulcer prevention, what are they key processes, policies, and practices that address skin care and pressure ulcer prevention? In this case, participants from the emergency department, inpatient units, dietary department, materials management, and wound care would be appropriate. The point is not to select people who are just willing and the most vocal about the topic. Find out who is involved in the daily operations related to this topic and actively seek them out.

Creating an agenda with ground rules is a simple yet very important part of catch-ball sessions. The agenda creates a sense of professionalism and importance about the work you are trying to accomplish. Meetings without agendas eventually suffer from lack of attendance and participation. An agenda, on the other hand, outlines specifically what is being addressed, who is participating, and what is expected of them. An example of an agenda is provided in Figure 6.4. This agenda is specific to developing strategic initiatives for the organization. Each organization will have their own organizational style to add to the agenda, but some key things will set each meeting in the right direction and eliminate confusion.

1. Date, time and location
2. Purpose of the meeting – a one-sentence explanation of why you are meeting
3. Attendees – list of those attending

Company Name
Strategic Initiative Determination

Date & Time: _____

Location: _____

Purpose of the Meeting: Determine the Two Strategic Initiatives to pursue for the current year.

Attendees

Agenda

	Topic	Leader	Time
1	Welcome, Background and Introduction		3 min
2	Company's Purpose		3 min
3	Worksheet: Current State: "Strategic Initiative Planning"		25-30 min
4	Identify Future State Catch Ball		25-30 min
5	Worksheet: "Initiative Overview" - Define Initiatives Catch Ball		25-30 min
6	Review scheduled future meetings and next steps		3 min

Catch Ball Rules:

Be Present
Participate by providing honest input
Say AND, not BUT
Think creatively
Be open minded

Expectations:

Cell Phones go to in the "Cell Phone Jail" basket (group consensus to allow individual deviation)
Be Present
Speak up and be heard: No silent objectors in the room

Figure 6.4   Catch-ball agenda.

4. Agenda topics with the facilitator for each topic and time allotted
5. Meeting rules
6. Meeting expectations – the expectations of the participants

Sharing relevant information prior to the meeting accompanied by the agenda can make your meeting more efficient. In the example utilized for pressure injury prevention, you may provide the relevant measures related to pressure injuries in your organization. This information can pro-actively address questions by participants who may wonder if there is a pressure injury problem or be unaware of any process issues leading to them.

CELL PHONE JAIL

A colleague of mine, Suzanne, came up with the concept of cell phone jail in the example agenda for catch ball. If you're bold enough to actually take a person's cell phone away for a meeting, your actions will help convey the importance of what you expect them to focus on and achieve.

The catch-ball process is easy! The facilitator starts the meeting by asking questions or request-ing feedback, then passes the "ball" to anyone in the room. The person with the ball is expected to add their input, then pass the ball either back to the facilitator who will designate another person or to another person in the room. The only person allowed to speak is the one with the ball. This can be a fun exercise involving a small ball or any object you wish to use. It can feel a bit awkward for teams who have never done this before, but once you establish this form of communication in meetings, it can become the norm – with or without a ball – because people quickly understand that we are trying to get everyone's input and realize the importance of letting our peers speak without interruption.

6.4 Standard Work

Standard work is the best way to safely complete an activity with the proper outcome and the highest quality. Taichi Ohno stated, "The first step toward improvement is standardization. Where there is no standard, there can be no improvement." This can be a very daunting state-ment for someone who desperately wants to improve quality yet realizes the processes are not defined, and everyone performs them differently. Taichi Ohno is right. How can you improve a process that is as variable as the people doing them? Which process is the correct one to improve? How does one impact the other? What change would you (or could you) make that would result in a different outcome? Standard work is the very foundation of process improvement. The first step of any process improvement initiative should be to assess the standard practice of the pro-cesses leading to the undesirable outcome. If the standard is not there, create the standard first. The then outcomes can be measured and improvements applied to the process that has been standardized.

Standard work has many names and interpretations. You may have heard of SOPs (standard operating procedures), organizational policies, or procedures. The reality is that companies have literally thousands of written policies and procedures, and we would be delusional to think people are religiously referencing these documents to perform their day-to-day work. So where does that leave us?

We need to remember that there are at least three ways in which work is defined:

1. The way the work *should* be done (typically found in the policies, procedures, and SOPs).
2. The way people *tell* you how the work is done (discussing with the people doing the work, keeping in mind that the reliability of the quality depends on how they were trained or obtained their information).
3. By watching how the work is *actually* done (observing someone competent or not).

In the book *The Elegant Solution*, author Matthew E. May[4] explains, "The thought of standards makes a lot of people cringe. That's because they confuse standardization with uniformity. They think standards somehow discourage creativity. They see standards as restrictive and rigid, even oppressive." The fact is that a standard is none of these things. A true standard is created by individuals doing the work. It is a dynamic exercise. A standard is an established best-known method or practice followed until a better way is discovered, tested, and accepted.

Following Matthew May's thought process on standard work, let's take a deeper look at how this dynamic process happens.

First and foremost, an idea is sparked in a person performing the work, and they determine that some definite standard would simplify the situation. Next, the individuals who are performing the work create step-by-step instructions as to how the work needs to be carried out. Each member of the care team who is actually providing the patient care determines how it should be administered. These standards are created by the people closest to the service delivery. They are not defined by administrators in far-off buildings who are removed from the patient care delivery process. Evidence-based practices are followed in many areas of healthcare, but they tend to lack exact specifications that can be applied to individual hospitals. Each hospital has different standards for documentation, electronic medical record (EMR) systems, job descriptions, facility layouts, etc. The standard for performing work (including evidenced-based practice) is defined by those who actually perform the work.

> Imagine that you are a patient in a hospital. Each nurse who comes in to care for you does things differently; one writes your medications on the white board religiously, another nurse never touches the white board. One nurse injects your medications fast (which makes you nauseous) while another injects them slowly. One nurse checks your wound dressing and uses rubbing alcohol to wipe the drain surface each time, yet other nurses don't even look at the dressing when they come into your room. One nurse looks to make sure your catheter is draining and peeks in the bathroom to make sure everything is shipshape; the nurse on the next shift does not look at anything. How confident are you about the care you are receiving? This has *nothing* to do with friendliness or personality and *everything* to do with standard care.

Second, standard work is only the standard until a better way is discovered. This can happen daily or hourly, but the key point is that the standard is followed by everyone performing the same task.

Healthcare is a service industry. The most important person is the customer/patient we are serving. If one nurse determines a safer, more efficient way to perform the work or a manner that provides superior customer satisfaction, wouldn't you want *all* the nursing staff to be aware of the procedure so they all can work in concert? In this way, a standard can be modified for all to see, follow, and benefit from.

Finally, as we finish our discussion, it is vital to understand that standard work is *not* a piece of paper that you carry around with you. Most standardized procedures are for repetitive and ongoing tasks that employees have experience doing. The people performing them do not need to read step-by-step instructions while doing the work. It is, by definition, second nature to them. What about people relatively new to the field? In the next section, we will describe a concept called training within industry, in which standard work is taught and memorized by those who do it.

Standard work is for the benefit of employees, customers/patients, and organizational leadership. The main job of leadership is to ensure standards are followed. The only way for leadership to know if tasks are being done properly is to read the written standard work while observing. Remember, we all have different strengths in our jobs; an administrator isn't the clinician providing care. If the standards are written correctly, leadership can address any deviations they may witness by asking employees why they are doing things differently from what is stated in the standard work. It is much easier to have conversations about deviations in standard work when it was the employees themselves who wrote the document and agreed to do things a certain way, rather than being forced to follow a rule that was created and mandated by people who don't even provide the care. It is in this way that we work together as a team, look out for each other, and ensure that the work is being done correctly to provide the best patient care possible.

6.5 Training within Industry

Training within industry (TWI) is a technique used to implement and utilize standard work. It was born out of World War II during a time when new approaches to support manufacturing and build infrastructure emerged. This section is a cross between standard work and training. Because TWI merges these two things, there are important aspects of each.

One of the key concepts of TWI is <u>if the worker hasn't learned, the instructor hasn't taught</u>. This methodology puts a huge emphasis and responsibility on the trainer to get their message across in a way the learner can understand. An instructor has a very large responsibility to get the knowledge and information across to the learner. We don't get to simply use one methodology for training and blame the learner for failing when they don't comprehend the message.

Within TWI is a component called job instruction. Under Job instruction has four main steps:

1. Prepare the worker
2. Present the operation
3. Tryout performance
4. Follow-up

The first step, <u>preparing the worker</u>, places an emphasis on consciously providing an environment that enables the learner to learn. You should put the person at ease, state the job, and find out what the person already knows. Get to know your learners and understand where they are coming from. The fact is, they may already know much more about the topic than you do. Give them an opportunity to express that. Other logistics in preparing the worker involve getting them interested in learning the job you are going to train and getting them in the correct position to see and hear the instruction.

Step two of job instruction is to <u>present the operation</u>. Here you tell, show, and illustrate one important step at a time as you go through the procedure. Go through the steps again and stress the key points. Lastly, demonstrate the process a third time after describing the reasons for each of the key points. Let's use an example. Suppose you need your charge nurse to fill out the staffing matrix on a document located on your shared drive for each shift. The key steps could be: 1) Open the staffing.xlsx file on the shared drive, 2) put in the number of nurses and techs you have for the day, and 3) save the document. Those three steps are easy to follow and simple to memorize. You demonstrate this process by mentioning those three key steps. Next, you will want to demonstrate the task again, but this time you will stress the key points and describe them further. An example may be 1) open the staffing.xlsx file located on the nurse-staffing X drive by double-clicking on the file, 2) obtain the staffing numbers from your unit and type them into the specific fields, and 3) save the file and close it. This seems fairly straightforward, but there is one additional step the instructor must take. They must emphasize the reasons for each key step. Adult learners want to know why they are doing something and want to understand the importance their work has for the task at hand. In this example, while demonstrating the steps for a third time, you may say something like 1) Open the file on the X drive. This is a location that is shared by all nursing leadership, and they can reference the information you put in this location. 2) Type in your staffing numbers. This information is combined with the staffing numbers from all other units and allows leadership to gage the hospital's capacity for new patients and additional needs. 3) Save the file. Because this is on our shared drive, it does not automatically save, so until it is saved, others looking at the file will not be able to see your additions.

The third step of job instruction is performance. It is in this phase that you have the person you just trained do the job. It is during this time that you observe what they learned and correct any errors. In the same manner that you taught the steps, have them perform the task three times, starting with them explaining each important step, then each key point, and lastly the reasons why. Here is where you make sure the person understands. Do not continue until you know that they are proficient and capable.

Lastly within job instruction is follow-up. This is the most important yet often overlooked step. Do not assume when someone leaves the instruction area that they have the knowledge and will follow those steps perfectly. That seldom happens. Follow-up requires the instructor to take the time after teaching the employee to observe and answer any questions regarding the training. Here, the person is on their own to perform the task. Designate someone they can go to for help who will check on them frequently. Encourage questions and provide support in performing the standard work in a real-world environment.

Figure 6.5 is an example of a standard work document. The procedure for hand hygiene was developed by Patrick Graupp and Martha Purrier, RN, at Virginia Mason.[5] They have extensive training and literature on training within industry and are an excellent source if you would like to "geek out" on training within industry in healthcare.

DcJ Solutions STANDARD WORK & JOB BREAKDOWN SHEET	Job Function: **Hand-Hygiene-Washing**		Date:	Sheet 1 of 1
	Area:		Prepared By:	
	Operation Name:		Approved By:	Dept:
			Revision Date:	Revision Level:

#	Work Elements / Important Steps	Key Points	Reasons Why	Sketch / Drawing / Picture
1	Wet Hands	1. Without soap	Rinses away	
2	Apply soap	1. Cover surfaces	Kills all germs	
3	Rub hands	1. Palm to palm 2. Palm to backs	Clean the entire surface	
4	Rub fingers	1. Thumbs 2. Interlocking 3. Backs of fingers to palm 4. Tips to palm	1. Most active part of hand 2. Sides of fingers cleaned at one time 3. Cuticles and knuckles 4. Under fingernails	
5	Rinse	1. Leave water on	Prevent recontamination of hand	
6	Dry	1. Use towel to turn water off	Prevent recontamination	

Figure 6.5   Hand hygiene standard work.

6.6 Summary

In this chapter, we covered the role of the quality professional, including their responsibility and accountability to provide training that is meaningful and results in improved patient care. Key concepts and techniques around employee engagement were outlined. We defined standard work and the reasons for it and introduced tools for implementing standard work practices.

6.6.1 Key Concepts

- Quality professionals must be able to engage and influence the quality agenda with those providing patient care.
- Every moment is a teaching moment.
- Understanding how employees are motivated is a prerequisite to engaging them.
- Intrinsic motivation involves autonomy, mastery, and purpose.
- Define ideal behaviors, practice them, and incorporate them into everything you do.
- Develop an intentional method for communication across the organization.
- Standard work is the current, single best way to safely complete an activity with the proper outcome and the highest quality.
- Training within industry is an effective way to combine standard work and training.

6.6.2 Areas You Can Geek Out On

- Daniel Pink, *Drive: The Surprising Truth about What Motivates Us* (Penguin Group) 2009.
- Simon Sinek, *Start with Why: How Great Leaders Inspire Everyone to Take Action* (Penguin Group) 2009.
- Matthew E. May, *The Elegant Solution: Toyota's Formula for Mastering Innovation* (Free Press) 2007.
- Patrick Graupp and Martha Purrier, *Getting to Standard Work in Health Care: Using TWI to Create a Foundation for Quality Care* (Productivity Press) 2016.

Notes

1 www.ramseysolutions.com/store/books/one-question-by-ken-coleman.
2 www.danpink.com/books/drive/.
3 https://simonsinek.com/books/start-with-why/.
4 https://matthewemay.com/.
5 *Getting to Standard Work in Health Care*, (2013) Patrick Graupp, Martha Purrier, RN.

Chapter 7

Project Management

In all my years working in healthcare and around different professionals in the industry, I've found that one of the most underrecognized yet profoundly important professionals is the project manager. As a quality professional, you must have skills in project management and be able to utilize some of the key components of project management. You do not need to be a certified professional in project management. If you have the luxury of working with such a person, mentor with them and go to them for support and advice. Good project managers have skills and techniques that often take a lifetime to master, and they can be a wealth of information.

7.1 Project Management in Quality

There are a lot of activities that take place in healthcare quality management. If you focus on all these tasks without organizing them, managing them will seem insurmountable.

The role of the quality director is to orchestrate these activities and see them through to completion. The more organized you are, the more amazed you will be by the progress made.

Orchestrate all the activities going on related to managing Healthcare Quality

✓ PDSA Action Items
✓ Meeting Minute Action Items
✓ Accreditation Planning and Organization
✓ Reporting Deadlines
✓ Process Improvement Schedules & Action Items
✓ Communication, Follow-up, Communication

Figure 7.1   Orchestrate project tasks.

DOI: 10.4324/9781003358404-8

Some of the areas managed by quality professionals are PDSA action items, meeting minute action items, accreditation planning and organization, reporting deadlines, process improvement schedules, and communication plans.

Communication is the most important aspect of project management. Find creative ways to communicate what is effective for your specific audience. For example, communication to nursing director leadership may be very different from communication to hospitalist physicians. The nursing directors may have a weekly or monthly meeting you can attend where most are present. The hospitalists may also have a weekly or monthly meeting; however, many may not always attend. You will need to be creative in finding ways to get information to everyone, even if that means one on one in the hallway while they are working.

John C. Maxwell, an author, speaker, and pastor who focuses primarily on leadership, stated, "Diligent follow-up and follow-through will set you apart from the crowd and communicate excellence." Regardless of how skilled or experienced in quality management you may be, one trait we all can possess is the ability to be organized and to follow up. Use this to your advantage in any scenario, and, as John C. Maxwell points out, doing so will set you apart from the crowd and communicate excellence.

As a quality professional, you will have many action items and deadlines to work with. With all these action items and deadlines, confusion and chaos can quickly set in. This is why having a place to manage them is critical. Although you don't need to be a professional in project management, a few skills in project management will provide significant management capabilities.

An insecurity that plagues quality leaders is the thought that reminding people of tasks and deadlines creates tension and the illusion of their being the task police, ensuring everyone is doing their job. To do this correctly, you should obtain action items, accountabilities, and timelines by engaging those who are actually going to be completing the work. Ask them what task they are going to do and when they will be able to have it done. Seldom does a task require an enforced timeline unless it is accreditation mandated. In this way, when you remind them to update the status of their action items, you are only reminding them to do what they already told you they would do. Many good leaders are thankful for the reminders and your diligence in keeping them on track. Those who don't appreciate the reminders probably won't be around long anyway.

Examples of tasks that a quality professional must manage are meeting minute action items, action plans from PDSAs and process improvements, and accreditation requirements.

The Complete Idiot's Guide to Project Management[1] provides some useful techniques for managing projects. The twelve rules of project management are listed in the book.

You should:

1. Always gain consensus on project outcomes – a.k.a. always engage people in the work they are going to do.
2. Build the best team you can. Team members who are knowledgeable, capable, and willing to make changes will see far more progress.
3. Develop a plan – a plan is only a plan until a better one is discovered, but not having a plan will lead to absolute failure. Always have a plan involving the action items, accountabilities, and timelines.
4. Determine how much "stuff" you really need to get things done. Ever heard that you don't need to boil the ocean? That applies here. Narrow down what needs to be done in the short term and introduce the larger, long-range activities *after* things are making progress and only when appropriate to do so.

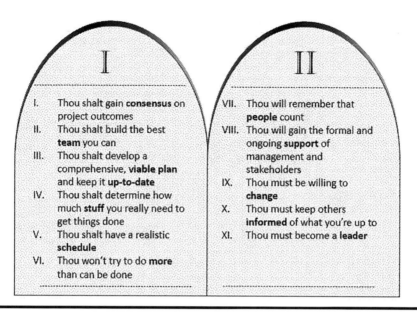

Figure 7.2 The 12 rules of project management.

5. Have a realistic schedule. This relates to the *R* in the SMART goal (relevant). Assess each task based on the capabilities of the people, timelines, organizational support, and commitment to get them done. Visionaries will want to see the perfect state right out of the gate. This can set your team up for failure and create a culture of failure that will actually harm your project management initiatives. We want a gradual, positive trajectory.

6. Don't try to do more than can be done. Much like the *S* in the SMART goals (specific), be careful not to allow a lot of "scope creep" on the project. For example, if the project is to improve patient flow in the general medical unit, you may be tempted to start your interventions hospital wide right away. By expanding the scope, your complexity is multitudes greater, significantly increasing the risk of failure in one or all areas of your plan.

7. Remember that *people* count! The project you are helping manage isn't yours – it belongs to the people doing the work. You, as project manager, cannot take the credit for the great work people do. Remember, the people doing the work are the ones who create the improvements. They have different personality traits, needs to engage, and ways they like to participate. A good project manager will the spend time to get to know every member of the team as an individual and engage them in ways that are meaningful to that person. This creates a lot of commitment to time and relationships, but it will never be time wasted.

8. Gain the ongoing support of management. Management can make or break your project. Communication with them through every step of the process is key, but it goes even deeper than that. You must understand what leadership needs, wants, and desires when it comes to project management change. Draw each of your interventions back to the things you know they are interested in and get their opinions and ideas along the way. The project manager is the go-between for the project team and leadership. In order to make things successful for your team, you must convey the work appropriately up and down the leadership chain.

9. Be willing to change. If a project manager is not willing to change, they are doing the wrong work. It is important that the members of your team are also willing to make changes. This important step appeared earlier as part of building a solid team.

10. Keep others informed of what you're up to. People get defensive when you go into their space and start making changes they are unaware of. You may have the best idea in the world, but if you show up in a department and start changing the layout of a director's area, you will make enemies, not allies. Work with the stakeholders of the areas where you are going to make changes. They must be allowed to contribute to the ideas, design, and concepts of that change along the way. You cannot inform people about the change you are going to make. You have to include them.

11. Become a leader. The definition of a leader does not come through the title. Please, stop and think about that for a moment – it's powerful. A leader is defined as one who has followers. I have seen leaders on a grade school playground. No, they are not the teachers. They are the kids who can organize or start a new game on the playground. In doing so, they may be ten years old, but they are already leaders.

Another general rule in project management is to <u>realize what is in your control</u>. Quality professionals tend to be very passionate about the work they do and become easily frustrated when they can't make something work. There are three things that you and your organization can control when it comes to project management: time, money, and resources.

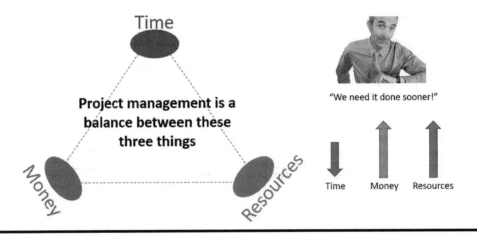

Figure 7.3   Project management time-money-resources.

When one of the three variables becomes mandated or static, you only have the other two to adjust. For example, if the customer states it has to be done sooner, they put a constraint on the time. With the original timeline now shortened, your option is to increase resources and/or money to get it done within the new time frame. If money is limited, resources and time will need to change to accommodate the contingency.

Knowing that there are three and only three variables within your control empowers you to negotiate and navigate the project management landscape. If you are given a constraint related to any of these three, your immediate response should be how to accommodate the constraint utilizing the other two variables.

You will quickly understand as a quality professional that collecting action items is a great habit to get into. Action items are those things that get people engaged and actually move the organization to a new level. In essence, collect action items as if they are gold coins!

Figure 7.4   Collecting gold coins.

When creating an action item, always use the concepts of a SMART goal described in Chapter 4 and identify what is to be done, who is going to do it, and when they will have it done. Getting to action items is harder than it seems, and you may feel awkward in meetings, especially if you haven't done it before. When you start asking questions of people to get to an action item, you will be asking questions that many people have never been challenged with before. Here is some sample dialogue:

You: "What are we trying to accomplish?"
Team: "Obtain reports on the medication reconciliation rates from our EMR."
You: "Great, who is going to do that?"
Participant: "I can reach out to clinical IT and work with them."
You: "Awesome! When will you have that done by?"
Participant: "I have no idea; it all depends on what IT can do for me."
You: "OK, but when will you reach out to them?"
Participant: "By the end of the day."
You: "Great, will you get a realistic deadline from IT to obtain the reports by that time?"
Participant: "Yes."
You: "After you find out, please notify the team so we can update the action item."

The initial action item requested in this dialogue was not completely formulated. In many situations, there are reasons for not being able to completely assign an action item. It would have been very easy to do nothing because the people who need to do the work (clinical IT) were not present. Assigning someone in the room to follow up with clinical IT actually created a manageable action item and allowed the action to move forward rather than becoming stagnant.

As important as action items are to you, remember, they are seldom as important to others. Everyone has additional job duties and expectations, so your action item is just another thing on a long list of duties. Reminders and follow-up on your part are necessary and will soon become appreciated by those managing multiple duties.

7.2 Action Item Tracking Tool

There are many tools out there to manage tasks and action items. Personally, I believe the simplest tool is Excel. Simply list the key elements of an action item in the action item tracker. (An example is shown in Figure 7.5.) The elements consist of the date the action item was initiated, the type of event it was obtained from (e.g., PDSA, quality committee, PDSA), the specific action item, who is accountable, due date, status, and days to due date. You can make this format consistent by using drop-down boxes for selections and conditional formatting colors in the status and days to due columns.

Quality Department Action Item List

Date	Event Type	Action Item	Accountable	Due Date	Status	Days to Due/ STATUS
8/18/2022	RCA	Process for wound management and assessment defined	Fred Smith	9/18/2022	Complete	
8/18/2022	RCA	Nurse led rounds in ICU	Joe Jackson	9/18/2022	Complete	
8/18/2022	QAPI Meeting	Make action item list available for all to view	Dan Dany	9/15/2022	Complete	
8/18/2022	QAPI Meeting	Discuss with hospitalists their needs from quality/data	John Smith	9/15/2022	Complete	
8/18/2022	QAPI Meeting	Get Case mix index information to Dr. Smith	Mary Robinson	9/15/2022	Complete	
8/18/2022	QAPI Meeting	Remove "temporary privileges" from medical staff scorecard, as this is not something tracked at this facility	Dan Dany	9/15/2022	Complete	
10/3/2022	PDSA	Uterine Rupture PDSA - Reiterate the escalation process for RNs	Jane Trainer	10/30/2022	Complete	
10/3/2022	PDSA	Uterine Rupture PDSA - Red phone investigation	Fred Johnson	10/15/2022	Complete	
10/3/2022	PDSA	Uterine Rupture PDSA - Initiate MTP code drill plan with education	Sherry Manger	4/15/2023	In Progress	29
11/22/2022	PDSA	ED boarders receive a hospital bed after admit orders received	Casey Jane	3/20/2023	In Progress	3
11/22/2022	PDSA	ED skin Assessment on Admit with picture of any findings.	Casey Jane	3/20/2023	In Progress	3
12/30/2022	PDSA	Investigate an increase in FTE of inpatient WCN coverage	Jane Doe	3/1/2023	In Progress	-16
12/30/2022	PDSA	MD education on WCN orders process	Jane Trainer	5/1/2023	In Progress	45
12/30/2022	PDSA	Role define for WC of primary RN with WCN	Joe Jackson	5/1/2023	In Progress	45

Figure 7.5   Action item tracker.

7.3 Action Item Standard Work

Develop standard work to manage your action item follow-up process. This standard work needs to include follow-up durations (e.g., weekly, monthly, etc.), escalation paths (e.g., quality council, leadership, etc.), who is going to do the follow-up, and how the follow-up is to be done (e.g., phone call, email, etc.). Without standard work and regular follow-up on action items, your action item tracker will soon become out of date and meaningless.

An example of action item standard work is seen in Figure 7.6. Here, there are five easy steps: 1) receive the action item, 2) enter the action item in the action item tracker, 3) update the action item list, 4) send out reminders monthly, and 5) issue monthly report-out.

This also creates a template that enables the quality professional to send consistent messages to accountable owners when action items are past due (Figure 7.7). Creating a template allows you to quickly perform the follow-up and to provide consistent feedback to colleagues that they can depend on.

7.4 Summary

Project management is a critical component of a quality professional's role. As a quality professional, you will be faced with many challenging activities to juggle and manage throughout the organization. If this area interests you, I recommend further education and study in project management. At the very least, ensure you have the skills and tools to manage the multiple action items as tasks for quality.

STANDARD WORK & JOB BREAKDOWN SHEET	Job Function: Quality Management Action Item Follow-up		Date: mm/dd/yyyy	Sheet 1 of 1
			Prepared By: John Doe	
	Area: Quality Department		Approved By:	Dept: Quality Department
	Operation Name: Action Item Management Process		Revision Date: mm/dd/yyyy	Revision Level: 2.0
# Work Elements / Important Steps	Key Points	Reasons Why	Sketch / Drawing / Picture	
1 Receive Action Item	Receive action item in one of the following areas: - RCA Action Plan - PDCA Action Plan - Process Improvement Initiative - QAPI - Mortality Reviews - Risk Events	Action items come to the Quality department in many ways. We, as a team, need to manage them to completion.		
2 Enter Item in the Action Item Tracking Tool	Enter the newly received action item in the All Action Items tab of the Action Item List workbook located in the Team site for quality ("Action Item Tracker.xlsx"	One central location will allow us to work from the same status.		
3 Update Action Item List	When updating information or a status for an already existing Action Item, make the appropriate updates within the Action Item List workbook.	Maintain the most accurate information in our shared list.		
4 Send Out Reminders Monthly	A designated associate from the Quality department will send out monthly email reminders to the accountable owner(s) of specific action items listed in red.	Managing action items to completion is a critical component of an ISO certified organization and leads to appropriate follow-through.		
5 Monthly Report Out	An action item summary will be reported out to Quality Committee Monthly. This report-out will contain: - Number of Action Items - Completed Action Items - Past due Action Items - Details of past due items	Engaging leadership increases the chances of accountability of completion of action items.		

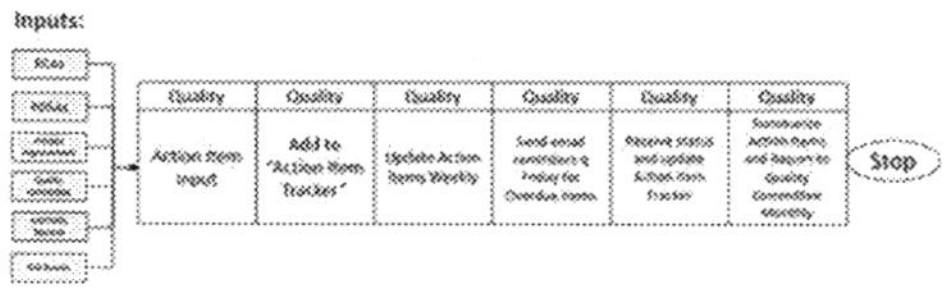

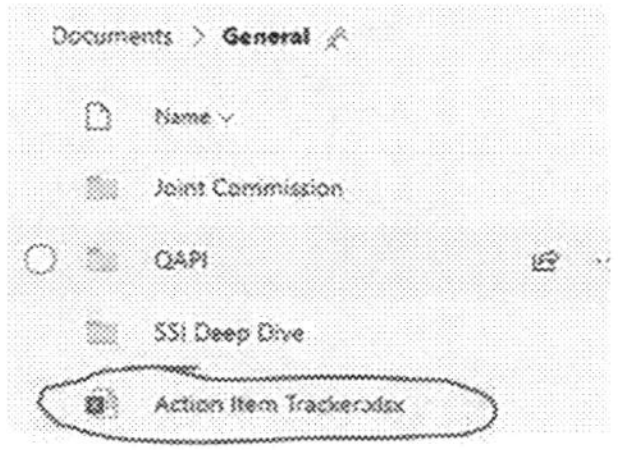

Figure 7.6 Action item standard work.

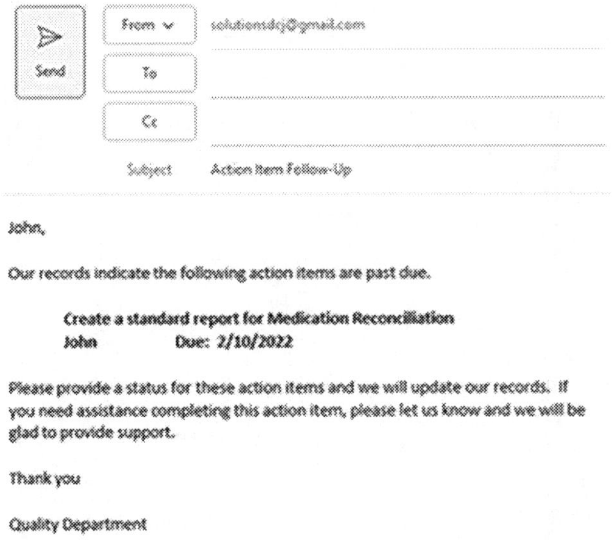

Figure 7.7   Action item email notification.

7.4.1 Key Concepts

■ Find those who are skilled or certified in project management and learn from them.
■ Always organize and track your action items and tasks for quality in a consistent format.
■ Set up processes through standard work to follow up with action items and report their status.

7.4.2 Areas You Can Geek Out On

■ Sunny Baker and Kim Baker, *Complete Idiot's Guide to Project Management* (Alpha) 2000.
■ Project Management Professional (PMP) Certification and Training through the Project Management Institute: www.pmi.org/.

Note

1 Sunny Baker and Kim Baker, *Complete Idiot's Guide to Project Management* (Alpha) 2000.

Chapter 8

Accreditation

This chapter will discuss accreditation and certification. Accreditation is often a dreaded term for hospitals and quality professionals, but it does not need to be. Accreditation and certification can be used as learning opportunities and chances to celebrate success.

Accreditation is an official authorization or approval, recognition for conforming to standards or being outstanding. Certification, on the other hand, is recognition for meeting special qualifications within a field. There are too many certifications to list here, but a few examples are chest pain certification, clinical laboratory improvement amendments (CLIA), left ventricular assist device (LVAD) certification, stroke management, and bariatric center certification. Certifications can be provided by either sector organizations or government agencies.

One of the most misinterpreted aspects of accreditation that it is compulsory. In fact, accreditation is considered voluntary; organizations volunteer to be accredited. The caveat, however, is that if you want to care for and receive revenue from patients who have payors like CMS, you must meet their accreditation standards. Based on the percentage of revenue you receive from CMS as a payor and the source of your customer base, you can develop your own definition of the word *voluntary*.

Accreditation starts with an application from the healthcare provider to the accreditation agency. These agencies were listed in Chapter 2, but most organizations utilize the Joint Commission or DNV. Once you've selected an agency, a business associate agreement must be completed with them. There are significant fees for accreditation ($10,000–$45,000 a year as of this writing), so you should make sure these fees are identified in your facilities budget.

8.1 Role of the Quality Professional in Accreditation

In most organizations, the quality department is significantly involved with accreditation. Because of its importance to the facility, it can be mistakenly felt to be the only focus of the quality department. Accreditation and quality improvement, however, do not need to be in competition with each other. The work for accreditation and quality improvement can be very complementary. In most situations, an accreditation standard is high level and vague enough to allow you to utilize your specific quality improvement techniques to achieve it. Aligning these standards with the

DOI: 10.4324/9781003358404-9

work you do every day enables you to merge the two and make accreditation just part of the way you do business.

The role of the quality department in accreditation may vary among organizations, but here are a few key things you should consider:

1. Manage the activities of the accreditation agency
2. Communicate all accreditation-related information to hospital employees and committees
3. Manage survey action plans
4. Manage survey readiness and preparation
5. Manage survey site visits

8.2 Managing the Activities of the Accreditation Agency

Managing accreditation agencies is not a difficult task, but it is an important one. Most accreditation agencies provide clear pathways for customer service and support. Even if your organization is already established with an accreditation agency, reach out to them to determine your main points of contact, determine annual accountabilities, and establish a communication pathway. Some key things to consider when managing the activities of your accreditation agency are:

■ Completing and submitting your organization's application[1]
■ Ensuring there are funds in the budget for accreditation
■ Communicating with your accreditation agency (blackout dates, dates for survey, serious reportable events, quality measures, etc.)
■ Managing survey action plans

Another role of the quality professional is to communicate all accreditation-related information to hospital employees and committees. If you established a communication pathway with your accreditation agency, you should be receiving information from them on a regular basis. It is your role to disseminate that information throughout the organization. It is important to note that forwarding an email from your accreditation agency to everyone in the organization does not fulfill this need. As discussed earlier, if the learner did not learn, the trainer did not train. **The quality professional's role is to decipher the information and get the right information to the right person(s) at the right time**. If, for example, you obtain a list of modifications to 20 different accreditation standards, you should first understand those modifications, identify what department(s) need to know about the modifications, deliver the message to the recipients, and ensure they understand the information. If you consistently send out global accreditation information to everyone in the organization and expect them to weed out the relevant information, you will quickly end up with zero communication or information transfer because people will grow accustomed to deleting your messages.

As the quality professional, you will also know the approximate time of a site survey. Although all surveys are considered unannounced, you will have a span of about three months when you know when they will arrive. This information should be communicated frequently to everyone in the organization so there are no surprises when they do show up. Most offer an opportunity to list some blackout dates. These are dates specifically listed by you and your organization when the surveyors are not allowed to show up. Although you might be tempted to tell them your blackout dates are the entire year, you are only allowed to have a couple of blackout dates for a set period of time. Ask your accreditation agency about current rules.

8.3 Manage Survey Action Plans

If you initiated an action item tracker (Chapter 7) and a process to manage survey readiness, adding to it will be very straightforward. Every survey typically ends up with some action items that need to be managed to improve performance. These action items can be incorporated into your action item tracker and will follow the same procedures and standard work developed for the process. The accountability for managing these action items to completion and communicating the action plans and results to your accreditation agency usually falls to the quality department and/or quality professional.

8.4 Survey Readiness and Preparation

Survey readiness and preparation are often referred to as continuous survey readiness (CSR). The goal is to break crisis-management cycles and just-in-time cultures to provide continuous, safe, high-quality patient care and sustained compliance with regulations, standards, evidenced-based practices, and professional standards. Continuous survey readiness program[2] requirements consist of:

1. Leadership commitment
2. Manager accountability
3. Survey readiness oversight
4. Requirement oversight
5. Organizational assessment
6. Staff education
7. Survey procedure planning
8. Pre-survey activities
9. Onsite survey activities
10. Post-survey activities
11. Staff recognition

8.4.1 Leadership Commitment

Leadership commitment involves leaders willing to change their organizational culture to one of readiness. Commitment is the most important step in this process. Without it, every other step will be difficult if not impossible to achieve. Begin by meeting with your leadership to understand their commitment to survey readiness. If you find they are lacking commitment, you must first work with them to obtain their required buy-in. Look for behaviors that support culture of leadership commitment. Some behaviors are:

- Survey readiness addressed at every daily huddle
- Survey readiness discussed by the governing board
- Standard agenda topic on the quality committee for survey readiness
- Survey readiness measured and quantified
- Leadership engagement, follow-up, and clearly defined expectations related to survey readiness

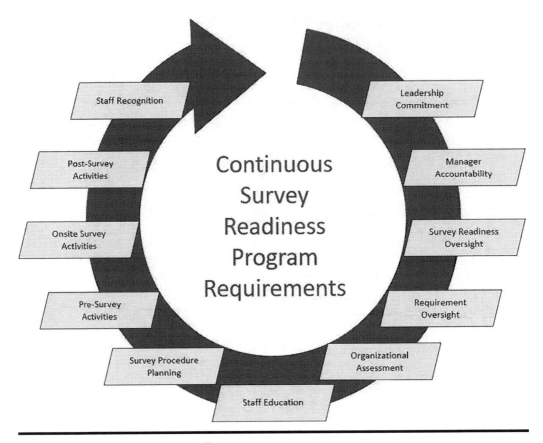

Figure 8.1 Continuous survey readiness.

Leaders must always impart the importance of survey readiness. This should happen weeks before an expected survey and not be a last-minute effort.

8.4.2 Manager Accountability

The manager's role in accreditation is complementary to their role in quality improvement. They should determine when practice and policies are inconsistent, understand root causes of variances, and take corrective action to make policy and staff adjustments. Managers must be trained in the expectations of daily management that lead to continuous survey readiness.

8.4.3 Survey Readiness Oversight

The oversight of survey readiness can be done by multiple methods, but oversight must be defined in your organization. I have found that, for many organizations, the term *survey oversight* was a foreign concept, or they had no evidence of doing such a thing. In pure terms, survey readiness is not a process; it is a goal. Achieving that goal will require many processes and interventions, but without the goal, busywork will prevail, and the goal may not be achieved.

Survey readiness is a team sport and should be owned by everyone in the organization. Because of this, your role as a quality professional is to bring together the people in the organization and facilitate the oversight. This can be done through a survey readiness committee. Involve nursing, medical staff, pharmacy, infection control, and leadership in this committee. Additional areas like facilities and lab may be important, depending on your organization's experience. Find people in these areas who are good at understanding standards and have accreditation experience. Pharmacy and lab are highly regulated areas; leaders in those areas tend to bring exceptional knowledge to an oversight committee. Once you establish this committee, set the frequency of your meetings and a standard agenda. If you have experience with developing a committee charter, this is usually a good way to initiate the committee and obtain their feedback and participation in creating the charter. Part of the committee's responsibility should be to develop internal survey schedules to assess the readiness of each area of the business and follow up on the findings. An example of a committee charter is in the appendix for this chapter.

Your accreditation agency should be able to provide you the tools to assess your survey readiness. Often called *tracers*, these tools guide you when assessing different areas of your organization. I suggest using these tools, survey results from other hospitals, and past survey findings to guide your areas of focus.

After you have your committee established and a plan in place to assess each area of the business over time, you now have a working agenda for your committee. A meeting may consist of reviewing the results of survey findings within the past month, developing action plans to mitigate problems, reviewing new accreditation requirements that have been published, and planning for next month's survey readiness assessments. Minutes from these meetings should be reviewed at your organization's quality committee and shared with leadership.

8.4.4 Requirements Oversight

Requirements oversight involves continual awareness of changes and emphasis in standards or regulations. Changes are usually well communicated by your survey vendor (e.g., JC, DNV). You should review these changes at your survey readiness committee and perform a gap analysis to understand the implication to the organization. A gap analysis (Figure 8.2) is used to understand how you currently perform the work, what is expected in the new standard, and whether your current process meets the new expectations. If it does not, you must determine what process changes you will perform to achieve that standard requirement. All these findings should be communicated throughout the organization, specifically to those areas of relevance.

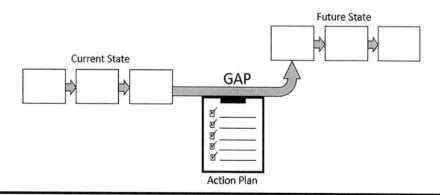

Figure 8.2   Gap analysis.

8.4.5 Organizational Assessment

Developing assessment processes, quantifying results, and creating action plans enable you to provide valid information leaders can use and keep you clear of subjective answers and questions. Organizational assessment is managed by the survey readiness committee mentioned earlier. Schedule and plan an annual organizational assessment. Typically, the assessment falls on the quality department and/or the survey readiness committee, but you can utilize outside sources such as corporate employees, vendors, temporary staff, etc. You should utilize the survey as a learning session and be encouraged by any findings that enable your organization to learn and grow. Now you can quantify results, create action plans, implement improvements from the findings, and summarize them in a survey readiness assessment dashboard (Figure 8.3).

Survey Readiness Assessment (SRA) Dashboard

Date:	2/14/2023

Total SRAs	259
Completed SRAs	256
Complete Percentage	98.8%

SAFER Classification Distribution	Scope		
Risk	Limited	Pattern	Widespread
High	3%	11%	25%
Moderate	2%	2%	7%
Low	9%	14%	27%

Percent Complete Classification	Scope		
Risk	Limited	Pattern	Widespread
High	100%	96%	97%
Moderate	100%	100%	100%
Low	100%	100%	100%

Figure 8.3   Survey readiness dashboard.

8.4.6 Staff Education

Healthcare employees are not accreditation experts, nor do they work every day to accommodate accreditation needs. The role of the quality professional is to translate the accreditation requirements into real work practice. For example, if an accreditation requirement changes, the quality professional should help the areas impacted by those changes: help them change policies, procedures, and training to accommodate the need for patient quality care. Reasons for change should always be communicated, but the reason for change should never be simply because it is an accreditation requirement. In essence, staff should be following accreditation requirements in every process they perform, but that should never be the sole purpose they do it.

8.4.7 Survey Audits

This section addresses the next two steps in the continuous survey readiness program: survey procedure planning and onsite survey activities.

The most important thing a quality professional can do for a site survey is to instill organization. If you start off the survey in total chaos, it will be viewed negatively by the surveyors. Most people think that when surveyors show up, it is the surveyor who is in charge. Not so. The quality leader has every opportunity to lead and guide the survey and the activities that happen. A well-organized survey conveys a competent organization that is not afraid to lead and guide the surveyors through the very complex work they perform. Surveyors appreciate a local leader setting up the structure, agenda, and process that enable them to complete their tasks efficiently.

> In business, organization is an absolute necessity, not an alternative.
> Larry Burkett

Preparation for a survey begins long before the surveyors show up. Preparation and the following steps will help you manage and organize a survey:

Step 1: Identify the people who will need to be part of the survey.
Step 2: Develop a communication plan.
Step 3: Create job descriptions for each of those involved in the survey and train them.
Step 4: Set up the process and structure for the survey.
Step 5: Create a survey ready box of all the required documents, office supplies, etc.
Step 6: Communicate and obtain approvals.

Note: If you already have a well-defined incident command system, you may be able to merge these steps into that design.

8.4.7.1 Step 1: Identify the People Who Will Need to Be Part of the Survey

There can be many roles required for a survey at your organization. The point here is to identify them. The following roles are critical:

■ Survey commander – This person makes all final decisions regarding the survey and oversees every function during the survey. This person is *not* the highest-ranking person (e.g., CEO) in the organization. In fact, those above the survey commander in rank must be willing to relinquish power to them.
■ Survey command room champion – This person stays in the survey command room and manages the activities of incoming and outgoing messages, delegates tasks, and communicates directly with the commander.

- Subject matter expert – Multiple subject matter experts are assigned according to the area they work in: for example, pharmacy director, nursing unit leader, facilities manager, etc. There are typically as many subject matter experts as there are departments in your organization. Find out who they are and list them.
- Electronic medical record expert – This person is assigned to navigate all areas of the electronic medical record for the surveyors. They should have the appropriate access and be well versed in where and how to find the information requested. Be aware, however, even though this person is an expert in the EMR, they are not the subject matter expert for the area(s) in which it is used. You should coordinate both subject matter experts and the electronic medical record expert to work together with surveyors.
- Survey escort – This is someone who is very familiar with the facility and can quickly escort surveyors to any location they request. Part of this role is communicating to every department head their planned arrival at the department.
- Survey scribe – The person assigned to every surveyor for the purpose of taking notes, listening, and collecting information to be reported back to the survey command room champion.

8.4.7.2 Step 2: Develop a Communication Plan

Create a communication plan that allows those with specified job duties to be immediately deployed for the survey. This plan should also address communication to notify all employees when surveyors arrive. Most organizations have some method for urgent and emergent communication, such as call trees, text message alerts, overhead pages, etc. Utilize these same techniques for initiating a survey. An example of a communication plan is shown in Figure 8.4.

Communication Method	How	Purpose
Initiate the company call tree	"We have initiated the call tree. Joint Commission surveyors are on site, please call and let the next person on your call tree know."	Notify all leaders that the surveyors have arrived.
Announce Survey at morning huddle	"The Joint Commission surveyors have arrived to do our _____ survey. The survey commander is _____ and can be reached by calling _____."	Communicate to the entire organization. Expectation that huddle leaders take this information to their unit huddles.
Survey Commander Team briefing	Show up at designated location. Quickly brief roles for every individual and initiate survey process.	Survey team show up at designated area to brief and ensure roles are delegated appropriately.
Survey Commander Call CEO	Survey commander call CEO to notify of surveyor arrival and current status of the team.	Specifically engage CEO and make them aware everything is in place.

Figure 8.4 Survey communication plan.

8.4.7.3 Step 3: Create Job Descriptions

The next step is to create job descriptions for each of those involved in the survey and train them. Put together an organizational chart with job descriptions. Figure 8.5 shows an organizational chart for the survey team. This identifies the reporting structure and location of each role during the survey.

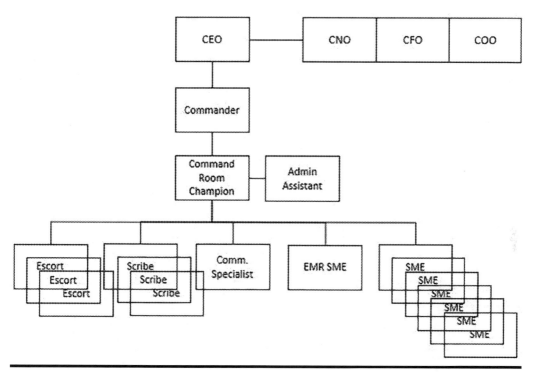

Figure 8.5 Survey organizational chart.

Job descriptions for a survey are nothing like your typical human resources job descriptions. A simple one-page document outlines the role, availability, reporting structure, and key accountabilities. A template is shown in Figure 8.6 and sample job descriptions are available in the appendix at the end of the book.

Survey Job Description

This job description is a temporary description of what is expected of you during an onsite survey. This enables each of us to perform our duties during a survey and work in unison with each person assigned a job description role. It is critically important that each person assigned a job duty perform the accountabilities listed here. Questions regarding these expectations and the role can be directed to the "Reports to" person identified below.

Role:	
Availability:	
Reports To:	
Accountabilities	

Figure 8.6 Survey job description template.

8.4.7.4 Step 4: Set Up the Process and Structure for the Survey

There are logistical aspects that need to be thought through and defined before surveyors show up. This will help prevent the chaos that results when things are not properly planned. First, define and designate a command center room and a surveyor room. These two are not the same. A command center room is a location where all internal survey employees come to coordinate activities, discuss survey needs, research policies and procedures, and prep materials for the surveyors. The surveyor room is a base for the surveyors to work from. If logistics allow, keep the surveyor room close to the command center. You will spend a lot of time going between these two rooms to deliver materials and coordinate with the surveyors.

SETTING UP THE STRUCTURE

1. Designate a command center and surveyor rooms
2. Create color teams
3. Create team badges for color teams
4. Create an inbox and an outbox
5. Develop management white board
6. Create agenda templates
7. Develop contact list

Next, set up survey teams based on colors (red, yellow, blue, green, etc.). The number of teams is dependent on the number of surveyors who show up. Usually four teams are sufficient. Each team will consist of a surveyor, a scribe, and an escort. Create three badges in each team color.

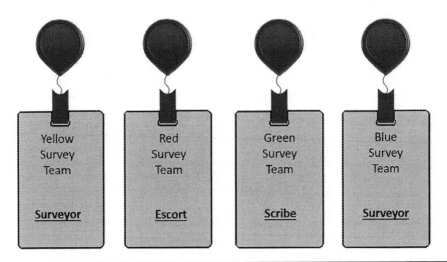

Figure 8.7 Survey badges.

Obtain and designate inboxes and outboxes. You will need an inbox and an outbox for the command center and an inbox for the surveyor room. If you want to make things even more organized, it is helpful to have a inbox in the surveyor room that separates the teams. This enables you to get the information specifically to the surveyor who asked for it.

Next, develop a survey management white board. This is the main tool used in the command center room that allows for visual management of all survey activities. If you have ever been through a survey, you know that many requests come in, and a lot of information goes out during the survey. Keeping track of this information is difficult without organization. Figure 8.8 shows an example of a white board. You can purchase a white board and put pin-striping on it to make it look like this figure, or you can repurpose a white board already in the room and draw the lines. Each team has their own section. When requests come in from that surveyor, use Post-It notes to record the request and place it on the board. As the requests are processed, move the Post-It notes to the appropriate location (open, completed, etc.). The board also has other sections on the right to add additional information about survey team members' availability, daily activities, etc. Visual management throughout a survey is critical. It provides efficiency in ways that you will not even realize until you start to use it. When leaders or other team members come into the command center to get information, they can look at the white board to get the answers without having to be briefed multiple times throughout the day. Also, there are usually many people working in the command center trying to coordinate efforts. The white board is a standard meeting place for all those people to come together and follow the same procedures, reducing confusion, rework, and missed communications. Lastly, it provides a tracking mechanism. When one surveyor has a request multiple times or another surveyor has the same request, you can see what has been requested and/or delivered previously so you can keep those messages consistent. It is never good to provide surveyors with different policies for the same request at different times. This opens up the risk of redundancy and error.

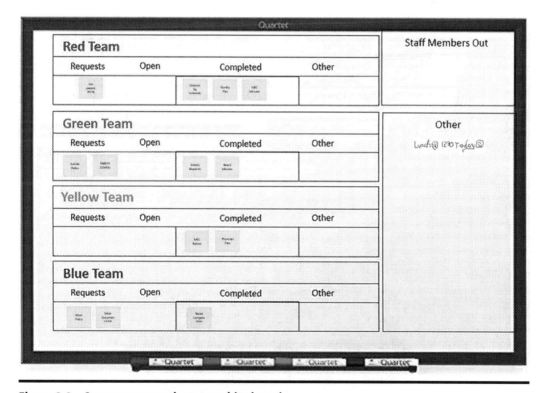

Figure 8.8 Survey command center white board.

Create agenda templates that can be updated ad hoc (Figure 8.9). It is good to set up an end-of-the-day briefing internally with those involved in the survey. Set up a template agenda so you can easily facilitate a meeting without having to prep while the surveyors are there. A typical agenda will include areas the surveyors inspected today, expectations for tomorrow, inspection trends (e.g., they are looking closely at suicide precautions and documentation), opportunities for improvement, changes you can make in the survey process to make it better, and what went well.

Date: _____

Time: _____

Attendees:			
Topic:	Briefing on Survey After day ___		
Agenda Topic	Facilitator		Time
Areas Inspected today			
Tomorrow's Expectations			
Survey Trends			
Opportunities for Improvement			
Survey Process Opportunities			
What went Well			

Figure 8.9 Survey briefing agenda.

The next area of preparation is developing a contact list. Create a list of all department directors, managers, leadership, and others who may need to be contacted during the survey. Since most are seldom available at their desks, ask each of them if you can list their cell phone numbers. This list of contacts will be very valuable and can be posted on the survey management board once

Figure 8.10 Survey ready box.

the survey begins. Once the survey starts, that is not the time to scramble to find phone numbers for those you need to reach.

8.4.7.5 Step 5: Create a Survey Ready Box

It is important to create a survey ready box for all the supplies you will need during a survey (Figure 8.10). It seems logical that there will be paper, pens, and Post-It notes around, but you will be surprised how much chaos will result if you don't have these materials ready and available at all times. A simple 15″ x 12″ x 10″ box (standard size of a copy paper box) is large enough for the supplies you will need. First, start with an inventory checklist and list all the items that should be in the box. Once you obtain those items, check them off on the checklist and tape the checklist to the top of the box. An example of a checklist is shown in Figure 8.11. Store the survey ready box in a location in the quality department and ensure the location is known by those who need to initiate the survey process.

Survey Ready Box Inventory Checklist

Color Badges (Red, Yellow, Green, Blue)	
Contact List	
Communication Plan	
Job Descriptions with Copies to hand out	
Printed Accreditation Standards	
Box of pens	
Dry Erase markers	
12-inch Notebook Paper	
"In" Basket	
"Out" Basket	
Post It Notes	

List assumes you have a laptop and network access to all related documents like policies, procedures, meeting minutes, organizational structure, etc.

Figure 8.11   Survey box inventory.

8.4.7.6 Step 6: Communicate and Obtain Approvals

Depending on your organizational culture and leadership, Step 6 may be Step 1. If approvals need to be made before taking steps to perform the work you may need to get approval from executive leadership before you initiate Steps 1 through 5. Regardless of the order, start with your CEO and executive leadership by describing your plan for survey readiness. Without their approval and understanding, this process will be circumvented and made irrelevant when surveyors show up. It will result in a chaotic environment where everyone leads and no one executes. Present the survey readiness plan to all leadership levels in your organization. It is through these presentations that you can obtain feedback, define expectations, and train people on the survey readiness process. It is also a great time to take that feedback and make modifications to meet your organization's needs.

A common challenge during a survey is "Who is in charge?" Different organizational leaders pop in at different times and may try to take control of the process. After all, they are leaders! Set up your processes early and clearly define the roles of every member of the organization before a survey begins so you can mitigate this confusion and misdirection if it begins.

8.5 Sample Case Study

Let's give our approach a test drive.

It's Tuesday morning, and you show up to work as the quality director. You start going through your daily tasks when the phone rings. It's the administration office. "Surveyors are here to do an inspection." You ask the person calling to escort the surveyors to the dedicated surveyor room. Now, immediately contact the administration assistant who has been briefed and trained in the survey readiness process and ask them to initiate the communication plan that is in place for surveys. From there, pick up the survey readiness box, take it to the surveyor room, and greet the surveyors. In their opening briefing, they will tell you who they are, why they are there, and what type of survey they are going to do.

Note: As the quality director, obtain their credentials and business cards to validate who they say they are. (If there is any speculation with regard to their credentials, follow up after the initial meeting by calling the agency they are from to validate them.)

Once the briefing is complete, take time to describe the survey process to the surveyors. Each will be assigned a color team and introduced to the scribe and escort assigned to them. The inboxes (already available in the survey ready box) are set up and described to the surveyors. Obtain a schedule of activities from the surveyors for the day. (Note: They should be able to tell you what areas they are going to tour for the day and what materials they will initially need.) With this information, go to the command center room and start updating the survey white board with the initial requests. If you are not the command center champion, brief that person. Do a quick command center huddle with the employees in the room and remind them of their roles. The communications person in the command room will call the leaders of each area the surveyors want to tour and let them know they will soon be in their area. The scribe assigned to each surveyor notifies the command room of their current whereabouts and areas they are planning to visit. The communication person continually calls or texts the leaders in those areas with that information. Requests throughout the day come into the command center through phone calls and texts from the scribes and/or the escorts. This information is added to the white board. The command center champion prioritizes and assigns tasks to obtain the information requested by the surveyors. Once obtained, the information is marked with the color of the team requesting it, placed in the outbox in the command center, and eventually delivered to the appropriate inbox in the surveyor room.

End of case study example.

An important point to note is document control. The command center controls all documents delivered to the surveyors. It is good practice to maintain a copy of what was provided to the surveyors so there is no question later as to what was delivered. The surveyors will typically request many documents. Some of these documents will be policies and procedures, meeting minutes for quality council, board meetings, and organizational charts. The command center champion should review all documents provided to the surveyors to determine that they are correct, valid, and not out of date. The command center champion does not need to be an expert in all areas but should reach out to subject matter experts familiar with the documents if there are any questions.

Keeping everyone informed throughout the survey is very important. This is done through the communications person, but it is good practice to set up a daily debrief with all the leaders in the organization. In this scenario, ask your administrative assistant to set up a 30-minute call at the end of each day and invite the leaders. Each day, open the call line and utilize your standard agenda template to go through the events of the day and answer questions for those participating.

At the end of the survey (usually in two to four days), the surveyors will typically offer to do a closing briefing. Work with the surveyors to obtain the date and time they would like to do this. Start this as early in the process as you can and get the meeting set up with all the leaders in the organization. When the surveyors leave, they will usually give some of their preliminary findings, the process of receiving the formal findings, and expectations to respond with an action plan.

8.5.1 Pre-Survey Activities

Pre-survey activities should be managed throughout the year to prepare for any future survey. Continuously look for opportunities from the last survey to determine whether they have been appropriately addressed, with solutions hardwired into your processes. Continually maintain improvements and corrective actions. This can easily be done by making these improvements and the processes for them measurable and including them on your quality oversight scorecard (Chapter 4). Keep staff apprised of key standards, regulations, and changes. Maintain the survey readiness oversight outlined earlier while performing self-assessment compliance status and gap analysis. Utilize educational programs for building skills related to regulatory, accreditation, and performance and quality improvement. Engage your clinical education department to help you get the appropriate regulatory and survey readiness activities deployed to everyone. Initiate activities to prepare staff and leadership for anticipated survey activities, and make sure your survey planning documents are current and relevant.

8.5.2 Post-Survey Activities

Post survey is all about learning from the opportunities for improvement found and applying process improvement to implement them. Since these are the deviations the surveyors found, the findings will be under a microscope well into the future. All surveys require you to create a corrective action plan for items cited. The format of the action plan varies depending on the surveyor's or agency's preference, but they all contain essentially the same basic elements:

- The topic or standard cited
- Compliance issues for correction
- Planned actions
- The target deadline for completion
- Name of person accountable for the action item

Figure 8.12 shows an example of a basic action plan. If not directed to use the surveyor's or agency's format, this can be utilized.

Survey Corrective Action Form

Survey:
Date:

Standard	EP	Compliance Issue	Planned Actions	Due Date	Person Accountable

Figure 8.12 Corrective action form.

8.5.3 Staff Recognition

Although it may be the last thing people think of after three days of grueling survey activities, it is important to take the time to recognize staff and celebrate the positive things that resulted from the work that was done. Regardless of the outcome of a survey, one thing that always holds true is the collaboration and teamwork of everyone involved. Survey days are hard, and it is a great time for people to put aside any differences they may have had and come together for a common goal in achieving success. This can always be celebrated after a survey. More than likely (depending on the surveyors), specific things are outlined as notable mentions. This means that your organization does particularly well in a specific area. These things should be celebrated with the entire organization. If they were notable, dig in a little deeper and understand why. It's these things that can be applied to other areas of the business to set them apart from the norm. As a quality professional with the responsibility of managing an organization through surveys, make sure you take the time to send personal words of thanks and appreciation to those supporting you in this endeavor. This will ensure those people continue to feel appreciated and will support you in the future.

8.6 Summary

Mentioning the word *accreditation* in healthcare typically elicits feelings of pain and discomfort, but it doesn't have to. An organization that is well organized and ready for an accreditation (one they already know will happen anyway) will start to embrace surveys and welcome them. They can actually be enjoyable in that they enable your organization to learn and grow while showcasing all the great things you have done. Overprepare for survey readiness and organization. If you currently experience pain and discomfort when thinking about accreditation, once these guidelines are in place, you may start to develop a significantly different outlook on it.

8.6.1 Key Concepts

- The combination of accreditation and quality can be a complementary relationship.
- Work with an accreditation agency and develop a relationship with those who support you.
- Communicate accreditation-related material to all areas of your organization in a way that is meaningful and that they can understand.
- Objectively define *accreditation readiness* so leaders can be confident in your current state of readiness.
- Organization and professionalism are critical to accreditation surveys.

8.6.2 Areas You Can Geek Out On

- Work with your accreditation vendor to obtain additional educational resources.
- Obtain survey tracers from your accreditation vendor and perform your own accreditation survey.
- Interview peers and/or leaders throughout the organization and find those with significant accreditation experience.

Notes

1 Request application from Joint Commission: www.jointcommission.org/accreditation-and-certification/health-care-settings/hospital/learn/learn-the-application-process/Application. For DNV: https://maritime.dnv.com/DocumentApprovalHelp/CMC_Application%20overview.html.
2 Luc R. Pelletier and Christy L. Beaudin, *HQ Solutions Resource for the Healthcare Quality Professional* (Wolters Kluwer) 2018.

Chapter 9

Sustaining Quality

Let's review the role of the quality professional with respect to sustaining quality, daily operations, communication, reporting, and standard work.

9.1 Role of the Quality Professional in Sustaining Quality

Although quality is part of everyone's job and should be instilled in all the work we do, the reality is that quality is not always on everyone's mind, nor is it comprehendible at the systems level when trying to do an individual task.

As a coach, teacher, and consultant, the quality director's role in sustaining quality involves:

- Overseeing all organizational metrics and outcomes related to patient safety and quality
- Communicating quality topics often to everyone in the organization
- Supporting quality strategy and initiatives that support the overall quality agenda
- Monitoring and maintaining quality tools that enable continuous quality control
- Continuously drawing connections between the work and processes performed every day and the outcomes they yield
- Simplifying all the complexities of healthcare quality management in a relevant way that enables those who need to participate in achieving quality to understand.
- Organize, organize, organize!
  - Quality committee
  - Survey readiness committee
  - Daily communications
  - Weekly leadership communications
  - Surveys

9.2 Daily Operations

To improve outcomes, start by improving the daily processes that yield those outcomes. Daily management means moving from the traditional <u>outcomes</u> monitoring and oversight to the daily

140

DOI: 10.4324/9781003358404-10

processes that produce those results. There are many examples, but let's explore the example of patients who left the emergency department without being seen. This is an outcome measure that most organizations review daily or monthly. It refers to the number of patients who checked in to the emergency department but left before they were called back to be seen. It is well known that extended wait times contribute significantly to patients leaving without being seen because they get tired of waiting. It may even be a standard line item in your daily operations huddle. "Yesterday we saw 102 patients in our emergency department, and we had 7% left without being seen." If anything is said about the 7% who left without being seen, it is usually only to explain away why the number was so high. The explanation might be "We had a lot of patients come in at the same time, and we were down a triage nurse." Although it is good to be cognizant of these outcomes, the reality is that what is done is done, and there is no going back to prevent the negative customer experience. Improving daily processes means looking at the real-time processes, measuring them, and reacting to them. If we know patients leave without being seen because of the time they spend in the waiting room, then monitoring wait times in real time will help reduce this outcome. Setting a goal to prevent patients from waiting over one hour in the waiting room would trigger interventions when a patient wait time exceeds that, thus preventing them from leaving before being seen. Interventions at this level will reap significant rewards in the outcome measures and eliminate the constant struggle to find excuses for those measures.

In Chapter 3, we covered daily management application. This is where you apply techniques to your operations. Through this process, outline in-process measures (from strategic initiatives, PDSAs, and process improvements) and monitor them daily through daily huddle agenda topics, quality and leadership rounds, and daily report-outs.

Another example showing the difference between outcome measures and in-process measures is pressure injuries. Every hospital measures the patient safety indicator 03 (PSI 03),[1] the number of pressure injuries. Evidence-based practice, policies, procedures, and nursing care outline the specific things that should be done to protect a patient's skin from pressure injury. When performing a root-cause analysis (RCA) on a Stage 3 pressure injury that already occurred, you would typically reference these guidelines to determine if these prevention measures were in place. Recognize that most RCAs performed for a pressure injury reveal missing documentation and/or action related to these guidelines. Basically, we failed to do the things that we said we were going to do to prevent a pressure injury. This sounds like a punitive statement directed at caregivers who didn't do their jobs. If you manage at the outcome level, you may easily come to that conclusion. If, however, you manage at the in-process level, you may find root causes that are more meaningful and enable you to implement better solutions. Managing to in-process measures related to pressure injuries may include looking at patients who have not had a skin assessment in the specified time after admission. For those identified as high risk for pressure injury, it may be patients were not turned within the last two hours, have not received a nutrition consult, or were not placed on the appropriate mattress. If you manage your daily operation at these levels and intervene, you will come to different conclusions. You may improve your in-process measures based on guidelines, thereby improving the outcome measure for pressure injuries. You may come up with very valid root causes and barriers that prevent employees from managing in-process measures. Examples include staffing shortages, complex electronic medical record documentation, a shortage of supplies (e.g., mattresses), and a lack of guideline understanding. Root causes managed at the in-process level will enable you to make real improvements before a patient is harmed with a pressure injury.

In summary, we are monitoring and managing the in-process measure(s), *not* the outcome measure PSI 03. If we take a look at the airline industry, the in-process measures they look to are near misses. All interventions to mitigate a near miss identify its root causes, and preventative actions are taken at the critical in-process level. If the professionals in the airline industry waited for the near miss to become an outcome measure (collision) before intervening, far fewer people would travel by air. We take for granted all the work we never see that goes into making our flights safe.

NEAR MISS!

Have you heard of the term *near miss*? We use it as a figure of speech when we have an event in our lives that is very close to resulting in a negative outcome. The Federal Aviation Administration (FAA) defines a near miss as an incident associated with the operation of an aircraft in which the possibility of a collision occurs as a result of proximity of less than 500 feet to another aircraft, or a report is received from a pilot or a flight crew member stating that a collision hazard existed between two or more aircraft.[2]

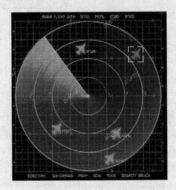

With 227 near misses reported in 2022,[3] chances are that if you traveled frequently, you might have been on one of those planes. You, however, would have never known the incident occurred. You landed not knowing that a stream of activity, paperwork, and focus occurred for the very flight you were on.

So, what happens behind the scenes with a near miss? The air traffic control equipment sounds an alarm, and all hands are on deck to avert the crises. Immediately after the incident, the investigation begins. The air traffic controller responsible for keeping the planes at a safe distance is removed from their current duties and put into a program for retraining.

The World Health Organization reports that one in every ten patients (10%) is harmed while receiving care.[4] Nearly 50% of these adverse events are preventable. With 36.2 million hospital admissions each year in the US, this equates to 1.8 million recipients of a harm that could have been prevented.

Comparing the FAA's near-miss numbers to healthcare harm events may not be appropriate. Fewer than 30,000 passengers would have been impacted by airline near misses, compared to the 1.8 million patients in hospitals. The comparison, however, leads to some discussion. In these two high-risk industries, what processes and procedures are different?

Although a plane crash in which lives are lost is a very significant event, this industry looks at near misses and crashes with the same level of diligence. Action plans are initiated as soon as a process failure exists to prevent the crisis from occurring. Healthcare, on the other hand, typically looks at this process failure differently. An event occurs that already harmed the patient, and a root-cause analysis is done to identify the reasons. Ninety percent of these root-cause analysis findings lead to a failure to adhere to the processes defined. We know what to do; we just don't know how to ensure that we do it.

In the airline industry, an investigation begins immediately, and, in some cases, the process is stopped until a cause can be mitigated. On October 29, 2018, a Boeing 747 crashed, followed by another on March 10, 2019. Every Boeing 747 Max was grounded for nearly two years. In 30 years of healthcare, I've yet to see a process be grounded for any reason.

The last comparison involves training. The training for air traffic controllers accompanies process deficiencies continuously throughout the year. Although, as in healthcare, annual training still exists, this training is revisited as often as necessary in response to adverse outcomes.

In healthcare, we identify competencies that are necessary for clinicians to safely perform their duties. Once a year, each employee is required to go through these competencies and demonstrate proficiency. This may be all well and good; however, it is unknown during the 364 days in between whether the employee is actually following the processes that were defined during the competencies. It is known, for example, that a patient should have a nursing assessment within four hours of admission, that they should be screened for suicide risk on every admission, and they should be repositioned every two hours if they are at risk of developing a pressure injury, yet we continually miss these standard of care steps. We wait for the pressure injury to exist, report it, and do a root-cause analysis on the case, only to find out the processes of evidence-based practice that were put in place to prevent such an occurrence never happened.

Although hospitals are now beginning to take on the challenge of moving to the concepts of high reliable organizations (HRO), the fact remains that the outcomes are not where they should be. Until a culture of zero harm is accepted in healthcare, and evidence-based processes are managed like near-miss airline occurrences, anything in between is nothing but lip service that results in 1.8 million people harmed by hospital errors each year.

9.3 Standard Work for the Quality Professional

Standard work was introduced and discussed in Chapter 6. This section covers using that standard work to define the work of the quality professional. As a leader, the quality director should have standard work. Multiple job duties can be difficult to remember, manage, and keep straight. Although the quality professional's role cannot be summed up in one simple standard work document, it is suggested that standard work be created to define routine activities. A good way to start standard work is to list all your tasks on a piece of paper and keep that list easily accessible, adding to it as you go. It may take up to a month to accurately list activities, tasks, and responsibilities. Anything that takes time should be included in standard work: for example, email management. As a leader, you are expected to read, work through, and respond to emails. This should not be overlooked and needs to be on the list. Once you feel your list is sufficient, separate the items into things that are done daily, weekly, or monthly. It may be more manageable to develop three standard work documents – one for daily, one for weekly, and one for monthly standard work. Figures 9.1 through 9.3 provide high-level examples.

STANDARD WORK & JOB BREAKDOWN SHEET	Job Function: Director Quality/Risk Daily Standard Work		Date: mm/dd/yyyy	Sheet 1 of 1
	Area: Quality		Prepared By: John Doe	
			Approved By: Jane Smith	Dept: Hospital Quality
	Operation Name: Daily Quality Activities		Revision Date:	Revision Level: 1.0

#	Work Elements / Important Steps	Key Points	Reasons Why	Sketch / Drawing / Picture
1	Email Management	Review/respond to email at least 1x per day	Stay up on communications with hospital teams	
2	Incident Review	Review incidents in Quantros. 1) Assign incidents to the appropriate director 2) Review incidents looking for SREs or any that need quality or Risk follow-up	Incidents are recorded ad hoc but usually show up daily. Reviewing the quality worklist daily is critical to ensure quality is engaged in all incidents in a timely manner	
3	Administrative Huddle	Daily administrative huddle held every day at 0800. Report out any fails or SREs. Phone conference number x1234	Communication of daily organizational needs and status.	
4	Action Item Management	Update and manage the Action Item list daily. These are the action items that are recorded for all quality and risk. Location: X:\departments\Quality\Action Items\Action Item Traker.xlsx	This is the main document for managing the action items	
5	RCA Events	Perform RCA events with applicable teams. A PDCA template is used as well as other RCA templates. These are found on the quality share drive x:\departments\quality\templates	Part of quality management functions to perform RCAs on all SREs.	
6	Ad Hoc Team Management Activities	Ad Hoc activities related to managing the quality team.	Ad Hoc request come to the quality director daily. Support team to remove barriers, prioritize work, and support quality initiatives.	
7	Team Management Activities	Goal setting, time card management, PTO requests, sick time off, scheduling, duty assignment.	Standard management activities.	
8	Invoice Management	XYZ is the invoice approval system for the Quality Budget. An email will come from XYZ letting you know you have an invoice that needs to be approved. Open XYZ, review the invoice, and approve or reject then send onto the next workflow group (finance) location: http://XYZ/portal/index.htm	Management of invoices and Quality budget.	

Figure 9.1 Quality director standard work – daily.

STANDARD WORK & JOB BREAKDOWN SHEET	Job Function: Director Quality/Risk **Weekly Standard Work**		Date: mm/dd/yyyy	Sheet 1 of 1
	Area: Quality		Prepared By: John Doe	
	Operation Name: Weekly Quality Activities		Approved By: Jane Smith	Dept: Hospital Quality
			Revision Date:	Revision Level: 1.0
# Work Elements / Important Steps	Key Points	Reasons Why	Sketch / Drawing / Picture	
1 Quality Team Huddle	Quality team huddle scheduled for 9AM every Monday. Huddle template is created and utilized for each meeting. The members of the quality team rotate responsibility for leading the huddle. Huddle Template: x:\departments\quality\templates\Weekly Huddle Template.doc	Weekly check-in to communicate weekly activities, support needed, and issues for the week.		
2 Leadership Meeting	Weekly leadership meeting at 0830 every Wednesday in the CCSR Conference room. Administrative huddle for the day will follow this meeting.	Communication of organizational needs and status.		
3 Weekly Leadership Report	Weekly leadership report to report out on Quality Status for: - SREs - Complaints - Risk Events Report out Template: x:\departments\quality\quality improvement department\Leadership Weekly Report out	Weekly report for communication of quality and risk activities		
4 Action Item Reminders	Quality has a action item list located under the quality share drive in Action Items>Action Item Tracker.xls. This is a list of all action items for quality initiatives. A reminder must be sent to the accountable owners through email every week for overdue action items. The process and standard work for managing Action Items is located in quality's standard work folder.	Keep people on track to complete their action items and demonstrate diligence in managing action items		
5 Bi-Weekly Timecard Approval	Time card approval for all employees by Monday 1000 for the week of a pay period close. Review each employee's time submitted in Kronos and approve/reject time card based on PTO entered, days/hours worked etc. Suggestion: Enter all PTO approvals on Outlook calendar so it can be cross checked when this approval process is done.	Stewardship in managing employees time and PTO.		
6 Employee Onboarding	Update and manage the employee onboarding for any employees in their 1st 9 months of hire.	Continued management of employees being onboarding will improve employee retention and department efficiency		

Figure 9.2 Quality director standard work – weekly.

STANDARD WORK & JOB BREAKDOWN SHEET	Job Function: Director Quality Monthly Work		Date: mm/dd/yyyy	Sheet 1 of 1
	Area: Quality		Prepared By: John Doe	
			Approved By: Jane Smith	Dept: Quality
	Operation Name: Monthly Work		Revision Date:	Revision Level: 1.0
# Work Elements / Important Steps	Key Points / Monthly Quality Activities	Reasons Why	Sketch / Drawing / Picture	
1 Quality Committee Meeting	Monthly meeting scheduled on the fourth Wednesday of every month at 12:30 - 2:00 PM. As part of the Quality Plan and the joint commission criteria as Quality Management oversight performed at regular intervals, at a minimum of once annually. Each department reports up to the Quality Committee at least 1x per year. See the presentation schedule located on the Quality Drive Committees and Councils)	Quality oversight of each area within hospital is vital to maintaining, reviewing, and improving quality processes throughout the organization. The Quality Committee is the sole venue to disseminate quality and regulatory information up through the leadership ranks.	2.	
2 Medical Executive Committee Attend	Monthly meeting scheduled on the third Thursday of every month. This meeting is managed and facilitated by the credentialing group. Quality participates each month to present the current quality scorecard. A template Word document is used to present the critical indicators score card, Serious Reportable Events, RCAs, Quality Improvement Scorecard, Current project status, and accreditation updates.	This is an informative discussion to keep the Medical Executive Team up to date on quality status throughout Trios	3.	
3 Board Committee	Monthly meeting. Prepare quality report out information. Information used for MEC can be used to support Board Report-out	This is close to the MEC template and used to keep the Board informed.		
4 Corporate Quality Meeting	Attend corporate scheduled quality team meetings.	This is a meeting to coordinate between all hospital's quality departments.	5.	
5 Employee 1:1 Meetings	Lead: One on one meetings for all direct reports done 30 minutes per employee per month. A template is utilized for the 1:1 meeting and stored in the employee file.	Coordinate department activities, goals, and check in with employee needs and performance.		
6 Mortality Review Chair	Chair the monthly Mortality Review Committee. Documents for this committee are located under the Quality share drive/Mortality Review Committee.	Process to review mortalities monthly.		
7 Infection Control Committee Meeting	Attend: Infection control committee is facilitated by the Infection Control team in collaboration with our infectious disease physician. This meeting outlines all hospital acquired conditions and improvements for IC issues.	Status updates on HAI.		
8 Safety Committee	Attend safety meeting	Status on safety initiatives.		
9 New Employee Orientation	New employee orientation is every other week on Mondays from 11 - 11:30 AM. Slides for this presentation are located under quality\New Employee Orientation	Engage new employees with the resources of the quality department.		

Figure 9.3 Quality director standard work – monthly.

Some key elements in quality director standard work are:

1. Daily
   a. Email management
   b. Incident review
   c. Safety huddle
   d. RCA management
   e. RCA events
   f. Team management activities
   g. Financial invoice management
2. Weekly
   a. Quality team huddle
   b. Administrative huddle
   c. Senior leadership report-out
   d. Weekly meetings
   e. Action item management
   f. Employee timecard approvals
   g. Employee onboarding
3. Monthly
   a. Monthly committee meetings
   b. Quality council facilitation
   c. Employee one-on-one meetings
   d. New employee orientation

9.4 Summary

The topic of sustaining quality is a large one. Many have seen quick wins or short-term improvements, but few experience long-term sustainability of those efforts. Sustainability requires an intentional effort to continually stay ahead of the curve. There are a multitude of books on sustainability. Every chapter in this book provides some foundational elements of achieving sustainability. It all links together.

As a quality professional, focus on supporting the daily management system. Move toward managing in-process measures that are meaningful to the patients you are caring for in the moment. Ask questions like, "How many patients are in the hospital today?" Of those patients, "How many have been assessed for risk of skin breakdown?" For those assessed as high risk for skin breakdown, "How many have been turned in the last two hours?" You may be lucky to get the answer to the first question. Finding these opportunities can help you lead the organization to focus on what matters most for your patients.

Standard work for the quality professional was introduced in this chapter. It is important to remain diligent and consistent in managing quality operations. Successfully managing to obtain quality outcomes requires all leaders in the organization to be diligent and consistent in managing **daily operations**. Although much of the quality professional's work is focused on outcomes or results, showing how you do this can provide an example of how others can utilize this method.

9.4.1 Key Concepts

■ A daily management system consists of managing in-process measures that prevent adverse events or poor outcomes.
■ Standard work for the quality professional demonstrates professionalism and commitment to managing daily operations.

9.4.2 Areas You Can Geek Out On

■ C. Protzman, G. Mayzell, MD, and J. Kerpchar, *Leveraging Lean in Healthcare: Transforming Your Enterprise into a High-Quality Patient Care Delivery System* (CRC Press) 2010.
■ Kim Barnas, *Beyond Heroes: A Lean Management System for Healthcare* (ThedaCare Center for Healthcare Value) 2014.

Notes

1 https://qualityindicators.ahrq.gov/Downloads/Modules/PSI/V60-ICD09/TechSpecs/PSI_03_Pressure_Ulcer_Rate.pdf.
2 faa.org, ENR 1.16 Safety, Hazard, and Accident Reports.
3 www.bts.gov/content/number-pilot-reported-near-midair-collisions-nmac-degree-hazard.
4 www.who.int/news-room/fact-sheets/detail/patient-safety.

Chapter 10

The Quality Plan

A quality improvement program is required by CMS conditions of participation (CoP) regulation.

§ 482.21 Condition of participation: Quality assessment and performance improvement program.

The hospital must develop, implement, and maintain an effective, ongoing, hospital-wide, data-driven quality assessment and performance improvement program. The hospital's governing body must ensure that the program reflects the complexity of the hospital's organization and services; involves all hospital departments and services (including those services furnished under contract or arrangement); and focuses on indicators related to improved health outcomes and the prevention and reduction of medical errors. The hospital must maintain and demonstrate evidence of its QAPI program for review by CMS.

The details of this regulation can be obtained at CMS.gov. If you follow the accreditation standards of the Joint Commission or DNV, the regulations are referenced there too (see Figure 10.1).

Quality Improvement

The Joint Commission:

- Performance Improvement 02.01.01
- Leadership 03.07.01

DNV:

- Quality Management System QM.1

Figure 10.1   Accreditation requirements.

Next, we will discusses one of the critical elements of managing quality for a hospital: the quality management plan. Any accrediting organization inspecting your facility will ask for the quality plan in order to determine how these regulations for quality performance improvement are followed.

The quality plan is a document that comprises of all the necessary elements to adhere to this regulation, but it should not be developed only for that purpose. A quality plan is a document that mirrors the strategic initiatives of your organization and applies the specific elements of quality and performance improvement. This document is one in which all members of the organization, up to the governing board, join forces to coordinate efforts for the common goals related to quality and performance improvement. Accreditation agencies want to ensure that the organization is unified and committed to continuous performance improvement.

The key elements of a quality plan should include (at a minimum):

1. Performance improvement priorities established by hospital leadership
2. Defined processes needing improvement, along with any stakeholder (for example, patient, staff, regulatory) requirements, project goals, and improvement activities
3. Method(s) for measuring performance of the processes identified for improvement analysis
4. Method(s) for identifying causes of variation and poor performance in the processes
5. Methods implemented to address process deficiencies and improve performance
6. Methods for monitoring and sustaining the improved processes
7. Leadership and governing board review and annual updates

If the organization already follows CMS's conditions of participation, there should be a quality plan on file. Start by locating the quality plan to determine the focus of past quality initiatives. Updating to make the plan current is much easier with a previous quality plan and helps keep the message consistent.

10.1 Components of the Quality Plan

Many organizations utilize the structure of their policies and procedures to complete a quality plan. Even if you choose to not use your organization's format for policies and procedures, keep the quality plan in the same location so it is accessible by anyone in the organization.

Purpose: State the purpose of the quality plan. Ensure that corrective and preventative actions are taken by the organization and objectives and goals are utilized as a means to coordinate and oversee the quality agenda.

Scope: The scope should outline the specific location and services accountable to the quality plan. If you have multiple hospitals and/or clinics, list all of them. List the departments and services in your organization: for example, oncology, surgery, emergency department, respiratory, etc.

Authority: This addresses who has authority over the quality plan. Because of the accreditation criteria, the authority should ultimately lie with the governing board. Under this umbrella, other authorities can be listed. Examples are the executive leadership, the medical executive committee, and the quality committee.

Organization: The organization of the components of the quality plan is managed through the quality committee. Here, activities to oversee, review, manage, and monitor should be detailed. For example, if the quality committee monitors the quality plan, outline the procedure(s) by which the quality committee does this. (See Figure 10.2.)

Organization: The Quality Council will meet at least eight times per year to accomplish the following:

1. Assure regulatory and accreditation standards are met by the hospital
2. Oversee and evaluate the effectiveness of the Quality Management System
3. Oversee patient safety initiatives
4. Oversee programs and projects aimed at achieving the organization's quality and safety goals
5. Determine annual quality and patient safety goals
6. Support the development, maintenance and monitoring of quality and patient safety goals
7. Provide administration, Medical Executive Committee, and governing Board with regular reports on quality of care

Figure 10.2   Quality plan organization.

Methodology: The methodology section of the quality plan describes how performance improvement is done. List and describe the techniques utilized to manage performance improvement. Examples may include PDSA, Lean, Six Sigma, RCA, etc. More is not better here. Have a standard methodology and describe it well.

Oversight: The oversight process of the governing board is described, with specific responsibilities listed. An example is provided in Figure 10.3.

Oversight:
The Governing Board, Medical Executive Committee, and Administration are responsible and accountable for promoting the organization's implementation and maintenance of an effective quality management improvement plan.
These duties are to:
• Promote the implementation and effectiveness of the Quality Management System
• Take action when reviewing the Quality Management improvement Plan to: Identify quality and performance problems
• Review corrective and preventative activities and evaluate for effectiveness
• Monitor the sustainability of those corrective and preventive activities
• Set priorities for improved quality of care and patient safety to include: Patient safety expectations
• Reduction of medical errors
• Eliminate preventable hospital acquired conditions (HAC)
• Eliminate preventable hospital acquired infections (HAI)

Figure 10.3   Quality plan oversight.

Communication: List the specific elements utilized to communicate initiatives throughout the year (e.g., the daily safety huddle, leadership meetings, the medical executive committee, and the governing board), those participating, the quality topic, and the frequency. (See Figure 10.3.)
Example:

Venue: Safety huddle
Frequency: Daily
Attendees: All leadership representation for each operational area of the business

Quality improvement program elements: The program elements of quality improvement can vary among hospitals. Now describe additional details about your program: process for identification, management, and improvement of quality incidents throughout the organization and quality incident definition with a list, if appropriate. Make clear to the reader how the organization defines a quality incident. Examples of quality incidents may be hospital-acquired conditions (HACs), harms, patient safety indicators (PSI), HIPPA incidents, EMTALA incidents, medication errors, operating room errors, patient complaints, unanticipated deaths, infection control incidents, or readmissions. The list of items to be managed through the quality plan can become quite extensive, so don't limit yourself to a specific list. Utilize wording such as "Quality indicator data should be presented at the quality committee and may include (but is not limited to . . .)" This allows you to provide the reader with specific information about quality incidents but does not limit your scope for quality review.

Performance improvement projects: If your organization has specific strategies related to quality, list those projects here. The quality plan is updated annually, so only those projects to be covered in the next 12 months would be listed here. Examples of projects could be hand hygiene compliance improvement, emergency department throughput initiative, readmission reduction, or pressure ulcer prevention. Limit the list to the top three or four to tackle for the upcoming year.

It is appropriate to use graphs and pictures in the quality plan. It is important that the quality plan be easy for everyone to understand. Include the elements required for accreditation, and make sure the plan is organized in a manner that can be readily understood. An example quality plan is provided in the appendix for this chapter.

Quality plan approval is critical. The plan should be reviewed and approved by the governing board. It is critical that the governing board document this approval in their minutes.

10.2 Summary

We outlined the format and structure for a quality plan. Developing one offers a great way to engage everyone in the organization and coordinate a consolidated approach to improving quality for the year. You can use the catch-ball sessions discussed in Chapter 6 to obtain necessary input. The more people engaged with the contents of the quality plan, the more likely they will be to participate in the initiatives supporting it throughout the year.

10.2.1 Key Concepts

- The quality plan is a condition of participation with CMS.
- Although the quality plan can be customized to meet your organizational needs, it must contain the key elements required in the CMS regulations.

10.2.2 Areas You Can Geek Out On

- § 482.21 Condition of participation: Quality assessment and performance improvement program
- Joint commission: Leadership and performance improvement
- DNV: Quality management system

Chapter 11

External Reporting

Although there are many different forms of reporting depending on the structure of your organization, most organizations are required to do some type of reporting to their state department of health, federal CMS, and the National Healthcare Safety Network (NHSN). Let's investigate who these entities are and their current reporting requirements.

11.1 National Healthcare Safety Network (NHSN)

NHSN is a tracking and reporting system for patient safety at the federal level. This organization promotes an effort for infection prevention working to achieve zero hospital-acquired infections (HAI) nationally. They have their own internet-based surveillance system for reporting.

NHSN reports on the following:

- National and state-specific standardized infection ratios
- Problem area data provided to facilities, states, regions, and nationally
- Tracking of blood safety errors and important healthcare process measures
- COVID-19 infection rates and status across the country

CMS reduces Medicare payments to hospitals in the worst-performing quartile with respect to hospital-acquired conditions (HACs). CMS utilizes the data from NHSN to help determine these rates.

BECKER'S
Hospital CFO Report

The 55 hospitals penalized by Medicare 8 years straight over patient complications

Ayla Ellison (Twitter) - Friday, February 18th, 2022 Print | Email

▭▭▭ ▭▭▭ ▭▭▭▭ Listen ▶ ᴀA TEXT

More than 2,000 hospitals have been penalized at least once in the eight years since the Hospital-Acquired Condition Reduction Program began. Fifty-five hospitals have been penalized all eight years, according to *Kaiser Health News*

Figure 11.1 Article hospital penalties.

DOI: 10.4324/9781003358404-12

11.2 Hospital Consumer Assessment of Healthcare Providers and Systems (HCAHPS)

HCAHPS (pronounced "H-caps"), also known as the CAHPS hospital survey, is a survey instrument and data collection methodology for measuring patients' perceptions of their hospital experience. HCAHPS has three broad goals:

1. Produce data about patients' perspectives on care that allow objective and meaningful comparisons of hospitals on topics that are important to consumers
2. Create new incentives for hospitals to improve quality of care
3. Enhance accountability in healthcare by increasing the transparency of the quality of hospital care provided

Figure 11.2   CMS five-star patient survey rating.

The HCAHPS survey asks discharged patients 29 questions about their recent hospital stays in nine categories.

- Communication with doctors
- Communication with nurses
- Responsiveness of hospital staff
- Cleanliness of the hospital
- Quietness of the hospital
- Communication about medicines
- Discharge information
- Care transition
- Overall rating of hospital
- Willingness to recommend hospital

A complete set of HCAHPS questions is available in the appendix for this chapter.

Since HCAHPS is a standard set of questions developed by the Centers for Medicare and Medicaid Services (CMS) and the Agency for Healthcare Research and Quality (AHRQ), there are a number of vendors that provide the HCAHPS service. An approved vendor list for HCAHPS can be found at https://hcahpsonline.org/en/approved-vendor-list/.

Vendors providing this service send out surveys to customers, collect the returned surveys, and store them in a database. They provide this information to CMS through the QualityNet portal (discussed later in the chapter) if your organization allows them to do so. There are some key things to understand about the configuration of HCAHPS data and your organization:

1. Vendors do not survey 100% of your customers. Find out what the sample methodology for your organization is from your HCAHPS vendor.

2. Does your vendor have access to load the HCAHPS data to the CMS portal for you?
3. How do you access the vendor's database to obtain your own HCAHPS results?

Any vendor providing this service for you should also provide you access to the survey results in real time. It is important to access and understand the HCAHPS results. This data should be utilized internally for quality scorecard reporting and organizational process improvements. Without this transparency, the results will be known only after CMS has published them.

11.3 QualityNet/HARP (CMS) Portal

There has been a lot of confusion around the terminology utilized for the CMS portal. Terms that are used often to mean the same thing are *HARP*, *QualityNet*, and *inpatient quality reporting* (IQR).

HARP is a CMS application that stands for HCQIS access roles and profile. This system is a secure identity management portal for CMS. In essence, it is the system that enables you to access, through an ID and password, all the other CMS applications. QualityNet is the CMS website for secure communications and healthcare quality data exchange. You must be credentialed through HARP to access the QualityNet application.

https://qualitynet.cms.gov/

Figure 11.3   QualityNet home page.

The QualityNet application contains information needed for the inpatient quality reporting (IQR) program for CMS. As a quality professional, you will need to create an account with the QualityNet system. It will guide you through the HARP registration process first and provide credentials to QualityNet.

QualityNet is a data-reporting program for inpatient hospital services implemented by CMS. From their website:

> Under the Hospital IQR Program, CMS collects quality data from hospitals paid under the Inpatient Prospective Payment System, with the goal of driving quality improvement through measurement and transparency by publicly displaying data to help consumers make more informed decisions about their health care.

Initially, CMS applied a 0.4-percentage-point reduction in payment to hospitals that did not successfully report. The Deficit Reduction Act of 2005 increased that reduction to 2.0 percentage points.

As a quality professional, be familiar with the QualityNet application. If you are new to this, here are a few things you should look into:

1. Sign up for a QualityNet/HARP account.
2. After signing up, you will receive email notifications when data needs to be updated on the site.
3. Log in and update measures requested/required by QualityNet.

You will also be notified through this site when quality rankings and results are available. When notified, go to the site and download the information. The information can be lengthy and time consuming to process, but familiarity alleviates that. Summarize the report findings to provide leadership. An example of a report sent to you through QualityNet is readmissions. The data will contain all the encounter-level detail on patients who were readmitted, the CMS methodology for calculating the results, actual readmission rates, benchmark comparisons, and potential penalties that will be applied to the organization. Create a simple graph as seen in Figure 11.4 to compare your rate to expected rates. This distills over 100 pages of information into a single picture that can be shared with leadership. The concept that if the learner did not learn, the trainer did not train applies here too. Simply forwarding many pages of information received from CMS to leadership does not align with the goal of providing meaningful information that everyone can quickly understand.

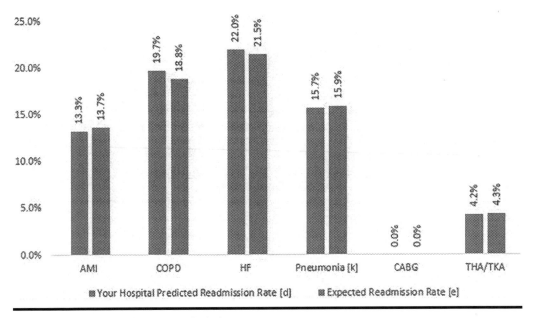

Figure 11.4 30 day all cause readmissions.

The data captured in QualityNet changes over time, but as of this writing, the following categories of data are in QualityNet:

■ Hospital inpatient measure sets
  • Electronic clinical quality measures (eCQM)
  • Healthcare-associated infections (HAI)

- Hospital consumer assessment (HCAHPS)
- Hospital-wide readmissions (HWR)
- Payment standardization
- Total hip arthroplasty/total knee arthroplasty (THA/TKA) patient-reported outcome-based performance measures
■ Claims-based measures
  - Complication measures
  - Disparity methods confidential reporting
  - Episode-based payment measures
  - Excess days in acute care (EDAC) measures
  - Hospital value-based purchasing (HVBP) mortality and complication measures
  - Medicare spending per beneficiary (MSPB) measure
  - Mortality measures
  - Patient safety indicators
  - Payment measures
  - Readmission measures
■ Hospital inpatient quality program measures
  - Hospital inpatient quality reporting (IQR) program measures
  - Hospital value-based purchasing (HVBP) program measures
  - Hospital-acquired condition (HAC) reduction program measures
  - Hospital readmission reduction program (HRRP) measures

As a registered user of QualityNet, you will receive detailed instructions when these measures need to be updated along with the reporting time frame parameters. Additional measure detail can be found at https://qualitynet.cms.gov/inpatient/measures.

11.4 Using Vendors for QualityNet Data

Many of the data elements uploaded to QualityNet can be done through vendors. A third-party vendor may submit data on a provider's behalf if previously authorized by the hospital. Hospitals utilizing a vendor must first complete the online vendor management application process via the HQR secure portal. Vendor authorizations remain in effect until the hospital modifies the authorization.

As a quality professional, understand which vendors you are utilizing to manage measures. There are many vendors that provide services for eCQM, HCAHPS, IQR, readmissions, complications, and patient safety indicators. A simple internet search for these services will provide a lot of information. It is unlikely that readers are starting at the beginning with little or no vendor support. Most organizations already have established programs in place, but few completely understand what those vendors are doing for them. As a quality professional, you have the opportunity to outline and understand these vendor partnerships.

Once you have access to QualityNet, open the Vendor Management section of the application. This will illustrate which vendors can update QualityNet information. If you are unsure of what they are doing for you, reach out to those companies and ask for clarification. Most are very willing to help you understand and partner to manage the metrics they are submitting. Figure 11.5 shows the QualityNet Vendor Management page.

CMS.gov | Hospital Quality Reporting

Vendor Management

Your Vendors

Search   Status

4 Vendors				Add Vendor
Name ▲		**Vendor ID**	**Status**	
HOSPITALS		H-0S4725	● Active	⋮
MEDISOLV, INC		V100359	● Active	⋮
PREMIER HEALTHCARE SOLUTIONS, INC		J051101	● Active	⋮
PRESS GANEY ASSOCIATES		V100063	● Active	⋮

Figure 11.5 CMS hospital quality reporting.

11.5 Updating Information in QualityNet

The data submission deadlines for QualityNet can be found on the CMS website at https://qualitynet.cms.gov/outpatient/data-management/data-submission/deadlines.

It is good practice at the beginning of the year to review deadlines and incorporate them into your quality management calendar (see calendar for reporting in Chapter 14), quality huddles, or other schedule you utilize to manage accountabilities.

[EXTERNAL] AutoRoute - Package 500053_2022_DRAH>

CMS-MFT <noreply@hcqis.org>
To Johnson Douglas

CMS.gov | MANAGED FILE TRANSFER

Figure 11.6 CMS hospital quality reporting email.

As a user of the QualityNet application, you will receive updates from the application when specific measures are requested (Figure 11.6). Click on the link provided or go to https://hqr.cms.gov/hqrng/login and log in to the system. Select each of the tabs located at the top of the page (eCQM, Web-Based Measures, Population & Sampling, Chart Abstracted, HCAHPS, and Structural Measures) to look for any measures that are available for update (Figure 11.7). CMS opens these measures for the period of time they are to be updated and closes them when the reporting opportunity is over. The email will initiate communication when those measures are open for update.

Figure 11.7   CMS hospital quality reporting structural measures.

QualityNet reporting is an important responsibility. It is important to become familiar with your hospital's practices to update this information. In most cases, this will be done through a combination of vendor-supported applications, data interfaces, and manual data entry. Additional information, training, and support can be found at QualityNet.CMS.gov.

11.6 COVID-19 Reporting

With the COVID-19 pandemic, CMS created a new condition of participation in October 2020 requiring hospitals to report hospital status measures to HHS daily. Many state departments of health require the same information.

DEPARTMENT OF HEALTH & HUMAN SERVICES
Centers for Medicare & Medicaid Services
7500 Security Boulevard, Mail Stop C2-21-16
Baltimore, Maryland 21244-1850

CENTERS FOR MEDICARE & MEDICAID SERVICES

Center for Clinical Standards and Quality/Quality, Safety & Oversight Group

Ref: QSO-21-03-Hospitals/CAHs

DATE: October 6, 2020

TO: CMS Locations State Agencies, Hospitals/CAHs, and other
           stakeholders

FROM: Director Quality, Safety & Oversight Group- Division of Continuing and Acute
           Care Providers

SUBJECT: Interim Final Rule (IFC), CMS-3401-IFC; Requirements and Enforcement
Process for Reporting of COVID-19 Data Elements for Hospitals and Critical Access Hospitals

5. Providers that have failed to meet the reporting requirements within 1 week following the
    second enforcement notification letter will receive a third and final enforcement
    notification letter. This notification will include a notice of termination to become
    effective within 30 days from the date of the notification. Failure to meet the reporting
    requirements within this 30-day timeframe may result in termination of the Medicare
    provider agreement.

Figure 11.8   CMS condition of participation COVID reporting.

The new data reporting requirements involve daily patient census, COVID- and influenza-positive patients, personal protective equipment inventories, ventilator inventory status, and others. At the time of this writing, there are 134 measures collected under this reporting condition of participation. If your state requires this information, they will also have a process and/or software for you to submit your data. A couple of software vendors used by states are Juvare EMResource, and ImageTrend. As a quality professional, determine what your state requirements are for reporting. Currently, there are 32 states certified to report information to HHS for the hospitals in their state. This means those states have the application or the means to report the information directly to the state, and they, in turn, send it to HHS. This eliminates the need to send the data to both the state and HHS. If your state does not submit data to HHS for you, you are required to update the data through HHS's application NHSN. The list of states certified to report COVID-19 data for their hospitals is located at https://healthdata.gov/stories/s/COVID-19-Hospital-Reporting-State-Certification-St/i62t-8mpj/.

Because reporting these measures 365 days a year is labor intensive, a software vendor has developed an automation application to update state and federal reporting requirements. Consulting Remedy, LLC (www.ConsultingRemedy.com) provides a solution that utilizes standard processes and information from your hospital's electronic medical record to update this data. In the interest of full disclosure, I am a part owner of this company. We have had a 100% compliance rate for all hospitals utilizing this service since its inception in 2020.

For additional information and a full detailed list of current measures for reporting, visit HealthData.gov.

11.7 Summary

There are many areas of external reporting for healthcare organizations. Reporting requirements vary significantly from state to state. The federal reporting requirements were outlined in this chapter. Work with your state's department of health to determine the specific reporting requirements for your organization. Proactively identifying reporting requirements will allow you to obtain access to the systems necessary, develop internal report collection methodologies to obtain the data, and set up a quality reporting calendar so department staff can be prepared to report on time.

11.7.1 Key Concepts

- QualityNet is CMS's application for collecting quality data.
- There may be many other external reporting requirements, depending on state requirements, corporate affiliation, and preference.

11.7.2 Areas You Can Geek Out On

- Review the data submission deadlines for QualityNet and incorporate them into a quality calendar for your department: https://qualitynet.cms.gov/outpatient/data-management/data-submission/deadlines.

Chapter 12

Patient Safety Organization, Quality Incidents, and Mortality Reviews

12.1 Patient Safety Organization (PSO)

This chapter will describe the patient safety organization (PSO), its purpose, and how a quality professional manages it.

The patient safety organization (PSO) was created out of the Patient Safety and Quality Improvement Act (PSQIA) of 2005. From HHS.gov:

> This act establishes a voluntary reporting system designed to enhance the data available to assess and resolve patient safety and health care quality issues. To encourage the reporting and analysis of medical errors, PSQIA provides Federal privilege and confidentiality protections for patient safety information, called patient safety work product. PSQIA authorizes HHS to impose civil money penalties for violations of patient safety confidentiality. PSQIA also authorizes the Agency for Healthcare Research and Quality (AHRQ) to list patient safety organizations (PSOs). PSOs are the external experts that collect and review patient safety information.

The PSO provides privilege and confidentiality protections for providers who choose to work with them. The intent is to promote shared learning from medical errors to improve patient safety across the nation.

Why is a PSO important? Prior to this act, clinicians and healthcare workers were not protected from sharing the truth about medical errors. For a quality professional trying to find root causes for medical errors, there was more of a disincentive by clinicians to share information and mistakes (because of potential lawsuits) than there was an incentive to share them. Under the protection of the PSO, information that is considered "nondiscoverable" in order to solve real issues related to patient harm can be shared confidentially now.

Figure 12.1   PSO seal.

Determine if your organization already participates in a PSO. If your organization is part of a larger system of hospitals, chances are they have this program in place. A list of active PSOs can be found on the AHRQ website.[1]

If your organization wants to become a PSO, the AHRQ website provides the instructions, requirements, and process to do so.[2]

The PSO benefits your organization by putting a spotlight on the importance of patient safety and quality care. As a quality professional, you will have the trust of more clinicians when they realize the reason for investigation is to get to the root cause of an issue in order to improve care for future patients. They'll realize participation is protected under the PSO.

Although it is beneficial to have a PSO, it comes with specific requirements:

1. The mission and primary activity of the PSO must be to conduct activities to <u>improve patient safety and the quality of healthcare delivery</u>.
2. The PSO must have appropriately <u>qualified workforce members</u>, including licensed or certified medical professionals.
3. The PSO, within the 24-month period that begins on the date of its initial listing as a PSO and within each sequential 24-month period thereafter, must have <u>two bona fide contracts</u>, each for a reasonable period of time, each with a different provider for the purpose of receiving and reviewing patient safety work product.
4. The PSO is <u>not a health insurance issuer</u> or a component of a health insurance issuer.
5. The PSO must make <u>disclosures</u> as required under the PSQIA.
6. To the extent practical and appropriate, the PSO must <u>collect patient safety work product</u> from providers in a <u>standardized manner</u> that permits valid comparisons of similar cases among similar providers.
7. The PSO must utilize patient safety work product for the <u>purpose of providing direct feedback and assistance to providers</u> to effectively minimize patient risk.

When performing a root-cause analysis or process improvement (PDSA or other) or discussing the medical error, all documents and discussions should be under the umbrella of the PSO. If you read the PSQIA in its entirety, you may be overwhelmed. Let's attempt to simplify the things a quality professional should do under the umbrella of a PSO.

1. PSO policy
    If you don't currently have a policy for the PSO, one will need to be created. An organization working under the aegis of a PSO must have a policy in place. The policy should provide

the scope, purpose, definitions, and details of your organization's PSO management. If you are already participating in a PSO, you should be able to obtain a template policy.

2. PSO documentation for patient safety work product (PSWP)

Utilize a standard confidentiality statement to be placed on all documents and materials related to the medical error under investigation. An example is:

> *This is a confidential patient safety work product document. It is protected from disclosure pursuant to the provisions of the Patient Safety and Quality Improvement Act (42 CFR Part 3) and other state and federal laws. Unauthorized disclosure or duplication is absolutely prohibited.*

Remember, emails that contain this information must include this statement. It's helpful to create a PSO signature in Outlook using this statement that can be easily selected before sending an email.

3. PSO confidentiality agreement

When discussing PSO-related information with employees, it is important to have a PSO confidentiality agreement signed. Having this agreement allows you to explain the importance of the PSO and their role in participating. If a person has signed one previously, before a new discussion, remind them that the information falls under the same confidentiality agreement. It is important to let anyone participating in PSO activities know that there can be no gossip, discussion, or sharing of the information outside the PSO event. If they do discuss information outside the PSO event, it will be deemed "discoverable" and can be used in punitive ways. An example of a confidentiality agreement is available in the appendix for your reference.

4. File storage for patient safety work product (PSWP)

Create an electronic file folder on a secure server in your organization to store all PSWP documents and related items. It becomes difficult to find PSWP documents when they are stored and saved randomly throughout the quality department. Having a separate location helps make them readily available and secure. Work with your information technology support department to set up the security requirements for the server location. Only members of the PSO should have access to the contents.

5. Reporting PSWP

After utilizing the PSO to perform a root-cause analysis or process improvement, the information should be submitted to your PSO for file storage. One of the requirements of a PSO is to collect PSWP in a "standardized manner that permits valid comparisons of similar cases among similar providers." If you don't currently have a PSO and are not able to find a standard, you can create a standard reporting mechanism by developing a Word document template.

In summary, PSO management can vary depending on your organization's policies, procedures, and processes. If you already have a PSO, reach out to the PSO champion to get information on defined procedures and practices. If you do not have a PSO for your organization, I encourage you to go to the Agency for Healthcare Research and Quality (AHRQ) and follow the steps to become one. Lastly, even if you don't fall under the umbrella of a PSO, these practices are a good way to manage patient safety–related work product within your organization.

12.2 Quality Incident Events

A quality professional will quickly get buried in terminology, acronyms, and differing definitions. There's a glossary of terms at the end of the book to reference when faced with yet another

Events...

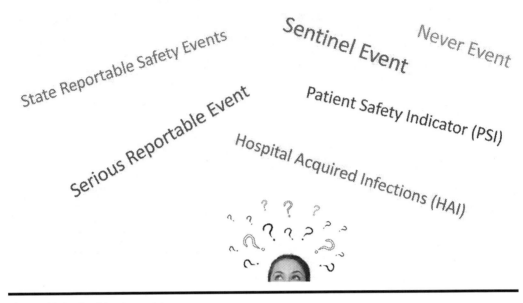

Figure 12.2   Incident event terms.

unfamiliar term. The terms describing quality incident events are no exception. This section attempts to distill the multiple terms used for a quality event and give you an understanding of where they came from, what they mean, and what that means to you. Some of the terms for quality events are:

- Serious reportable events (SRE)
- State reportable safety events (SRSE)
- Sentinel events (SE)
- Never events (NE)
- Patient safety indicators (PSI)
- Hospital-acquired infections (HAI)
- Hospital-acquired conditions (HAC)

People use terminology in different ways at different times, creating a lot of confusion. One person may use the term *SRE* for everything while another person will use the term *never event* when they are both actually talking about the same thing. As a quality professional, I encourage you to standardize your terminology and familiarize people with how to use it.

12.2.1 Serious Reportable Events (SRE)

The National Quality Forum developed and endorsed a set of serious reportable events (SREs) This is a compilation of serious, largely preventable, and harmful clinical events, designed to help the healthcare field assess, measure, and report performance in providing safe care. A list of SREs defined by the National Quality Forum can be found on their website.[3] These events are well defined, with a classification system that enables you to compare classifications across the industry.

For example, under SREs, classification 1A is a surgical or invasive procedure event that results in a procedure performed on the wrong site. If other organizations utilize the same SRE criteria, you can compare the duration and frequency of their 1A events to yours.

12.2.2 Sentinel Events (SE)

A sentinel event is the Joint Commission's version of the patient safety event.[4] A sentinel event is a patient safety event that results in death, permanent harm, or severe temporary harm where intervention is required to sustain life. Detailed information on sentinel events can be found on the Joint Commission website.

12.2.3 Never Events (NE)

You may find healthcare employees using the term *never event*. The good news is that this term has the same meaning as serious reportable event (SRE). The term *never event* was first introduced in 2001 by Ken Kizer, MD, former CEO of the National Quality Forum (NQF), in reference to particularly shocking medical errors that should never occur.[5] Over time, the term's use has expanded to signify adverse events that are unambiguous (clearly identifiable and measurable), serious (resulting in death or significant disability), and usually preventable. Since the initial never event list was developed in 2002, it has been revised multiple times and is now referred to as serious reportable events.

12.2.4 Patient Safety Indicators (PSI)

PSIs were discussed in Chapter 2, but it is important to mention them again in this context. Although it's unlikely people use the term *PSI* solely to describe a quality incident, I am beginning to see it happen more frequently. Patient safety indicators are a set of 26 indicators (including 18 provider-level indicators) developed by the Agency for Healthcare Research and Quality (AHRQ)[6] to provide information on safety-related adverse events occurring in hospitals following operations, procedures, and childbirth. The PSIs were developed after a comprehensive literature review, analysis of available diagnosis codes, review by a clinician panel, implementation of risk adjustment, and empirical analyses. **It is important to note that patient safety indicators are determined based only on claims billing data submitted**. It would not be appropriate to use the term *PSI* to describe all quality incident events.

12.2.5 Hospital-Acquired Infections (HAI)

The term *hospital-acquired infection* specifically relates to detailed criteria defined by the CDC[7] for central line–associated infections (CLABSI), catheter-associated urinary tract infections (CAUTI), surgical site infections (SSI), and ventilator-associated pneumonia (VAP). Although these events can be classified as quality incident events, they are managed under their own classifications.

12.3 Quality Incident Summary

What does all of this terminology mean to the quality director? First of all, find out which classifications you need to follow based on your organizational policies and procedures, PSO policy, state requirements, and accreditation agency requirements. If, for example, you utilize the Joint

Commission for accreditation, the terminology and associated classification system for sentinel events would need to be used. Some states require that events be reported to the department of health. Their classification systems generally follow one of those listed earlier. I found it helpful in organizations that use multiple classification systems to create a cross-reference grid for each one. Figure 12.3 represents a portion of a checklist that contains both SRE and SE criteria. The entire checklist is available in the appendix for this chapter. This enables the user to utilize the checklist and quickly identify whether something is an event and what classification(s) it falls under. This tool is very helpful in educating, reducing confusion, and initiating the reporting requirements, depending on which classification it falls under.

Event Checklist		SRE	SE
SURGICAL OR INVASIVE PROCEDURE EVENTS			
Wrong Site	SRE1A Wrong Site SE11 Surgery or other invasive procedure performed at the wrong site, on the wrong patient, or that is the wrong (unintended) procedure for a patient regardless of the type of procedure or the magnitude of the outcome	X	X
Wrong Patient	SRE1B Wrong Patient PC18 Procedure or surgery on wrong patient, wrong site, or wrong (unintended) procedure SE11	X	X
Wrong Procedure	SRE1C Wrong Procedure SE11	X	X
Retained Object	SRE1D Retained Foreign Object PC3 Object inadvertently left in after surgery SE16 Unintended retention of a foreign object in a patient after an invasive procedure, including surgery	X	X
OR Death	SRE1E Intra-Op or Immediate Post-Op Death of ASA Class 1 patient PC15 Unexpected death, suicide, or death occurring in the operating room	X	
PRODUCT OR DEVICE EVENTS			
Medications	SRE2A Death or serious injury associated with contaminated drugs, devices or biologics provided by the healthcare setting	X	
Device	SRE2B Death or serious injury associated use or function of a device in patient care	X	
Air Emboli	SRE2C Death or serious injury associated intravascular air embolism that occurs while being cared for in a healthcare setting PC3 Air Embolism	X	
PATIENT PROTECTION EVENTS			
Discharge	SRE3A Discharge or release of a patient/resident of any age, who is unable to make decisions, to other than an authorized person	X	
Discharge	SE12 Discharge of an infant to the wrong family		X
Elopement	SRE3B Patient death or serious injury associated with patient elopement (disappearance) PC23 Elopement leading to death or permanent injury or severe temporary injury SE14 Any elopement (that is, unauthorized departure) of a patient from a staffed around-the-clock care setting (including the ED), leading to death, permanent harm, or severe harm to the patient	X	X
Suicide	SRE3C Patient suicide, attempted suicide, or self-harm that results in serious injury, while being cared for in a healthcare setting SE1 Suicide of any patient receiving care, treatment, and services in a staffed around-the clock care setting or within 72 hours of discharge, including from the health care organization's emergency department (ED)	X	X

Figure 12.3 Event classification guide.

Because there are many different classification systems and rules related to quality events, remember you can always do a process improvement event containing a root-cause analysis on anything you feel is amiss. Having a standard process improvement methodology (like PDSA) and using that methodology for all of them is critical. Additional tools and techniques can be utilized if necessary; when you initiate every one with a standard process, it will serve well in standardization, training, documentation, and accreditation. Classify and track all events regardless of whether they meet one of the classification events. If it is in question, classify it. Recorded documentation showing classification determination and decision making is important.

12.4 Mortality Reviews

Mortality rates are among the top measures utilized in healthcare for comparisons and benchmarks. As mentioned in Chapter 2, mortality rates are used as part of the CMS five-star criteria for quality performance. Mortality rates are an important measure and contribute significantly to hospital-based reimbursement. The CMS measures look for 30-day mortality rates for these specific diagnostic categories: congestive heart failure (CHF), acute myocardial infarction (AMI), pneumonia, stroke, and chronic obstructive pulmonary disease (COPD). The 30-day mortality rate is an important point to understand. Since most hospitals look at fatalities occurring in the hospital, CMS analyzes mortality rates based on patients who died while hospitalized <u>and</u> within 30 days of their discharge. You may or may not know whether a patient dies after discharge through the use of your electronic medical record resources, but Medicare (as a health insurance provider) has the larger picture of the patient's progress post discharge. For this reason, it is unlikely you will be able to match the results for Medicare mortality rates. Hospitals can look at in-hospital mortality and estimate 30-day mortality rates. That's as close as you'll get.

Reviewing mortalities in your organization is more than just good practice. Those who take this review seriously believe that we save lives by studying deaths. On the other hand, I have also heard "We are a hospital, and in hospitals, people die." Although this is true, the goal of hospitals is to treat people and to every extent possible keep them from that final outcome. It is our duty to those patients and their families to review these cases to understand whether we could have done anything to prevent the mortality.

It seems every hospital in the country has their own custom process for reviewing mortalities. Regardless of the specified process at your institution, performing mortality reviews will enable your organization to identify trends and focus improvement efforts.

In this chapter, I will suggest a process for performing mortality reviews and my thoughts on these processes that result from my experiences.

My first thought regarding mortality reviews is that they must be significantly supported with <u>participation from a physician medical director or similar</u>. Many organizations attempt to have nurses or staff in the quality department perform all mortality reviews with no input from physicians. This is a critical mistake. When it comes to decision making, diagnoses, and treatment of complex patients, physicians are the professionals we look to. Second-guessing whether they made the right decisions, diagnoses, or treatment should also remain with them. This does not mean we should have physicians review their own cases and make an after-the-fact recommendation of their findings. Rather, we should utilize the knowledge of other physicians to make those determinations.

My second thought when it comes to mortality reviews is that <u>one person should not make the final determination of the findings</u>. I suggest having a mortality review committee that includes at least one physician, quality personnel, and subject matter experts who can review each mortality.

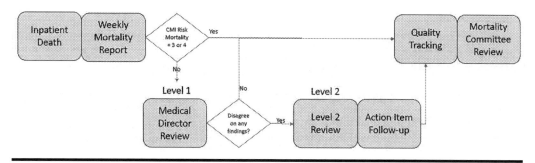

Figure 12.4   Mortality review process.

It may seem impossible to review all mortalities. With all the other quality demands, adding this one may seem like too much. The good news is that you don't need to review all mortalities. Figure 12.4 provides a sample flowchart to utilize for reviewing mortalities.

When a patient dies in the hospital, they are coded with a discharge disposition of "expired." This enables most organizations to run a simple report from their electronic medical record to search for any patients with that discharge disposition within the last week. Another common coding summary found in your electronic medical record is the case mix index (CMI) risk of mortality. This risk is determined through diagnoses codes and procedures for the hospitalized patient.

This flowchart works initially to separate those at high risk for mortality from those with low risk. Remember, we are looking after the fact, so we already know whether there are any patients classified with a lower risk of mortality who died. A patient with an extreme or major risk of mortality (3 or 4) is one who has a very complex condition and is at a high risk of mortality. Those with less than a 3 risk of mortality are not considered to be at high risk. This flowchart separates the 1- and 2-risk from the 3- and 4-risk patients. If the patient had a 1 or 2 risk of mortality, they are sent to a physician medical director to review.

Patient Initials:		MR#		Encounter#	
Admit Date		Death Date		Unit	
Certified Cause of Death					

	Agree	Disagree
I am satisfied with the cause of death as listed above		
To my knowledge, there were no significant errors of omission / commission from one week prior to admission to the time of death		
To my knowledge, no clinical incidents or adverse events occurred during the course of the admission (such as a fall, unexpected return to theatre, unexpected readmission, prescribing error)		
To my knowledge, there were no issues in relation to negative patient experience raised by the patient or family, or known to me (such as a complaint)		
I consider this death to have been unavoidable		

If you disagree with any of these statements, a formal mortality review must take place	
This death should be reviewed more fully	
I do **not** consider that this death requires further review	

Name/Signature		Date	

Figure 12.5 Mortality level 1 review form.

In order to help standardize these reviews and remind the reviewer what to address, an initial review template is utilized. Figure 12.5 provides an example of this Level-1 review form that should be completed by a physician. Issues addressed are:

1. I am satisfied with the cause of death as listed above.
2. To my knowledge, there were no significant errors of omission/commission from one week prior to admission to the time of death.

3. To my knowledge, no clinical incidents or adverse events occurred during the course of the admission (such as a fall, unexpected return to theater, unexpected readmission, prescribing error).
4. To my knowledge, there were no issues in relation to negative patient experience raised by the patient or family or known to me (such as a complaint).
5. I consider this death to have been unavoidable.

If the reviewer disagrees with any of these statements, the case should go to further review.

A Level-2 review is more detailed and involves additional work. By the time a patient review gets to this level, the number of reviews is usually very small. They were already narrowed down significantly by selecting only 1 and 2 CMI risk of mortality cases, then narrowed down again after the initial Level-1 review.

A Level-2 review involves significant chart review, data gathering, and sometimes interviews with the clinicians involved in the case. All reviews and their findings should be tracked on a quality tracking form and taken to the mortality review committee for one final review and recommended next steps. Next steps may include further investigation, physician peer review, process improvement initiatives, or documentation and closure. In any event, tracking all mortalities and managing them in this way will enable you to trend them using a holistic view. For example, if data shows that a large majority of low-risk mortalities followed a specific procedure type, yet all Level-1 reviews came back as "no need for further review," the trending of these mortalities may still lead you to further investigation. Figure 12.6 provides an example of a quality mortality tracking form utilized for this process. Level-1 and Level-2 review forms are provided in the appendix.

Mortality Review Log															
							Level 1 Review		Review Responses					Level 2 Review?	
Patient Initials	MR#	Date Admit	Date Death	Attending Provider	Unit	CMI Risk	Reviewed Date	Reviewed by	Q1	Q2	Q3	Q4	Q5	Level 2 Review?	Date	Actions

Figure 12.6   Mortality review log.

The key thing to remember about mortality reviews is standard process. There are many ways to review mortalities. How to manage mortality reviews is up to each organization. Having a process in place will enable you to collect information and initiate process improvements with your findings. Chapter 4 outlined measurement and analytics and gave ideas on how to analyze data. Mortality review data allows you to do the same thing by looking for trends and different groupings and classifications that can lead to opportunities for improvement.

12.5 Summary

As with many things in healthcare quality, topics discussed merge together and should work cooperatively. The patient safety organization is the defining body that encompasses the information necessary to manage quality incidents and mortality reviews.

Your organization may have standard procedures and software for managing quality incidents. Identify these sources in your organization and maximize their effectiveness. You may have a tool that is available to anyone in the organization to report quality incidents. Determine the effectiveness of this tool, whether people are aware of it, and whether they use it. If you can get the organization to report quality incidents when they occur, the ability to manage the quality of these incidents will be significantly increased.

Lastly, although mortality review processes vary among hospitals, ensure you have a program in place to review them and obtain opportunities for improvement. Engage your physicians and leaders to provide a physician champion to lead the reviews.

12.5.1 Key Concepts

- The PSO provides privilege and confidentiality protections for providers who choose to work with them. The intent is to promote shared learning from medical errors and improve patient safety across the nation.
- There are many terms used to describe a quality incident. Identify terms used in your organization and standardize their meanings. Continually train and mentor employees in your organization on how to use the terms.
- You should have a process in place for reviewing inpatient mortalities. Make sure you have physician leadership in making judgments about mortalities.

12.5.2 Areas You Can Geek Out On

- Study the instructions, requirements, and processes for becoming a PSO: https://pso.ahrq.gov/become.
- Identify the types of quality events your organization uses for classification and create your own event classification guide like that found in the appendix for this chapter.
- Mortality review study material:
  - Duke Health:
    https://ja.dh.duke.edu/sites/default/files/Sea%20Pines%20Mortality%20Review%202017-05-23_for_upload.pdf.
  - National Library of Medicine: Quality Gaps Identified through Mortality Review
    www.ncbi.nlm.nih.gov/pmc/articles/PMC5284344/#:~:text=Hospital%20mortality%20rate%20is%20a,problems%20associated%20with%20patient%20deaths.

Notes

1 https://pso.ahrq.gov/pso.
2 https://pso.ahrq.gov/become.
3 List of SRE by National Quality Forum: www.qualityforum.org/Topics/SREs/List_of_SREs.aspx.
4 www.jointcommission.org/resources/sentinel-event/.
5 https://psnet.ahrq.gov/primer/never-events.
6 https://qualityindicators.ahrq.gov/measures/psi_resources.
7 www.cdc.gov/hai/index.html.

Chapter 13

Managing Hospital-Acquired Conditions (HAC) and Harms

13.1 Role of the Quality Professional in HACs and Harms

As a quality professional, you would think that all complications, harms, and hospital-acquired conditions would come in through the incident management system, awareness, or self-reports. The fact is that things happen in a hospital that sometimes you are never aware of. It is particularly difficult being unaware of incidents only to find out later when they show up in public reporting by way of claims data.

This section discusses steps a quality professional can take to be aware of hospital-acquired conditions and harm events and review them for appropriateness before they are reported externally.

To understand a HACs and harms review, one must first understand a little about billing in a hospital claim system. Hospitals have entire departments of people educated and certified in managing and processing claims. It is good to get to know these people and utilize their talents to assist you in managing healthcare quality. For the purpose of managing hospital-acquired conditions and harms, however, there are some basics to understand. After a patient is discharged from the hospital, the claims department summarizes the admission and submits a bill to the insurance carrier utilizing a health insurance claim form that has a required list of data elements for the hospital to get paid for the service. The form has multiple fields for information about the patient's hospitalization. The fields that we are concerned with for this discussion are <u>procedures</u> and <u>diagnoses</u>. Attached to each of a patient diagnoses is an indicator that specifies whether the patient came to the hospital with that diagnoses. This indicator, called the **present on admission flag (POAF)**, identifies whether the specific diagnosis for the patient was present on admission, not present on admission, or unknown. <u>A diagnosis of "not present on admission" or "unknown" is considered a hospital-acquired condition and/or harm caused by the hospital.</u> Figure 13.1 represents a hospital encounter with three diagnosis codes. In this example, the Stage-4 pressure ulcer is listed as *N* or not present on admission. It is through these indicators that hospitals are ranked (by claims data) on quality indicators such as pneumonia, aspiration, pressure injuries, etc. Patient safety indicators (PSI), listed and discussed in Chapter 2, are the primary quality measures that are ranked through this methodology.

Diag Code 0	Diag Desc 0	POAF 0	Diag Code 1	Diag Desc 1	POAF 1	Diag Code 2	Diag Desc 2	POAF 2	Diag Code 3	Diag Desc 3	POAF 3
R53.1	WEAKNESS	Y	L89.154	PRESSURE ULCER OF SACRAL REGION, STAGE 4	N	E43	UNSPECIFIED SEVERE PROTEIN-CALORIE MALNUTRITION	Y	I63.40	CEREBRAL INFARCTION DUE TO EMBOLISM OF UNSPECIFIED CEREBRAL ARTERY	Y

Figure 13.1 Present on admission flag.

Why does the quality professional care about the processing of a claim? The answer is simple: it is through those claims that incidents you may be unaware of get reported as quality outcomes nationally. If a patient's claim form includes a diagnosis of pressure injury associated with the POAF indicator "not present on admission," you need to be aware of this hospital-acquired condition. It will be reported that the hospital is accountable for not preventing the pressure injury because it was not present on admission.

This chapter provides a process that can be used to review HACs and harms. Working with the claims and information technology departments, obtain regular reports of patients who have been classified in the billing system with an NPOA flag of "no" or "unknown."

A review of all "not present on admission" indicators in claims data before the bill is sent to the insurance carrier will provide multiple benefits:

1. Awareness of these quality incidents will help you manage quality in your organization.
2. You can confirm accurate coding before the data is published publicly.

The second point requires explanation. As a quality professional, your job is to try to improve the reality of what is happening as it relates to quality. The root cause of a HAC or harm can start with many different things. The first and most obvious is that the HAC or harm is just that – a patient HAC or harm. But it is not always that simple. Sometimes there are coding errors and misunderstandings that result from pure coding quality issues. The reality of the care provided may be exceptional, but the coding of the claim does not represent that. In these cases, you wouldn't want to go to clinicians and ask them to participate in improving their HACs and harms when they had nothing to do with them; the problem was with the way they were coded. Thirdly, a HAC or harm can occur when there is poor or inaccurate documentation. Remember what we are discussing; if the documentation in the medical record does not describe what was found on admission, it is impossible for the person coding the bill to know if condition was present on admission. This results in a "not present on admission" or "unknown" indicator. The "unknown" indicator in analysis of these HACs and harms is equally damaging to the hospital's measurement rates and reputation. Lastly, if clinicians not only missed the documentation but also missed actually doing the assessment on admission, the result is the same.

Although the issues outlined result in the same outcome for HAC and harms measurement and rankings, the process improvement initiatives to identify and solve root causes are many. Some should be directed at improving coding and billing processes, some at documentation, some at admission assessments, and some at actual patient prevention and care. As a quality professional, understand what you are trying to improve before you begin.

There is no prescriptive standard for reviewing HACs and harms. Develop a process so they can be managed and reviewed. Most insurance companies have a time limit on submitting claims. Because of this, reviewing HACs and harms for claims before they are billed requires strict management to a timeline. The following process for reviewing HACs and harms is recommended:

1. Get to know the claims department and understand the processes they have for submitting a claim. Explain why you are engaging them and what you are trying to accomplish.
2. Working with the claims department, create a process by which they can trigger a claim with a "not present on admission" or "unknown" indicator and forward that claim to the quality team for review.
3. Standardize a weekly process whereby claims are reviewed and provide recommendations to the claims department. Either you agree with the findings or you suggest they look at additional documentation to thoroughly investigate them.
4. Use your findings to implement quality improvement projects directed at the true source of the HAC or harm findings.

In summary, it is important to understand what you are trying to accomplish by reviewing HACs and harms. The goal is never to try and find ways not to report true quality of care; however, it is critical to work to report the reality of care. If you have a significant problem with nurses not performing skin assessments on patients when admitted, and it is found that all diagnosis codes of pressure injury are classified as "not present on admission," your patient safety indicator rate for this condition is going to be very poor. Don't go out and try to improve hospital-acquired pressure injuries until you first improve admission assessments. When you're confident patients are assessed as not having a pressure injury on admission, yet they still end up with one, you can address the issues of skin care management to prevent them. In this way, you are attacking the root cause of the issues. I have never met a clinician who was not willing to support improvement on a real issue. I have, on the other hand, found it extremely difficult, if not impossible, to engage a clinician in an improvement project that was not directed at the right root cause. Try telling a cardiologist that they need to improve their practice because their AMI mortality rates are bad and later finding out that it was a coding error and had nothing to do with them. The next time you need their support to improve quality outcomes, you may find yourself alone in a room.

13.2 Summary

Quality measurement takes on a lot of different analytic forms. This chapter outlined the procedure for defining quality based on claims data submitted for billing purposes. Although it does not reflect everything known about patient care in the hospital, it is important to understand how quality is measured and compared nationally. Quality professionals can apply quality and improvement skills toward these measurement methodologies to improve care, documentation, and coding. The fact is this data is used for defining some portions of quality for customers. The best thing that can be done is to ensure it matches the reality of care.

13.2.1 Key Concepts

- HACs and harms are major indicators of quality reflected on external quality scorecards.
- The root cause of a HAC or harm showing up in claims data may not accurately reflect patient care.
- HACs or harms can be the result of poor patient care, poor documentation, poor process, or coding errors.

13.2.2 *Areas You Can Geek Out On*

■ Meet with coding experts in your organization. Ask them to share their experiences with accurately coding claims. What are their frustrations and pain points when it comes to selecting the appropriate NPOA classification?

Chapter 14

Managing the Quality Team

Lastly, we will discuss an approach to managing the quality team. The quality team is not much different from any other team.

First and foremost, the quality team is made up of individual people. Individuals bring unique education, experience, and skills to the team. There is no one-size-fits-all approach when managing a team. Work to understand each person's strengths.

14.1 Developing the Quality Team

14.1.1 Interviews

When starting a new position, managers sometimes appear to do nothing for the first week or so of employment. Observation and understanding of the people on a team are critical first steps. The team was making things work before the new manager arrived, so they should have some respect for what was being done already.

Start by listing questions you'd like team members to answer and schedule individual one-on-one meetings with each of them. In the meetings, ask these questions and record the answers:

- What does *quality* mean to you?
- What are your top three quality concerns?
- What are your recommendations for me in this role?
- What can I do to support you in this role?
- What are your expectations of me?

Open-ended questions are better than specific questions. Asking someone to describe their perception of the work experience, for example, will elicit more information than asking "Do you like your job?" Always avoid questions that lead to a yes or no response.

Be sure to take good notes during the interview and record promptly to ensure completeness and accuracy.

DOI: 10.4324/9781003358404-15

14.1.2 Summarize the Findings

After all the interviews, review the answers and summarize them by key themes. Key themes are one- to four-word phrases that express the context of the answer. There can be multiple key themes to one answer. For example, when asking someone what their expectations of their leader are, they may say something like, "To be available when I need you and clearly let me know what I need to do, how well I am doing, and if I need improvement." Key themes that could be pulled from this statement are "be available," "communicate," and "feedback." If multiple interviews result in some of the same key themes, it is easy to identify areas of concentration. Figure 14.1 provides some examples of interview statements aligned to key themes.

What does quality mean to you and your area?	Key Themes
Consistent care that is transparent to the patient. We must be open to feedback, education and seek knowledge	QA Education Consistency
Consistency of care, Low HAIs, High reliability principles in place	Consistency Good Outcomes High Reliability
Defined quality metrics with outcomes as well as high patient satisfaction	Measurement Good Outcomes Patient Sat
Quality is the product output to a patient in all aspects and providing good Customer service	Patient Sat Good Outcomes
A safe environment for our patients where they can trust the care they receive. Communicating effectively with our patients and sharing information.	Safety Trust Transparency Communication
Making sure we distribute products safely (Quality = Safety)	Safety
Data for provider feedback, High quality of care by those MDs	Data Reporting
Quality = clinical data. Trending/tracking, fraud, waste, abuse	Data Reporting
High standards, consistent with care and quality of care Measures in place - doing PDSA to get something changed Be aware of and watch for gaps	Consistency Data Reporting Gap analysis
Providing best patient care possible. Providing what the patient wants and needs	Patient Sat Good Outcomes
Quality staff who meet expectations while following best practice	Quality Staff Best Practice

Figure 14.1 Key themes grouping.

14.1.3 Prioritize Your Key Themes

Once you have all your key themes, rank them in order of frequency and prioritize them. Count the number of times a key theme came up for each question and rank them in descending order. Depending on the number of key themes, first focus on the top three or four.

14.1.4 Present Your Findings to the Group

Combine all your findings and present them to the group, assuring them, "I heard what you told me, and this is what I understood you to say." Anonymity is key. As everything has been wrapped up into key themes and prioritized, it is quite easy to do that. A simple PowerPoint presentation with one slide for each question asked during the interview works well (see Figure 14.2). Because key themes are listed and ranked, your audience can either agree or disagree with the findings. They may add additional explanation but will seldom disagree with the overall content.

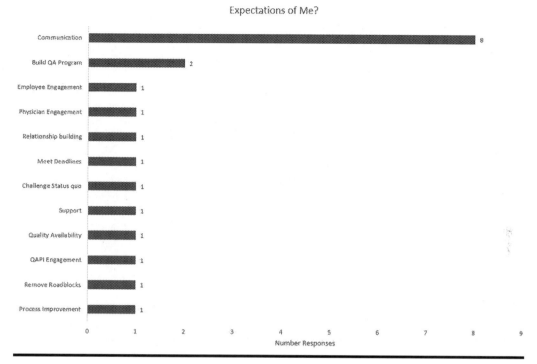

Figure 14.2 Expectations – grouping of key themes.

14.1.5 Provide a Plan

After presenting your findings, it is important to let the team know what you plan to do about them. Choose the top themes from your presentation and describe the things you plan to do to address them. For example, responses to the question asking what quality means to them may be very random and hard to bring together. In this case, it's appropriate to suggest bringing the group together to develop a single mission statement for the department and work with customers to define quality. Communication may be a key theme of each person's answers, so address it by setting up weekly huddle meetings with the team and bi-weekly one on ones and provide easy ways for them to contact you. You don't need to have the solution to addressing each key theme, but you should have a plan for how you will guide the team to solutions. Ignoring a key theme is very dangerous. You would be better off not doing the survey at all.

14.1.6 Personality Assessment

Recognizing that each person comes to the group with a different background and different experiences is essential to understanding them and developing a team that has synergy. There are a multitude of tools that can be utilized to learn about your team's personality types and learning styles. A good, inexpensive tool is Don Clifton's StrengthsFinder (Figure 14.3). His technique recognizes that every person has strengths and suggests focusing more on strengths than on weaknesses. Chances are you've been told to work on a weakness. If you were poor at public speaking, sales, or interacting with people, the message was to continue to practice until you improved. This instruction is somewhat misguided. If a person does not possess these strengths, they might end up working a lifetime to get better, only to become barely capable of them. With so much time

Figure 14.3   Clifton strengths.

spent on weaknesses, they've potentially missed the opportunity to excel in their strengths. Tom Rath states in the *Next Generation StrengthsFinder 2.0*:

> We were tired of living in a world that revolved around our weaknesses. Society's relentless focus on people's shortcomings had turned into a global obsession. What's more, we had discovered that people have several times more potential for growth when they invest energy in developing their strengths instead of correcting their deficiencies.

Clifton's *StrengthsFinder* is a short assessment that attempts to categorize people by their top five strengths. This tool is a great way to bring a team together and have dialogue about each of them. It shows that, as a leader, you care about who they actually are, and it introduces some great camaraderie among the team that may last well into the future. The goal is to find out what each individual's strengths are and place them in roles that align with those strengths as much as possible. It's equally important not to tell the members of the team that you only want them working in their areas of strength. This can send a message that they don't need to do things that are not strengths or things they don't want to do. In order to function in life, we all need to do things we don't like to do but still must be done. If, however, you require someone on the team to present information to all new employees every month, do not select an employee who is extremely afraid of talking in front of groups for that task.

14.1.7 Outline the Work of the Department

Collaborating with team members in a group session, list the work that needs to be done in the department. Get as specific as you like with this exercise, but start with high-level categories. Figure 14.4 lists some examples of the work done by one quality team. There are many duties in a quality department, and each organization has a unique set of accountabilities, but this illustrates a few of them.

Quality Committee – prepare, manage, and facilitate

Medical Executive Committee – prepare, present, and participate

Scorecards – Update quality measures

Staff meetings – Present quality status at staff meetings

Physician OPPE scorecards – create and update OPPE scorecard

Leapfrog – Manage Leapfrog data and update

State Reporting – Perform analysis and report state data

Complaints – Manage patient complaints

Provider Peer Review – Manage the peer review process

CMS Reporting – Update and manage the QualityNet reporting

HACs and Harms – Manage the process for reviewing HACs and harms in claims data

Metrics and Analytics – Provide ad hoc analytics for quality

Safety Huddle – Present daily quality message at the Safety Huddle

PDSA/RCAs – Perform process improvements

Accreditation – Manage the accreditation committee and activities

Figure 14.4 Quality team tasks and accountabilities.

14.1.8 Assign Primary and Secondary Owners

Once the work of the department is outlined and understood, it is easy to assess what a team member is doing and balance the workload. Assess the level of effort for work activities and get very specific work load analyses from employees if necessary. For example, if managing patient complaints takes three hours a day, that is significantly more work than preparing and attending the monthly medical executive committee meeting. Just because one member of the team has a greater number of tasks than another does not mean they have more work.

At this point, bring the team together with the work activities listed and the StrengthsFinder results for each individual. You can assign people to work activities or share your department goals and give them the opportunity to assign. Those who have been solely responsible for doing one task with no backup will appreciate that they have a secondary person to back them up when needed. There are training needs that will have to be implemented so that everyone assigned to a work activity can be trained to perform it. Utilize those who already have that knowledge to train the others, and if the work isn't defined, allow the newly assigned person to do the research and suggest an approach to managing the work.

14.2 One-on-One Meetings

Telling employees you have an open-door policy does not meet the need for employee one on ones. Stating you have an open door policy is a cop-out and puts the responsibility on the employee to come to you to discuss any issues that may arise. As a leader, it is your responsibility to engage with employees. Keep a strict schedule of one-on-one meetings at least monthly. They need to understand that in these meetings, they will have your undivided attention. One-on-one meetings should be intentional and focused. Create a template and utilize it every time so employees know what to expect. An example of a one-on-one template is shown in Figure 14.5. Each section is described next.

1:1 Meeting Template

Employee		Date	
Previous Action Item Review:			

Current Work	Issues/Barriers

Review Goals	

Ideas for Improvement	

Fun Factor	

Needs from Director	

Action Items	

Other	

Figure 14.5 Employee one-on-one template.

Previous action item review – Review any action items that were previously listed, and discuss the status and next steps if necessary.

Current work – List the activities the employee is currently working on and specifically inquire if there are any issues or barriers.

Review goals – Goals that align with the strategies of the organization should be outlined for every employee annually. Review these goals during one on ones. If you do this every time, there will be no surprises about their performance towards these goals when it comes time for their annual performance review.

Ideas for improvement – People bring a unique set of skills and value to your team. Always take the opportunity to solicit their input on ideas for improvement. You will be surprised how much value that brings to a team. I once had a quality department that had a credibility problem with the other departments in the organization. The departments in the hospital did not know who the people in the quality department were or what they did. Employees knew that quality incidents were reported to the quality department, but they never received feedback about how they were handled. During a one-on-one session, an employee suggested attending unit staff meetings for other departments and providing them with the quality agenda and feedback on quality incidents reported in their areas. It proved to be a great way to collaborate and obtain quality engagement with employees throughout the organization.

Fun factor – This is a feeling question intended to get to the soul of your employees. Asking your employees if they like their jobs does not help you understand how someone feels. Employees are people, and people are complex. How they feel is based on a multitude of things and is not always associated with work. They have family lives, work lives, social lives, illness, peace, etc. throughout the year. The intent behind a fun factor is to assess them as whole human beings and reach a part of their mind that relates to something more substantial – "On a scale of one to ten (ten being best), how much fun are you having?" This number can be used as a comparison from past one-on-one meetings and give you an idea of where they are today. Many times when a low fun factor is reported, it has nothing to do with work. It could be a sick child at home, stress with a spouse, or anxiety about an upcoming event. Use the fun factor as an opportunity to understand employees and help in any way possible.

Needs of the director (or you) – This is a specific question to find out if they have any needs from you. Employees will quickly realize that you will ask this question during every one on one. Rather than coming to you each day with things they need that are not significantly important and can wait, they can use this venue to discuss them. In my experience, most will communicate that they need nothing, then pause for a moment, and they often come up with something. It is a great way to show your focus on them and that you truly want to make their life easier at work. Follow up on the things they need from you. If you don't intend to follow up with them, avoid asking the question.

Action items – Summarize action items from the meeting. This is where you agree on what you are going to do and when it needs to be done. This section also feeds the initial section of the one on one by looking back to previous meetings to follow up on action items.

Other – Other things that need to be covered by you or the employee. A one-on-one template is nice to provide consistency, but it won't cover everything needed.

14.3 Huddle Meetings

Huddle meetings are set times for the team to come together and discuss the work department. Rapidly changing areas (like the operating department) should have daily huddle meetings because of the vast difference in work done daily. Quality departments do quite well with weekly huddle meetings. It is in these meetings that you'll discuss the weekly activities. A sample huddle template is shown in Figure 14.6. Similar to the one-on-one template, this provides consistency for the team.

Quality Weekly Team Huddle

| Purpose: Collaborate as a team, manage weekly activities, and review measures of success |

Date: _____   Huddle Leader: _____

Next Week's Huddle Leader	

Weekly Activities/News:	

Any roadblocks, barriers, resources, help needed?	

Any Opportunities for improvement?	

Metric Review/Adjust	

Recognitions:	

New Action Items		
What	Who	When

Figure 14.6   Quality team huddle template.

Next week's huddle leader – The weekly huddle is not an exercise for the leader of the organization to speak to employees. It is a team collaboration of weekly activities. For this reason, the first task in every huddle is to ask for a volunteer to lead the next week's huddle. Utilizing the template, any member of your team can lead the huddle. Try to do this without an assigned schedule. You may be amazed at how quickly team members will volunteer to lead this task on their own.

Weekly activities/news – This is when the huddle leader announces any special activities that will be happening during the week. An example would be that MEC is on Thursday, action items are due to the department of health on Friday, or there's a birthday celebration for Joe on Wednesday.

Any opportunities for improvement – A leader is always soliciting ideas for improvement. Recent obstacles, failings, or difficulties all come with potential opportunities. By asking people about opportunities for improvement, you reiterate the importance to the team and set the example to look for and act on quality improvement opportunities.

Metric review/adjust – The metric review is an opportunity to discuss the measures important to the quality department. Quality requires all departments to have a scorecard with metrics aligned with strategic initiatives. Quality is not exempt from this. Review quality measures so that every member of the quality team is aware of what is important and measured.

Recognitions – This is a great section that points out the importance of recognizing team members and others in the organization. Allow people to praise their peers and thank them for a job well done. If a team member wants to thank someone outside the team, keep thank-you cards available to sign and send out as a team.

New action items – As with any meeting, end the huddle with the action items discussed and list them. This template specifically outlines who is accountable and a completion date for the action item. It is rare to witness an organization so disciplined that they naturally create SMART goals when setting up action items. The tool is intended to remind people of key elements.

Lastly, it is helpful to have a huddle board for the quality department. It is utilized during the huddle but managed and used throughout the week to list all the department's activities. Figure 14.7 shows an example of such a board. It has a lot of information and may even look messy but is intended to be a great visual tool for those using it.

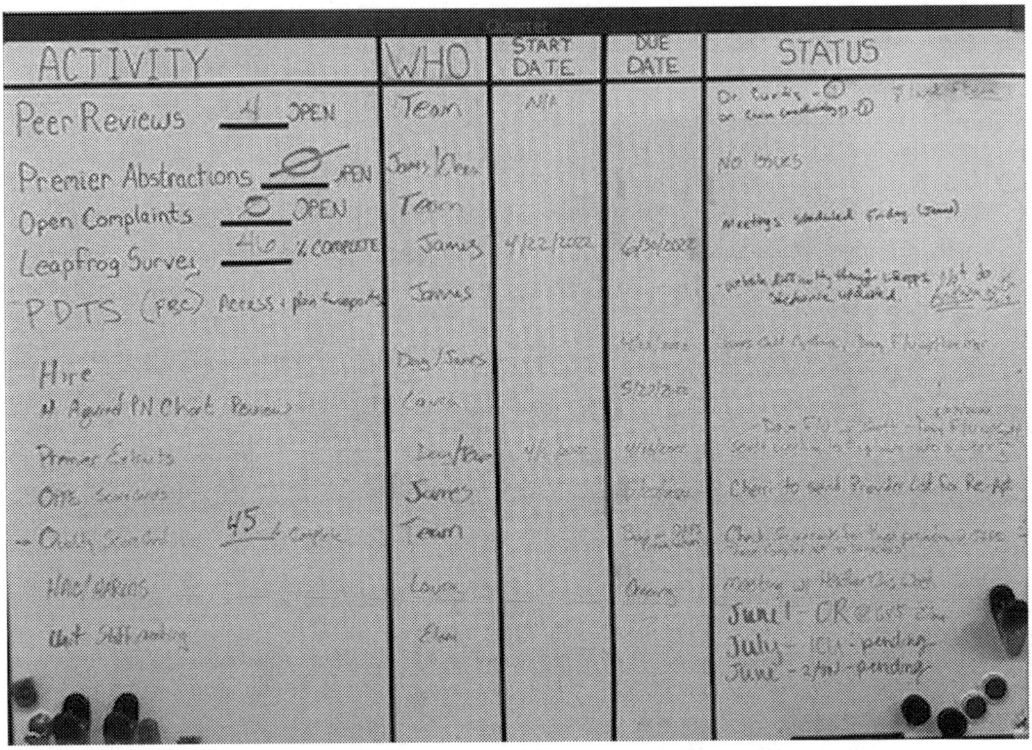

Figure 14.7 Quality team huddle board.

14.4 Calendar for Reporting

Another great tool that keeps the team on track is a calendar for reporting. This calendar was referenced in Chapters 2 and 11 in the context of CMS-required reporting requirements. Quality teams have many deadlines and reporting requirements throughout the year. Having a calendar posted in the department and visible to the entire team helps them to be proactive and meet reporting requirements without surprises. This should be customized for your department due to local, state, federal, and corporate requirements. Start with a basic calendar. The tasks will evolve and become more concise over time.

An sample calendar is seen in Figure 14.8. In this example, each reportable item is listed, and a column represents every week of the year. During team huddles, the team can quickly reference the current week to see if there are any items due.

Figure 14.8 Quality department due date calendar.

14.5 Support, Support, Support

As a quality leader, your primary responsibility is to support those you serve. First, you serve your team by providing them the tools, support, and ability to perform their jobs. Second, you provide support to everyone in the organization trying to perform quality patient care. Quality leaders don't "do quality." Quality is done at the point where employees interface with patients to do their jobs. Your role is to support them so they can do their jobs well. I have heard it said that leadership is a thankless job because you don't get credit for great things that are done. I disagree with this statement. Try to find joy in seeing your employees excel, learn new things, and succeed! Past leaders throughout my career taught me that I was capable of doing things greater than I could even imagine. The biggest rewards come when you know that you had the same impact on someone else, and that feels incredible.

14.6 Summary

I was hesitant to include this chapter in the book because I initially thought anyone in a leadership position probably already has the skills, techniques, and ability to manage a team. Although this may be true for you, I also believe employees who work in a quality department are unique. They come with vast differences in knowledge, background, and experiences. Some consider this a difficult combination to manage, but I see it as a great opportunity for success. Quality professionals seldom start out in a quality role in their career. They are highly educated and experienced professionals driven heavily by intrinsic motivation. You have the opportunity to embrace and harness their capabilities and passion and meld that into a team that has the potential to achieve success greater than you ever expected.

14.6.1 Key Concepts

■ Observe the work of the team – Remember, they were successfully doing this before you arrived.
■ Understand every employee individually.
■ An open-door policy does not constitute an employee one on one.
■ A leader is defined as a person who has followers – You have no control over their choice to follow.

14.6.2 Areas You Can Geek Out On

■ *StrengthsFinder Assessment*: Purchase the book on Amazon and use the code in the back of the book to do your own assessment.
■ Don Clifton's *Strengths-Based Leadership*: Leadership book to help you with leading individuals and teams based on their strengths.

Chapter 15

Summary: Bringing It All Together

15.1 Quality Professional Next Steps

The healthcare and quality industries have many training and certifications available to you. Referencing Chapter 14, where I present the concept of identifying the strengths of your team members, it's important to identify your own strengths to determine the best plan forward. Find the path(s) you feel will propel you forward with your interests and career. Some certifications and/or trainings available are:

- Certified professional in healthcare quality (CPHQ)
- Certified professional in patient safety (CPPS)
- Six Sigma yellow, green, or black belt
- Lean certification
- Project management professional (PMP)
- International Organization for Standardization (ISO) 9001 certification
- American Society for Quality (ASQ) certification

There are many additional certifications and training programs available. Each can provide the training and concepts behind their methodology, but few enable you to actually take that knowledge and implement it in your day-to-day work. It is up to you to take the concepts learned and apply them for organizational success. Although the certifications are helpful and add new acronyms to your resume, healthcare organizations desperately need people who can actually implement these concepts to improve their quality.

Throughout this book, many procedures and details on how to initiate and run a quality management program have been laid out for you. The real art in these techniques, however, is how they work together to create synergy. Following these baseline structures in your quality management program will allow flexibility for changing needs and provide the ability to sustain and evolve.

I'd like to close with a real-life scenario and demonstrate how all these techniques work together to create a sustainable quality management program. Although this scenario excludes many of

DOI: 10.4324/9781003358404-16

the change management processes, emotions, and dramatic discussions, information found in Chapters 14 (Managing the Quality Team), 9 (Sustaining Quality), 7 (Project Management) and 5 (Quality Improvement) are all applicable.

15.2 Sample Scenario

Scenario: The state department of health (DOH) visits the organization in response to a patient complaint. The complaint involved the death of a patient requiring emergent dialysis services.

- The survey team readiness process is implemented (Chapter 8 Accreditation) for the survey.
- After the DOH survey is completed, they present three findings:
  1. Delay from emergency department to dialysis for emergent cases
  2. Poor handoff from the emergency department to dialysis
  3. Dialysis nurses working outside the scope of the physician orders
- The action plan due dates are added to the quality department's due date calendar (Chapter 14 – Managing the Quality Team).
- PDSA events are scheduled, assigned to quality team members, and added to the quality huddle board (Chapter 14 – Managing the Quality Team).
- The quality team pulls together three teams to perform PDSA events for each of the findings (Chapter 5 – Quality Improvement), using the confidentiality and foundation of a patient safety organization (Chapter 12 – Patient Safety Organization, Quality Incidents, and Mortality Reviews).

The following action items were obtained from the three PDSA events performed:

1. Delay from emergency department to dialysis for emergent cases
   a. Update the policy and procedure for expected time frames and educate ED and dialysis nurses with updated policies/procedures by mm/dd/yyyy.
   b. Update the electronic medical record with expected time frames for each dialysis order type (routine, urgent, emergent) by mm/dd/yyyy.
   c. Monitor ED order time to initiate dialysis time for emergent dialysis orders by mm/dd/yyyy.
2. Poor handoff from ED to dialysis
   a. Develop situation-background-assessment-recommendation (SBAR) handoff standard report by mm/dd/yyyy.
   b. Implement SBAR handoff standard by mm/dd/yyyy.
   c. Create, measure, and monitor handoff reports for dialysis by mm/dd/yyyy.
3. Dialysis nurses working outside the scope of the orders
   a. Provide education for dialysis nurses by mm/dd/yyyy.
   b. Acknowledge dialysis order prior to starting dialysis by mm/dd/yyyy.
   c. Implement audit and measurement for dialysis orders by mm/dd/yyyy.

- The action item tracker is updated with the agreed action items (Chapter 7 – Project Management).
- An action plan is put together and submitted to the DOH (Chapter 8 – Accreditation).

- Education and standard work are created and implemented for the dialysis findings (Chapter 6 – Quality Training).
- The dialysis score on the quality oversight scorecard (Chapter 4 – Quality Measurement and Analytics) is updated with the following measures:
  1. Percent of patients receiving appropriate handoff from the ED
  2. Percent of order compliance
- The ED score on the quality oversight scorecard (Chapter 4 – Quality Measurement and Analytics) is updated with the following measures:
  1. Percent of patients receiving appropriate handoff from the ED (same as for dialysis but located on both scorecards)
  2. Percent of ED order time to initiation of dialysis time expectations met.
- The standard agenda template for the quality committee (Chapter 3 – Managing Quality) is updated to include discussion and measure review for the dialysis finding action items.
- The board and MEC standard report-out templates (Chapter 3 – Managing Quality) are updated for the dialysis finding action items.
- The next scheduled quality committee report-outs by the ED and dialysis involve discussions of these findings, progress towards improvement, and deep-down review of the measures and any barriers to success (Chapter 3 – Managing Quality).

Measures are monitored and transparent throughout the entire governance structure. At any point along the way, the governance structure can initiate another PDSA to improve or sustain the results.

When the DOH comes back to the facility in 6 to 12 months, they see that every member of the governance structure and those participating in emergent dialysis are aware of the findings and action items to improve them. There are visual measures being tracked and managed for these findings and evidence of discussions through PDSA, quality committee, board, and MEC minutes. Progress toward these findings had improved, and it is clear the organization takes quality seriously from their implementing programs and improving on these findings.

As you can see from this summary of a very realistic scenario, the techniques covered in this book complement the ability to operationalize quality improvement techniques across most challenges. Imagine operationalizing this scenario without some of the techniques listed here. If there were no quality oversight scorecard, yet another individual scorecard would need to be created for dialysis, and people would need to remember to update it and use it to report out. No foundational standard would be in place to track these measures. If no standard was in place for process improvement techniques, action plans would be developed as a best guess and probably not involve the people doing the work. Without a defined governance structure, the quality committee, board, and MEC might or might not discuss or be aware of the findings. Without a well-defined action item tracking and follow-up process, action items might or might not be completed. Following up on these action items would not be part of standard practice and would be a randomly defined effort to get them accomplished.

Many other tools and techniques described in this book were not used in this scenario, but I hope that you can see how applicable they all are. The catch-ball sessions used to engage your staff and get their input would have been part of the process improvement initiatives to obtain root-cause analysis and solutions to the findings. Standard work would have been developed to ensure there were auditable and standard ways to manage emergent dialysis procedures. Communication plans would be in place to share the findings, action plans, progress, and expectations through safety and department huddles.

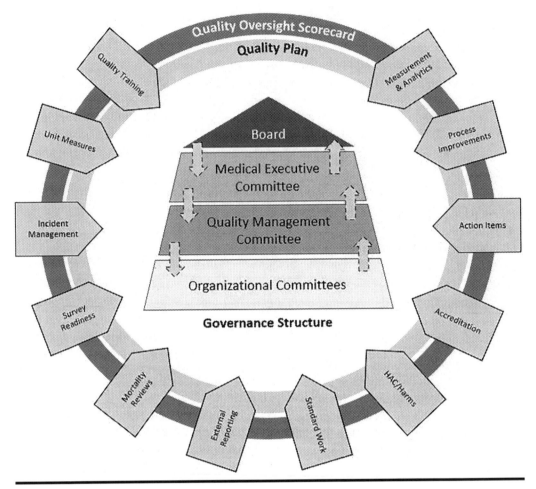

Figure 15.1   Quality management program.

15.3 Summary

The concepts, tools, and techniques described in this book were developed over time through trials and errors experienced along the way. Early in my career, I was faced with an insurmountable number of things to oversee, manage, and organize. It was through one of my mentors who always told me "The devil is in the details" that I was able to learn to break things down into their smaller components. Only then could I start to create the relationships and synergies between them. Over the years, I've built the components, studied how each relates to the others, and learned on a trial basis how well the process worked. The quality management foundation described here will prevent you from having to reinvent quality management every day to accommodate the randomness of the things thrown at you. Proactively set standard quality management operating principles that enable structure, flexibility, standardization, and professionalism, and you will create the benchmarks others aspire to achieve. Chase the grade, and you will find yourself up to your eyeballs in chaos and, eventually, burnout. Get ahead of it, get organized, and follow the foundational elements illustrated in this book to take your organization to new heights.

Appendix

Chapter 2 Appendix

Hospital Consumer Assessment of Healthcare Providers and Systems (HCAHPS) Questions
Your Care from Nurses:
• During this hospital stay, how often did nurses treat you with courtesy and respect?
• During this hospital stay, how often did nurses listen carefully to you?
• During this hospital stay, how often did nurses explain things in a way you could understand?
• During this hospital stay, after you pressed the call button, how often did you get help as soon as you wanted it?
Your Care from Doctors:
• During this hospital stay, how often did doctors treat you with courtesy and respect?
• During this hospital stay, how often did doctors listen carefully to you?
• During this hospital stay, how often did doctors explain things in a way you could understand?
The Hospital Environment:
• During this hospital stay, how often were your room and bathroom kept clean?
• During this hospital stay, how often was the area around your room quiet at night?
Your Experiences in This Hospital:
• During this hospital stay, did you need help from nurses or other hospital staff in getting to the bathroom or in using a bedpan?
• How often did you get help in getting to the bathroom or in using a bedpan as soon as you wanted?
• During this hospital stay, were you given any medicine that you had not taken before?

(Continued)

(Continued)

Hospital Consumer Assessment of Healthcare Providers and Systems (HCAHPS) Questions
• Before giving you any new medicine, how often did hospital staff tell you what the medicine was for?
• Before giving you any new medicine, how often did hospital staff describe possible side effects in a way you could understand?
When You Left the Hospital:
• After you left the hospital, did you go directly to your own home, to someone else's home, or to another health facility?
• During this hospital stay, did doctors, nurses, or other hospital staff talk with you about whether you would have the help you needed when you left the hospital?
• During this hospital stay, did you get information in writing about what symptoms or health problems to look out for after you left the hospital?
Overall Rating of Hospital:
• Using any number from 0 to 10, where 0 is the worst hospital possible and 10 is the best hospital possible, what number would you use to rate this hospital during your stay?
• Would you recommend this hospital to your friends and family?
Understanding Your Care When You Left the Hospital:
• During this hospital stay, staff took my preferences and those of my family or caregiver into account in deciding what my healthcare needs would be when I left.
• When I left the hospital, I had a good understanding of the things I was responsible for in managing my health.
• When I left the hospital, I clearly understood the purpose for taking each of my medications.
About You
• During this hospital stay, were you admitted to this hospital through the emergency room?
• In general, how would you rate your overall health?
• In general, how would you rate your overall mental or emotional health?
• What is the highest grade or level of school that you have completed?
• Are you of Spanish, Hispanic, or Latino origin or descent?
• What is your race? Please choose one or more.
• What language do you mainly speak at home?

Chapter 4 Appendix

Obtaining Standard Deviation in MS Excel	
1. List your data in a column in Excel. This example uses number of patients.	
2. Select any cell without data in the spreadsheet.	
3. Under Home, select the AutoSum dropdown.	
4. Select More Functions from the dropdown.	
5. Select STDEV from the function list.	
6. The next box will ask you what range of cells you want the standard deviation calculation derived from.	
7. Highlight the cells with your data or type in the cell numbers and click OK.	
8. The standard deviation will show up in the cell you selected in Step 2.	

Chapter 8 Appendix

Job Descriptions for Survey Readiness

Admin Assistant

This job description is a temporary description of what is expected of you during an onsite survey. This enables each of us to perform our duties during a survey and work in unison with each person assigned a job description role. It is critically important that each person assigned a job duty perform the accountabilities listed here. Questions regarding these expectations and the role can be directed to the "Reports to" person identified below.

Role:	Survey admin assistant
Availability:	24/7 while assigned surveyor is onsite
Reports to:	Survey command room champion
Accountabilities	• Organize schedules and documentation during the survey • Provide office supplies and necessary materials • Support command room champion and survey commander in communications • Create/update survey agendas • Make copies and print materials • Arrange food and snacks for command center and surveyors

Command Room Champion

This job description is a temporary description of what is expected of you during an onsite survey. This enables each of us to perform our duties during a survey and work in unison with each person assigned a job description role. It is critically important that each person assigned a job duty perform the accountabilities listed here. Questions regarding these expectations and the role can be directed to the "Reports to" person identified below.

Role:	Survey command room champion
Availability:	24/7 while surveyor is onsite
Reports to:	Survey commander
Accountabilities	• Manage all activities in the survey command room • Manage the contact list for all survey roles and surveyors (name, phone number, email, etc.) • Oversee all input requests from surveyors • Oversee all output answers to surveyors • Stay in the command room 24/7 while surveyors are present or delegate someone while stepping away • Communicate with and brief the survey commander regularly • Provide an organized structure for information coming in and information going out • Ensure responses to surveyors are delivered in a timely manner

Command Room Communication Specialist

This job description is a temporary description of what is expected of you during an onsite survey. This enables each of us to perform our duties during a survey and work in unison with each person assigned a job description role. It is critically important that each person assigned a job duty perform the accountabilities listed here. Questions regarding these expectations and the role can be directed to the "Reports to" person identified below.

Role:	Survey command room communication specialist
Availability:	24/7 while surveyor is onsite
Reports to:	Survey command room champion
Accountabilities	• Maintain the contact list for all survey roles and surveyors (name, phone number, email, etc.) • Answer and record all phone calls coming into the command center • Call appropriate departments and/or contacts throughout the survey to notify location of surveyors, needs, and requests • Communicate regularly with the survey command room champion on current status and needs as they arise • Record all communications with date, time, and person(s) involved

Survey Commander

This job description is a temporary description of what is expected of you during an onsite survey. This enables each of us to perform our duties during a survey and work in unison with each person assigned a job description role. It is critically important that each person assigned a job duty perform the accountabilities listed here. Questions regarding these expectations and the role can be directed to the "Reports to" person identified below.

Role:	Survey commander
Availability:	24/7 while surveyor is onsite
Reports to:	CEO
Accountabilities	• Lead all survey activities • Make final decision for all survey-related needs • Communicate and update the CEO and senior leaders regularly throughout the survey • Manage the activities and needs of the survey command room champion • Initiate the communication plan • Facilitate opening and closing survey meetings • Support the management of staffing needs with the survey command room champion

EMR Subject Matter Expert

This job description is a temporary description of what is expected of you during an onsite survey. This enables each of us to perform our duties during a survey and work in unison with each person assigned a job description role. It is critically important that each person assigned a job duty perform the accountabilities listed here. Questions regarding these expectations and the role can be directed to the "Reports to" person identified below.

Role:	Survey EMR subject matter expert
Availability:	24/7 while surveyor is onsite
Reports to:	Survey command room champion
Accountabilities	• Available during the survey to guide staff and surveyors through the electronic medical record to answer questions, find information, or describe documentation processes • Liaison to IT and analytics to request specific reports or information from all electronic data sources • Liaison to specialty areas (e.g., ICU) to identify and seek information related to EMR functions • Travel throughout the organization as needed, but check in with the command room champion often and notify them of their location

Survey Escort

This job description is a temporary description of what is expected of you during an onsite survey. This enables each of us to perform our duties during a survey and work in unison with each person assigned a job description role. It is critically important that each person assigned a job duty perform the accountabilities listed here. Questions regarding these expectations and the role can be directed to the "Reports to" person identified below.

Role:	Survey escort
Availability:	24/7 while assigned surveyor is onsite
Reports to:	Survey command room champion
Accountabilities	• Assigned to a specific surveyor • Guide the assigned surveyor throughout the day through the facility • Communicate often through phone or text with the command room communication specialist to provide exact location • Submit requests of the surveyor to the command center as they come up • Communicate regularly with the survey escort to validate information, summarize, and manage requests

Survey Scribe

This job description is a temporary description of what is expected of you during an onsite survey. This enables each of us to perform our duties during a survey and work in unison with each person assigned a job description role. It is critically important that each person assigned a job duty perform the accountabilities listed here. Questions regarding these expectations and the role can be directed to the "Reports to" person identified below.

Role:	Survey scribe
Availability:	24/7 while assigned surveyor is onsite
Reports to:	Survey command room champion
Accountabilities	• Assigned to a specific surveyor • Follow assigned surveyor throughout the day and record all activities, discussions, and questions from the surveyor • Provide a summary of daily notes to the survey command room champion at the end of every day • Communicate regularly with the survey escort to validate information, summarize, and manage requests

Subject Matter Expert

This job description is a temporary description of what is expected of you during an onsite survey. This enables each of us to perform our duties during a survey and work in unison with each person assigned a job description role. It is critically important that each person assigned a job duty perform the accountabilities listed here. Questions regarding these expectations and the role can be directed to the "Reports to" person identified below.

Role:	Survey subject matter expert
Availability:	Available as needed
Reports to:	Survey command room champion
Accountabilities	• Subject matter expert for the specified area of responsibility (e.g., ICU, materials management, facilities, lab, biomed, etc.) • Available 24/7 while surveyors are onsite to answer questions, present department processes and policies, and escort them through the area(s) they are responsible for • Provide contact information and be available to the survey command room at all times • Provide appropriate backups when not available while surveyors are onsite

---

Committee Charter Example

Team Charter: Cardiovascular quality workgroup
Date: MM/DD/YYYY
Definition:
The cardiovascular quality workgroup is an interdisciplinary team that oversees the quality initiatives, scorecards, and improvements for the other cardiovascular committees, including:
- Cardio-thoracic committee
- Emergency department committee
- Electrophysiology committee
- Intensive care unit committee
- Inpatient committee
- Invasive committee
- Vascular committee

Purpose:
1. To review quality activities of the cardiovascular committees including action plans, progress, and improvement outcomes
2. To ensure cardiovascular committees are meeting on a regular basis
3. To help remove roadblocks and barriers to improvement for all cardiovascular committees
4. Oversee cardiovascular quality scorecards and assist in measurement definitions and criteria
5. Oversee nationally reported data as it relates to cardiovascular activities including but not limited to CMS measures for hospital comparison, Leapfrog ratings, and critical indicators scorecard
6. Review summary and action items related to serious reportable events
7. Delegate quality initiatives to cardiovascular committees
8. Serve as a venue to raise quality issues, solicit feedback and support from other cardiovascular committee chairs, and provide a systemic view of quality across all cardiovascular areas
9. Oversee accreditation status and activities

Quality Indicators:
Members of the group will review specific oversight quality measures that ensure the progression of the quality review activities of the cardiovascular committees.
1. Cardiovascular meeting status
2. Serious reportable events (SREs)
3. Hospital-acquired conditions (HACs)

Member Responsibilities Include:
Members of the group represent each cardiovascular subcommittee and are empowered to provide best-practice expertise related to the transformation of patient care processes. Specifically, this group will:
1. Set the strategy for systemic improvement across all cardiovascular committees and areas
2. Make decisions that remove roadblocks and help facilitate the improvement of outcomes in critical care clinical quality measures
3. Ensure that best evidence and practice are incorporated into the protocols, pathways, and workflows developed by the teams
4. Ensure that workflows and other outputs are interdisciplinary in nature, transforming from the silo processes of the past into top performing cardiovascular service lines
5. Adopt evidence based best practices as the model for decision-making process

---

Committee Charter Example

Team Core Principles:
1. Attendance of meetings by subcommittee chairs to represent the status, work, and progress of the committee they represent
2. Consensus decision making based on the desired benefit for all hospitals incorporating feedback from a majority of the facilities
3. Active participation by all team members to ensure that best practice expertise and perspectives are represented
4. All members agree to represent the work of the team in a positive manner
5. The cardiovascular quality workgroup will support DNV accreditation readiness activities

Meeting Members:

Executive Owner: _____   Clinical Owner Invasive: _____
Clinical Owner CT: _____   Clinical Owner Vascular: _____
Clinical Owner ED: _____   Clinical Owner Quality: _____
Clinical Owner EP: _____   Clinical Owner STEMI: _____
Clinical Owner ICU: _____   Quality Director: _____
Clinical Owner Inpatient: _____

Meeting Logistics/Reporting:
1. Monthly for one hour
2. A conference line/WebEx provided to the group for remote participation
3. A scribe assigned to document minutes and requests
4. Cardiovascular committee scorecards reviewed monthly;
action plans for underperforming measures reviewed monthly

Chapter 10 Appendix

Example Quality Improvement Plan

Site: Medical Center   **Title:** Quality Improvement Plan
Approved Date: dd/mm/yyyy   **Effective Date:** dd/mm/yyyy
Document Number: 1234   **Next Review Date:** dd/mm/yyyy
Approved: Document control committee, governing board, MEC

Purpose: The Medical Center quality improvement and patient safety process ensures that the organization:
1. Has a system to ensure that corrective and preventive actions taken by the organization are implemented, measured, and monitored
2. Provides objectives, goals, and direction to help focus the hospital's continuous process improvement through measuring and monitoring improvements in health outcomes
3. Oversees quality functions for all services and departments, including those provided under contract, to ensure that they are managing under the same quality management improvement plan

Scope:
1. Medical Center consists of two acute-care hospitals geographically located in City, State at 1234 Long Drive and 4321 Short Drive.

(Continued)

(Continued)

Example Quality Improvement Plan

2. Our mission is to be the best place to care and be cared for, and our values consist of respect, responsibility, accountability, and compassion.
3. Our services include emergency services, cardiovascular, general medical, intensive care, surgery, gastrointestinal, imaging services, orthopedics, bariatric, stroke care, adult psychology, and neuroscience.

Authority: The governing board is ultimately responsible for the quality of care provided at Medical Center. The board shall review and approve the hospital's quality improvement plan annually and when significant changes to the plan are proposed. The board delegates oversight authority for the hospital quality improvement functions and patient safety to the medical executive committee (MEC) and quality council.

Organization: The quality council serves to provide oversight for the quality management system in conjunction with medical executive committee and an integrated set of committees and teams to assure representation, input, and involvement from key functional areas. These areas consist of administration, nursing, pharmacy, ancillary services, information management, risk management, safety management, the management representative, and other disciplines as needed to achieve the objectives of the plan.

1. The council will meet at least eight times per year to accomplish the following:
   1.1. Assure regulatory and accrediting standards are met by the hospital
   1.2. Oversee and evaluate the effectiveness of the quality management system
   1.3. Oversee patient safety initiatives
   1.4. Oversee programs and projects aimed at achieving the organization's quality and safety goals
   1.5. Determine annual quality and patient safety goals
   1.6. Support the development, maintenance, and monitoring of quality and patient safety goals
   1.7. Review and assess all components of the quality improvement function, including alignment to the quality improvement organization (QIO) measures
   1.8. Commission quality improvement teams to provide guidance and support for opportunities for improvement
   1.9. Provide administration, medical executive committee, and board with regular reports on the quality of care

Approach: The quality management system aligns specifically to the quality pillar on the organization's five-pillar balanced scorecard (service, financial, growth, quality, and people).

The organizational strategy under the quality pillar is to be a nationally ranked healthcare provider in quality and safety. Our objective is to achieve a CMS five-star rating.

The foundations for the quality improvement plan utilize the principles of the Shingo model Lean management system, Lean Six Sigma, ISO 9001:2015 quality management system, and plan-do-study-act (PDSA) to develop a culture of operational excellence throughout all layers of the organization.

Example Quality Improvement Plan

Methodology: The hospital's quality and patient safety process is rooted in operational excellence principle-based behaviors of the Shingo model. These principles, aligned with behavioral standards, consist of the following:

1. Enable
   a. Respect every individual by approaching every relationship with a willingness to listen without bias
   b. Lead with humility through authentic servant leadership
   c. Learn continuously by empowering and involving everyone, going to the GEMBA (actual workplace), and assuring a safe environment
2. Align
   a. Create a constancy of purpose through long-term strategy and goal development by cascading and gathering input at all levels
   b. Think systemically by eliminating barriers that prevent the flow of ideas, communication, and collaboration, implementing flow and pull processes where needed
3. Excel
   a. Focus on process
   b. Embrace scientific thinking
   c. Flow and pull value
   d. Assure quality at the source
   e. Seek excellence
   f. Manage variation
4. Results
   a. Create value for the customer

Utilizing those foundational elements, the quality plan aligns all areas of the organization through aligned strategies and goals through a data-driven approach. Organizational strategies developed at the leadership level through the balanced scorecard are cascaded down into all areas of the organization. The performance measures are updated on the quality oversight scorecard and reported to the quality committee at each meeting. Each measure is aligned with the CMS criteria and is accompanied by the owner, executive champion, and target goal.

Oversight: The governing board, medical executive committee, and administration are responsible and accountable for promoting the organization's implementation and maintenance of an effective quality management improvement plan. These duties are to:

1. Promote the implementation and effectiveness of the quality management system
2. Take action when reviewing the quality management improvement plan to:
   a. Identify quality and performance problems
   b. Review corrective and preventative activities and evaluate for effectiveness
   c. Monitor the sustainability of those corrective and preventive activities
3. Set priorities for improved quality of care and patient safety to include:
   a. Patient safety expectations
   b. Reduction of medical errors
   c. Eliminate preventable hospital-acquired conditions (HAC)
   d. Eliminate preventable hospital-acquired infections (HAI)
4. Allocate adequate resources for measuring, assessing, improving, and sustaining the hospital's performance and reducing risk to patients
5. Evaluation of all performance improvement activities
6. Management of the follow-up of action items related to root-cause analysis associated with serious reported events

(Continued)

(Continued)

Example Quality Improvement Plan

Communication: Management reviews occur at multiple levels throughout the organization. The following oversight processes are in place:
1. Administrative huddle
    a. Frequency: Daily
    b. Attendees: Leader representation from all operational areas
    c. Quality topic(s): Patient safety issues
2. Senior leadership team
    a. Frequency: Weekly
    b. Attendees: Senior leadership
    c. Quality topic(s): Serious reportable events (SRE), root-cause analysis (RCA), quality committee action items, days since last patient safety issues, process improvement project status, accreditation status
3. Quality committee
    a. Frequency: Monthly at least eight times per year
    b. Attendees: Senior leadership, nursing, pharmacy, compliance, hospitalist, medical director, risk, human resources, emergency department
    c. Quality topic(s): Review reporting committee minutes, Department-specific quality reviews, accreditation, patient safety measures, mortality reviews, process improvement reviews, review of corrective/preventive actions taken, serious reportable events (SRE), root-cause analysis (RCA), quality action item status
4. Medical executive committee (MEC)
    a. Frequency: Monthly
    b. Attendees: Members of MEC and medical staff
    c. Quality topic(s): Quality scorecard, serious reportable events (SRE), mortality reviews, quality improvement project status, accreditation status report, quality committee minutes
5. Governing board
    a. Frequency: Monthly
    b. Attendees: Members of board and administration
    c. Quality topic(s): Quality scorecard, serious reportable events (SRE), mortality reviews, quality improvement project status, accreditation status report

Quality Improvement Program Elements:
1. Variations, deficiencies, or non-conformities should be identified and addressed.
2. Corrective and preventive actions should be implemented and documented.
3. PDSA (plan, do, study, act) documentation of these activities should be reviewed by the quality committee.
4. Nonconformities should be corrected, and measurable improvements should be demonstrated and sustained.
5. Quality indicators scorecard should be measured, analyzed, and tracked.
6. ISO audit (internal review of key processes) results and corrective action plans should be conducted quarterly or when issues need to be addressed.
7. Regulatory and/or accreditation requirements should be incorporated.
8. Quality indicator data should be presented at the quality committee to include (but not limited to):
    a. Threats to patient safety (e.g., fall, patient identification, injuries)
    b. Medication therapy/medication use, to include medication reconciliation, high-risk drugs, look alike/sound alike medications, and the use of dangerous abbreviations.
    c. Operative and invasive procedures, to include wrong site/wrong patient/wrong procedure surgery

Example Quality Improvement Plan

    d. Anesthesia/moderate/deep sedation adverse events
    e. Blood and blood components – adverse events/usage
    f. Restraint use/seclusion
    g. Effectiveness of pain management system
    h. Infection prevention and control system, including hospital-acquired infections (HAI)
    i. Utilization management system
    j. Patient flow issues, to include reporting of patient held in the ED or the PACU for extended periods of time
    k. Customer satisfaction, both clinical and support areas
    l. Discrepant pathology reports
    m. Unanticipated deaths
    n. Adverse events/near misses
    o. Readmissions and unplanned returns to surgery
    p. Critical and/or pertinent processes, both clinical and supportive
    q. Medical record delinquency
9. Physical environment management systems.
10. Use the data collected to monitor the effectiveness and safety of services and quality of care.
11. Use the data to identify opportunities for improvement and changes that will lead to improvement.

Performance Improvement Projects:
1. The number and scope of performance improvement projects are aligned with the strategic initiatives of the quality pillar strategies and are reviewed annually.
2. Participate in quality improvement organization (QIO) requirements for the state.
3. Participate in the patient safety organization (PSO).

Department/Program Review Areas:
The following departments and programs are reviewed by the quality committee at least annually utilizing the quality oversight scorecard:

1. Ambulance Service
2. Anesthesia
3. Bariatric Program
4. Behavioral Health
5. Biomed
6. Blood Product Administration Management (BPAM)
7. Cardiovascular Lab
8. Dialysis
9. Dietary Services
10. Donor Services
11. Emergency Department
12. Employee Safety
13. Environmental Services
14. General Medical Unit
15. ICU1
16. ICU2
17. Imaging Nuclear
18. IMC Unit
19. Infection Control
20. Information Technology
21. Lab
22. LVAD Program
23. Materials Management
24. Medical Records
25. Medical Staff
26. Medication Management
27. Neuro Unit
28. Operating Department
29. Pathology
30. PCU Unit Heart
31. Physical Environment
32. Post-Surgical Unit
33. Radiation Oncology
34. Rehabilitation
35. Respiratory Care
36. Restraint Audits
37. Risk Management
38. Safety

(Continued)

(Continued)

Example Quality Improvement Plan	
39. Security 40. Sepsis Management 41. Staff Management	42. STEMI Program 43. Stroke Program 44. Utilization Review/Discharge
Exemptions from quality improvement plan: The quality improvement plan does not cover design and development.	

Chapter 12 Appendix

Patient Safety Organization Confidentiality Agreement
PSO, LLC CONFIDENTIALITY AGREEMENT POLICY ACKNOWLEDGEMENT AND COMPLIANCE ATTESTATION

PSO, LLC (the "PSO") is a component Patient Safety Organization that has been federally certified under the Patient Safety and Quality Improvement Act of 2005 and its attendant regulations ("PSQIA"). The PSO provides operational support and assistance to its member providers in matters relating to the improvement of patient safety and health care quality. Certain healthcare providers affiliated with _____ have elected to join the PSO for the purpose of conducting activities to improve patient safety and the quality of healthcare delivery.

The PSO's member providers have created a protected space to conduct patient safety activities known as the "Patient Safety Evaluation System" or "PSES." "Patient Safety Work Product" or "PSWP" is defined as any data, reports, records, memoranda, analyses or written or oral statements which are assembled or developed for reporting to the PSO; or are developed by the PSO to conduct patient safety activities; and which could result in improved patient safety, healthcare quality or healthcare outcomes; or which identify or constitute the deliberations or analysis of, or identify the fact or reporting pursuant to a PSES.

The Individual executing this Confidentiality Agreement is a member provider, quality or risk manager, patient safety task force member, authorized PSO contact at a member provider site, affiliated provider, contractor, or other authorized individual performing patient safety work. He or she has access to PSWP, including information related to peer review and quality assurance records.

By executing this Confidentiality Agreement, I understand that:
1) Effective patient safety activities cannot be achieved unless the confidentiality of all discussions, deliberations, records, and other information generated in connection with these activities is maintained.
2) Confidentiality of PSWP is necessary to ensure candid participation in PSO activities, which are critically important for the evaluation, review, and improvement of the quality of care provided by the member providers.
3) PSWP is generally not subject to subpoena or discovery in state or federal court, in administrative proceedings or pursuant to the Freedom of Information Act, and cannot be disclosed except as permitted under the PSQIA.

Patient Safety Organization Confidentiality Agreement

By executing this Confidentiality Agreement, I agree to:

1) Keep information learned through participation with the PSO/PSES confidential. I will not disseminate it outside the authorized recipients without the express permission of the PSO.

2) To mark all data submitted or received through participation in the PSO/PSES with the following notation: "*This is a confidential patient safety work product document. It is protected from disclosure pursuant to the provisions of the Patient Safety and Quality Improvement Act (42 CFR Part 3) and other state and federal laws. Unauthorized disclosure or duplication is absolutely prohibited.*"

3) To handle PSWP in a secure manner to ensure that the information is treated as confidential and to cooperate with established procedures to ensure the protection of the PSO documents.

4) To immediately notify the PSO if a request is received either by subpoena or other legal process to obtain access to PSO information. I agree to cooperate with all reasonable efforts to resist or narrow the disclosure and/or obtain a court order or other reasonable protection for such information. No information will be released without the written permission of the PSO.

5) Not to disclose any PSO records or information to anyone, except to persons authorized to receive such records or information. Specifically, I agree to limit dissemination of PSWP to employees, medical staff members, contractors, or other individuals entitled to receive/access such information under the PSQIA in furtherance of patient safety activities.

6) Acknowledge that any and all information gained through experience or association with the PSO/PSES is strictly confidential. I agree not to release, relay, transcribe, photocopy, retain or in any manner disseminate this information, either orally or in writing, to any person or organization without the express consent of the PSO Director.

7) Upon the expiration or termination of this Agreement for any reason or on demand, no matter when in the course of the relationship, I agree to promptly return any and all written materials containing or reflecting any PSWP or other related documentation and will not retain copies, extracts or other reproductions in whole or in part of such information.

By signing this form, I acknowledge and agree to comply with the above-stated requirements. I understand that the PSO and its member providers are entitled to undertake such action as deemed appropriate to ensure that this confidentiality is preserved. Any breach of this agreement, or threatened breach of this agreement, may subject me to legal action to prevent disclosure, civil or criminal penalties, corrective action or disciplinary action, as appropriate. I acknowledge that any questions I have regarding this agreement and confidentiality of PSO information may be directed to the PSO.

Employee/Physician/Consultant/Contractor Signature	Facility	Date
Employee/Physician/Consultant/Contractor Printed Name and Title		

(Continued)

Quality Incident Comparison Checklist		
Event Checklist	*SRE*	*SE*
SURGICAL OR INVASIVE PROCEDURE EVENTS		
Wrong Site — **SRE1A** Wrong site **SE11** Surgery or other invasive procedure performed at the wrong site, on the wrong patient, or that is the wrong (unintended) procedure for a patient regardless of the type of procedure or the magnitude of the outcome	X	X
Wrong Patient — **SRE1B** Wrong patient **PC18** Procedure or surgery on wrong patient, wrong site, or wrong (unintended) procedure **SE11**	X	X
Wrong Procedure — **SRE1C** Wrong procedure **SE11**	X	X
Retained Object — **SRE1D** Retained foreign object **PC3** Object inadvertently left in after surgery **SE16** Unintended retention of a foreign object in a patient after an invasive procedure, including surgery	X	X
OR Death — **SRE1E** Intra-op or immediate post-op death of ASA Class 1 patient **PC15** Unexpected death, suicide, or death occurring in the operating room	X	
PRODUCT OR DEVICE EVENTS		
Medications — **SRE2A** Death or serious injury associated with contaminated drugs, devices, or biologics provided by the healthcare setting	X	
Device — **SRE2B** Death or serious injury associated use or function of a device in patient care	X	
Air Emboli — **SRE2C** Death or serious injury associated intravascular air embolism that occurs while being cared for in a healthcare setting **PC3** Air embolism	X	
PATIENT PROTECTION EVENTS		
Discharge — **SRE3A** Discharge or release of a patient/resident of any age who is unable to make decisions to other than an authorized person	X	
Discharge — **SE12** Discharge of an infant to the wrong family		X
Elopement — **SRE3B** Patient death or serious injury associated with patient elopement (disappearance) **PC23** Elopement leading to death or permanent injury or severe temporary injury **SE14** Any elopement (that is, unauthorized departure) of a patient from a staffed around the-clock care setting (including the ED), leading to death, permanent harm, or severe harm to the patient	X	X

Quality Incident Comparison Checklist		
Event Checklist	SRE	SE
Suicide **SRE3C** Patient suicide, attempted suicide, or self-harm that results in serious injury while being cared for in a healthcare setting **SE1** Suicide of any patient receiving care, treatment, and services in a staffed around-the clock care setting or within 72 hours of discharge, including from the health care organization's emergency department (ED)	X	X

CARE MANAGEMENT EVENTS

	SRE	SE
Medications **SRE4A** Patient death or serious injury associated with a medication error (e.g., errors involving the wrong drug, wrong dose, wrong patient, wrong time, wrong rate, wrong preparation, or wrong route of administration) **PC9** Medication error resulting in the need for significant additional treatment	X	
Blood **SRE4B** Patient death or serious injury associated with unsafe administration of blood products **PC5** Blood incompatibility **SE15** Administration of blood or blood products having unintended ABO and non-ABO incompatibilities, hemolytic transfusion reactions, or transfusions resulting in death, permanent harm, or severe harm	X	X
Labor & Delivery **SRE4C** Maternal death or serious injury associated with labor or delivery in a low-risk pregnancy while being cared for in a healthcare setting **SE5** Any intrapartum maternal death	X	X
Labor & Delivery **PC12** Severe maternal morbidity when it reaches a patient and results in permanent harm or severe temporary harm **SE6** Severe maternal morbidity (leading to permanent harm or severe harm)		X
Labor & Delivery **SRE4D** Death or serious injury of a neonate associated with labor or delivery in a low-risk pregnancy **SE2** Unanticipated death of a full-term infant	X	X
Fall **SRE4E** Patient death or serious injury associated with a fall while being cared for in a healthcare setting **PC8** Fall resulting in fracture, intracranial bleed, or significant trauma **SE21** Fall in a staffed around-the-clock care setting or fall in a care setting not staffed around the clock during a time when staff are present resulting in any of the following: 1) Any fracture, 2) Surgery, casting, or traction, 3) Required consult/management or comfort care for a neurological or internal injury, 4) A patient with coagulopathy who receives blood products as a result of the fall, 5) Death or permanent harm as a result of injuries sustained from the fall	X	X

(Continued)

(Continued)

Quality Incident Comparison Checklist			
Event Checklist		*SRE*	*SE*
Pressure Injury	**SRE4F** Any Stage 3, Stage 4, and Unstageable pressure ulcers acquired after admission/presentation to a healthcare setting **PC6** Hospital-acquired Stage 3 and Stage 4 pressure ulcers	X	
Insemination	**4G** Artificial insemination with the wrong donor sperm or wrong egg	X	
Specimen	**4H** Patient death or serious injury resulting from the irretrievable loss of an irreplaceable biological specimen	X	
Laboratory	**4I** Patient death or serious injury resulting from failure to follow up or communicate laboratory, pathology, or radiology test results	X	
Disability	**PC7** Substantial disability – fractures, amputation, or disfigurement		
APGAR	**PC10** Birth-related injuries, maternal or fetal death, newborn fractures or dislocations, Apgar score below 5 at 5 minutes		
Spinal Cord	**PC14** Unanticipated neurological or spinal cord injury, permanent paralysis, partial or complete loss of sight or hearing, or anoxic brain injury		
Hyperbiliru-binemia	**PC19** Severe neonatal hyperbilirubinemia **SE17** Severe neonatal hyperbilirubinemia (bilirubin >30 milligrams/deciliter)		X
Internal Injury	**PC22** Severe internal injury, reproductive organ loss/impairment, or infectious process		
ENVIRONMENTAL EVENTS			
Electric Shock	**SRE5A** Patient or staff death or serious injury associated with an electric shock in the course of a patient care process in a healthcare setting	X	
Medical Gas	**SRE5B** Any incident in which systems designated for oxygen or other gas to be delivered to a patient contains no gas, the wrong gas, or are contaminated by toxic substances	X	
Burn	**SRE5C** Patient or staff death or serious injury associated with a burn incurred from any source in the course of a patient care process in a healthcare setting **PC13** Burns – thermal, chemical (including IV extravasations), radiological, or electrical	X	
Restraints	**SRE5D** Patient death or serious injury associated with the use of physical restraints or bedrails while being cared for in a healthcare setting	X	

Quality Incident Comparison Checklist			
Event Checklist		*SRE*	*SE*
Fire	**PC20** Fire, flame, or unanticipated smoke, heat, or flashes occurring during an episode of patient care **SE20** Fire, flame, or unanticipated smoke, heat, or flashes occurring during direct patient care caused by equipment operated and used by the organization		X
RADIOLOGIC EVENTS			
MRI	**SRE6A** Death or serious injury of a patient or staff associated with the introduction of a metallic object into the MRI area	X	
Fluoroscopy	**PC21** Prolonged fluoroscopy with cumulative dose >1500 rad to a single field or any delivery of radiotherapy to the wrong body region or >25% above the planned radiotherapy dose		
Fluoroscopy	**PC24** Radiation therapy to wrong body part or radiation therapy 25% or more above planned dose **SE19** Any delivery of radiotherapy to the wrong patient, wrong body region, unintended procedure, or >25% above the planned radiotherapy dose		X
Fluoroscopy	**SE18** Fluoroscopy resulting in permanent tissue injury when clinical and technical optimization were not implemented and/or recognized practice parameters were not followed		X
POTENTIAL CRIMINAL EVENTS			
Medical License	**SRE7A** Any instance of care ordered by or provided by someone impersonating a physician, nurse, pharmacist, or other licensed healthcare provider	X	
Abduction	**SRE7B** Abduction of a patient/resident of any age **PC11** Infant abduction or release of infant to incorrect family **SE13** Abduction of any patient receiving care, treatment, and services	X	X
Sexual Abuse	**SRE7C** Sexual abuse/assault on a patient or staff member within or on the grounds of a healthcare setting **PC16** Sexual allegations arising out of patient/healthcare provider relationship **SE7** Sexual abuse/assault of any patient receiving care, treatment, and services while on site at the organization or while under the care or supervision of the organization	X	X
Sexual Abuse	**SE8** Sexual abuse/assault of a staff member, licensed independent practitioner, visitor, or vendor while onsite at the organization or while providing care or supervision to patients		X
Assault	**SRE7D** Death or serious injury of a patient or staff member resulting from a physical assault (i.e., battery) that occurs within or on the grounds of a healthcare setting	X	

(Continued)

(Continued)

Quality Incident Comparison Checklist			
Event Checklist		SRE	SE
Assault	**PC17** Rape, assault (leading to death, permanent harm, or severe temporary harm), or homicide of any patient, visitor, or vendor while onsite **SE3** Homicide of any patient receiving care, treatment, and services while onsite at the organization or while under the care or supervision of the organization		X
Staff Assault	**SE4** Homicide of a staff member, licensed independent practitioner, visitor, or vendor while onsite at the organization or while providing care or supervision to patients		X
Assault	**PC1** When an event occurs that results in physical, mental, or emotional injury to a patient or visitor, or the loss of personal property of a patient or visitor where the injury/loss poses a threat of loss, liability, or exposure to the subsidiary. **SE9** Physical assault (leading to death, permanent harm, or severe harm) of any patient receiving care, treatment, and services while onsite at the organization or while under the care or supervision of the organization		X
Assault	**SE10** Physical assault (leading to death, permanent harm, or severe harm) of a staff member, licensed independent practitioner, visitor, or vendor while onsite at the organization or while providing care or supervision to patients		X
Legal	**PC2** When a letter from an attorney is received by a subsidiary or employee of a subsidiary asking the recipient to notify its/his/her insurance carrier.		

SRE = Serious reportable event (National Quality Forum criteria)
SE = Sentinel event defined by the Joint Commission

Mortality Review Forms

Mortality Level 1 Review Form

Patient Initials:		MR#		Encounter#	
Admit Date		Death Date		Unit	
Certified Cause of Death					

	Agree	Disagree
I am satisfied with the cause of death as listed above.		
To my knowledge, there were no significant errors of omission/commission from one week prior to admission to the time of death.		
To my knowledge, no clinical incidents or adverse events occurred during the course of the admission (such as a fall, unexpected return to theater, unexpected readmission, prescribing error).		
To my knowledge, there were no issues in relation to negative patient experience raised by the patient or family or known to me (such as a complaint).		
I consider this death to have been unavoidable.		
If you disagree with any of these statements, a formal mortality review must take place.		
This death should be reviewed more fully.		
I do **not** consider that this death requires further review.		
Name/Signature		Date	

Mortality Level 2 Review Form

Patient Initials:		MR#		Encounter#	
Admit Date		Death Date		Unit	
Certified Cause of Death					
DEMOGRAPHICS					
Date of Review			Lead Reviewer		
Patient's Age			Responsible Consultant		
Month of Admission			Age at Death		
Location of Death					

GENERAL INFORMATION	Yes/No	Brief Comment
Working diagnosis on admission		
Working diagnosis following initial clerking by inpatient team		
Working diagnosis following consultant review		
Was this diagnosis supported by tests?		
Did a hospital internal post mortem take place?		
Documented cause of death (MCCD)		

Charlson Index Comorbidities					
Acute myocardial infarction		Connective tissue disorder		Congestive cardiac failure	
Diabetic complications		Peripheral vascular disease		Severe liver disease	
Peptic ulcer disease		Pulmonary disease		Metastatic cancer	
Stroke		Paraplegia		Dementia	
Diabetes		Renal disease		Liver disease	
Cancer		HIV			
Other co-morbidities					

Was the patient identified as actively dying within 12 hours of admission?		If **yes**, you may proceed directly to "TERMINAL PHASE"

ADMISSION	Yes/No	Brief Comment
Route of referral (ED, GP, or Other)		
Admitted weekend or bank holiday?		
Time of arrival/admission (24h clock)		
Time from arrival to clinical attention (triage)		
Time from arrival to first recorded observations		
Time from arrival to first doctor review		
Grade of first doctor seen		
Time from arrival to first review by ST3+		
Time from arrival to first consultant review		

Was the patient admitted from an assessment area to ICU (including via operating theater)?		
Was the patient prescribed intravenous antibiotics within six hours of admission?		
Time from prescription to administration of antibiotics?		
FIRST 24 HOURS		
Was there evidence of a clear management plan?		
Essential investigations obtained without delay?		
Were the initial management steps appropriate?		
Were there any omissions in initial management?		
Is an online VTE risk assessment documented?		
Was the VTE recommendation followed?		
Was a MUST score undertaken (nutrition)?		
Was the patient weighed during the admission?		
Was a pressure sore assessment undertaken?		
Was a falls risk assessment undertaken?		
DURING THE INPATIENT STAY		
Was the patient admitted to the appropriate ward directly from an assessment area?		
How many wards was the patient admitted to altogether (excluding assessment areas)?		
Did medical staff write in the notes every weekday?		
Was there any period when the patient was not reviewed by a consultant for > 96 hours?		
GENERAL CARE		
Did a fall occur during the admission?		
Did a pressure sore occur post-admission?		
Did thrombosis (DVT/PE) occur during admission?		
Was hypothermia observed at any point?		
Was track & trigger undertaken appropriately?		
Was a track & trigger threshold met?		
If so, was appropriate action taken?		
Was there appropriate consultant supervision of junior staff?		
Could fluid balance have been better managed?		
Could nutrition have been better managed?		
ESCALATION OF CARE		
Was the patient admitted to ICU?		
If discharged, was a clear plan in place regarding appropriate ceiling of care?		
If discharged, was a handover of care to an ST3+ doctor documented?		
If discharged, was the patient readmitted to ICU?		

(Continued)

(Continued)

INVESTIGATION RESULTS		
Severe electrolyte abnormality (Na <120 or >150, K<2.5 or >5.9)		
Raised troponin		
Acute renal failure		
Hypoglycemia (<3mmol/l)		
Drop in hemoglobin of >2.9 g/dl over 24h		
INR>5		
HEALTHCARE-ASSOCIATED INFECTION		
Any evidence of HCAI (including HAP, bacteremia, Clostridium diff, SSI, wound infection, norovirus)?		
VIP (visual infusion phlebitis) score >2?		
Was the VIP score documented appropriately?		
Was a urinary catheter inserted?		
Indication for insertion documented & appropriate?		
SURGERY OR PROCEDURE		
General anesthetic?		
Conscious sedation?		
Unplanned return to theater (or procedure room)?		
Change in planned procedure?		
Unplanned removal/injury/repair of organ?		
MEDICATION		
Prescribed medications not available ("4" in drug chart)?		
Vitamin K, glucagon, 50% dextrose, naloxone, or flumazenil prescribed > six hours following admission?		
NEVER EVENTS/SREs		
During admission, did any never events or SREs take place?		
TERMINAL PHASE		
Was a decision made to limit treatment?		
Was resuscitation status documented in the notes?		
Is there evidence of discussion with the patient or family?		
Was it documented that the patient was dying and management modified accordingly?		
Did the palliative care team see the patient?		
Were pre-emptive end-of-life medications		
Was organ and tissue donation discussed?		

LEARNING DISABILITIES		
Did the patient have a learning disability? (Please tick.) **No** indication of a learning disability. (Please stop here.)		
Yes clear or possible indications from the case records of a learning disability. (Please provide assessments on the following specific criteria.)		
Delays in access		
Delays in access to treatment		
Dysphagia		
Hydration		
Nourishment		
PEG insertion		
Best interests assessment		
CONCLUSION/OVERALL VIEW	Yes/No	You MUST provide narrative to support any "YES" answer
Was there an undue delay in diagnosis?		
Was there an undue delay in delivering care?		
Was communication with patient/family poor?		
Was communication between professionals poor?		
Suboptimal care, but different management would have made NO DIFFERENCE to the outcome (death unavoidable).		
Suboptimal care – different management MIGHT have changed outcome (avoidable death possible).		
Suboptimal care – different management WOULD PROBABLY have changed outcome (avoidable death probable).		
Was there anything that could have been done differently?		
Was death explainable?		
Was death anticipated?		
Highlight notably good elements of care.		
Score for standard of documentation (please score 1 to 7; 1 = very poor, 7 = excellent).		
OTHER COMMENTS		
Name/Signature		Date	

Glossary of Acronyms

AHRQ – Agency for Healthcare Research and Quality. The lead federal agency charged with improving the safety and quality of healthcare for all Americans.

CAUTI – Catheter-associated urinary tract infection. A urinary tract infection associated with catheter usage.

C-Diff – Clostridioides difficile. A bacterium that causes diarrhea and colitis.

CMS – Centers for Medicare and Medicaid Services. The federal healthcare insurance provider for Medicaid and Medicare beneficiaries.

Cuff – Conditions for coverage. CMS develops conditions of participation (CoPs) and conditions for coverage (CfCs) that healthcare organizations must meet in order to begin and continue participating in the Medicare and Medicaid programs.

CLABSI – Central line bloodstream infection. Occurs when bacteria or other germs enter the patient's central line and then enter their bloodstream.

CLIA – Clinical Laboratory Improvement Amendments of 1988. This law requires any facility performing examinations of human specimens (e.g., tissue, blood, urine, etc.) for diagnosis, prevention, or treatment purposes to be certified by the secretary of the Department of Health and Human Services.

CoP – Conditions of participation. CMS develops conditions of participation (CoPs) and conditions for coverage (CfCs) that healthcare organizations must meet in order to begin and continue participating in the Medicare and Medicaid programs.

CPHQ – Certified professional in healthcare quality. CPHQ is a certification provided by the National Association for Healthcare Quality (NAHQ) for those seeking accreditation in quality.

CPPS – Certified professional in patient safety. CPPS is a certification provided by the Institute for Healthcare Improvement (IHI) for those seeking accreditation in patient safety.

DIKW – Data, information, knowledge, wisdom. The DIKW model or DIKW pyramid is an often-used method, with roots in knowledge management, to explain the ways we move from data (the D) to information (I), knowledge (K), and wisdom (W) with a component of actions and decisions.

eCQM – Electronic clinical quality measures. Tools that help measure and track the quality of healthcare services that eligible hospitals provide, as generated by a provider's electronic health record (EHR).

EMTALA – Emergency Medical Treatment and Labor Act. EMTALA was enacted in Congress in 1986 to ensure public access to emergency services regardless of the ability to pay.

HAC – Hospital-acquired condition. A HAC is a medical condition or complication that a patient develops during a hospital stay that was not present at admission.

HAI – Healthcare-acquired infections. An HAI, sometimes called a healthcare-associated infection, is an infection acquired while receiving treatment at a healthcare facility, like a hospital, or from a healthcare professional, like a doctor or nurse.

HARP – HCQIS access roles and profile, a secure identity management portal provided by the Centers for Medicare and Medicaid Services (CMS)

HCAHPS – The Hospital Consumer Assessment of Healthcare – Provider and Systems. This data contains the results of customer satisfaction surveys sent to patients who have utilized your healthcare system.

HCQIS – Health care quality information systems. Used interchangeably with HARP, a secure identity management portal provided by the Centers for Medicare and Medicaid Services (CMS).

HHS – Health and Human Services. A cabinet-level government department that provides health and human services and promotes research in social services, medicine, and public health.

HQR – Hospital Quality Reporting. CMS quality reporting platform.

IPPS – Inpatient Prospective Payment System. The IPPS pays a flat rate based on the average charges across all hospitals for a specific diagnosis, regardless of whether that particular patient's treatment cost more or less.

IQR – Inpatient quality reporting. Under the Hospital Inpatient Quality Reporting Program, CMS collects quality data from hospitals paid under the Inpatient Prospective Payment System, with the goal of driving quality improvement through measurement and transparency by publicly displaying data to help consumers make more informed decisions about their healthcare.

MEC – Medical executive committee. The MEC includes elected or "volunteered" surgeons from each specialty the facility performs, including anesthesia, the medical director of the facility, the administrator, and the nurse manager of the hospital department. The committee makes recommendations on matters that affect quality of care, including staffing, equipment, space planning, credentialing, medical staff appointment and reappointment, and clinical privileges.

MEDPAR – The Medicare Provider Analysis and Review. A MEDPAR file contains records for 100% of Medicare beneficiaries who use hospital inpatient services.

NE – Never event. First introduced in 2001 by Ken Kizer, MD, former CEO of the National Quality Forum (NQF), in reference to particularly shocking medical errors – such as wrong-site surgery – that should never occur.

NQF – National Quality Forum. A not-for-profit, nonpartisan, membership-based organization that works to catalyze improvements in healthcare

PSI – Patient safety indicator. A PSI provides information on potentially avoidable safety events that represent opportunities for improvement in the delivery of care.

PSO – Patient safety organization. The PSO was created out of the Patient Safety and Quality Improvement Act (PSQIA) of 2005.

PSQIA – Patient Safety and Quality Improvement Act. The PSQIA establishes a voluntary reporting system designed to enhance the data available to assess and resolve patient safety and healthcare quality issues.

PSWP – Patient safety work product. The PSWP is the information protected by the privilege and confidentiality protections of the Patient Safety Act and Patient Safety Rule.

QAPI – Quality assurance and performance improvement. QAPI is often referred to as the quality program in your organization and is often mistakenly used to refer to your quality committee. It is an acronym used for this purpose throughout CMS's conditions of participation.

RCA – Root-cause analysis. An RCA is defined as a factor that caused a nonconformance and should be permanently eliminated through process improvement.

SAFER – Survey Analysis for Evaluating Risk. Joint Commission's matrix to provide healthcare organizations with the information they need to prioritize resources and focus corrective action plans in areas that are most in need of compliance activities and interventions.

SE – Sentinel event. A patient safety event that results in death, permanent harm, or severe temporary harm.

SIR – Standardized infection ratio. An SIR is a statistic used to track healthcare-associated infection (HAI). It is calculated by dividing the number of observed infections by the number of predicted infections.

SRE – Serious reportable event. A compilation of serious, largely preventable, and harmful clinical events, designed to help the healthcare field assess, measure, and report performance in providing safe care.

SSI – Surgical site infection. An infection that occurs after surgery in the part of the body where the surgery took place.

VAP – Ventilator-associated pneumonia. A lung infection that develops in a person who is on a ventilator.

Index

Note: Pages numbers in *italics* indicate a figure on the corresponding page.

A

abdominal hysterectomy surgical site infections, 17
accountability
    accreditation and, 124, 125, 126, 131, 137
    admin assistant and, 194
    command room communication specialist and, 195
    defined, 84
    EMR subject matter expert and, 196
    HCAHPS and, 154
    individual actions or tasks and, 57
    manager, in survey readiness and preparation, 126
    managing hospital-acquired conditions (HAC) and
        harms and, 172
    post-survey activities and, 137
    process improvement and, 92, 94
    project management and, 116, 120
    quality improvement and, *83*, 84
    quality plan and, 150
    quality professional in training and, 101, 105, 108
    quality team and, 179, *179*, 184
    room champion and, 194
    subject matter expert and, 197
    survey action plans and, 125
    survey audits and, 131
    survey commander and, 195
    survey escort and, 196
    survey scribe and, 197
    updating information in QualityNet and, 158
    updating the quality oversight scorecard and, 79
accreditation, 123–139, *see also* survey readiness and
        preparation
    accreditation agency, managing activities of, 124–125
    agency documentation, 11
    application to accreditation agency, 123
    certification differentiated from, 123
    CMS accreditation process, *11*
    CMS approved accreditation agencies, 10–11
    compulsory *vs.* voluntary, 123
    corrective action form, 137, *138*
    DNV (*see* DNV accreditation)
    Joint Commission (*see* Joint Commission
        accreditation)
    post-survey activities, 137
    pre-survey activities, 137
    quality plan and, requirements for, 149, *150*
    quality professional in, role of, 123–124
    sample case study, 136–138
    staff recognition, 138
    survey action plans, managing, 125
accreditation readiness activities, 38–39, *see also* survey
        readiness and preparation
action items
    asking questions of people to get, 119
    collecting, 118, *119*
    creating, 119
    email notification, *122*
    standard work, 120, *121–122*
    tracking tool, 119–120, *120*
action item standard work, 120, *121–122*
action item tracking tool, 40, 119–120, *120*
acute myocardial infarction (AMI), 14, *49*, 49–54, *50*,
        58–59, 72, 78, 167, 173
admin assistant, 194
Agency for Healthcare Research and Quality (AHRQ),
        18, 154, 161, 162, 163, 165
airline industry, near-miss events in, 142–143
American Nurses' Credentialing Center (ANCC), 18
American Society for Quality (ASQ) certification, 187
analytics, 47, 48–49, *see also* quality measurement
authority, in quality plan, 150
autonomy, in intrinsic motivation, 104

B

Baker, Kim, 122n1
Baker, Sunny, 122n1
Baldridge Excellent Framework, 32
bariatric center certification, 123
behaviors, defining ideal, 105–106

bell curve, *see* normal distribution
billing data, 14
Burkett, Larry, 129

C

calendar for reporting, 18, 158, 184–185, *184*
cancer care, 16
carrot-and-stick management style, 103, *103*
cascading measures, 68–72, *69*, *70–71*, *72*
    achieving five-star status under CMS, 69–71, *70*
    cascade measure mapping, *71*
    on the front line, 68, *69*
    visual presentation, *72*
cataract surgery outcome, 15
catch-ball sessions, 107–109, *109*
catheter-associated urinary tract infections (CAUTI), 17, 165
cell phone jail, 108
Centers for Disease Control and Prevention (CDC)
    hospital-acquired infections (HAI) defined by, 165
    role of, 8
Centers for Medicare and Medicaid Services (CMS), 8–18, *see also* five-star quality rating system; QualityNet/HARP
    approved accreditation agencies, 10–11
    calendar for reporting, 18, 158, 184–185, *185*
    certification, achieving, 9
    conditions for coverage (CfCs), 9
    conditions of participation (CoPs), 9, 11, 29, 30, 72, 149–150, 159, *160*
    COVID-19 reporting, 159–160, *160*
    deeming process, 9
    governance structure required by, 29, 30
    Hospital Consumer Assessment of Healthcare Providers and Systems (HCAHPS), 154, *154–155*, 191–192
    hospital quality reporting (HQR), *158*, *159*
    importance of, 9
    National Healthcare Safety Network (NHSN), 153
    non-participating providers, 10
    opt-out providers, 10
    participating providers, 10
    quality assessment and performance improvement (QAPI) program, 29, 34, 149
    quality penalties, 5–6, *6*
    value-based purchasing model, 5
central line–associated infections (CLABSI), 17, 165
certification(s)
    accreditation differentiated from, 123
    CMS, 9
    examples of, 123, 187
    to report COVID-19 data, 159
certified professional in healthcare quality (CPHQ), 187
certified professional in patient safety (CPPS), 187
change management, *96–97*, 96–99, *99*
chest pain certification, 123

chronic obstructive pulmonary disease (COPD), 14, 167
claims-based measures, 157
claims data, 14
Clifton, Don, 177–179, *178*
clinical laboratory improvement amendments (CLIA), 22, 123
clostridioides difficile (C-Diff), 17
Coleman, Ken, 102
colonoscopy follow-up, 15
colon surgical site infections, 17
command room communication specialist, 195
committee charter example, 198–199
communication
    plan, employee engagement and, 106–107, *107*
    in project management, 115
    in quality plan, 151
competencies, 143
The Complete Idiot's Guide to Project Management (Baker and Baker), 116–118
conditions for coverage (CfCs), 9
conditions of participation (CoPs), 9, 11, 29, 30, 72, 149–150, 159, *160*
confidentiality agreement, patient safety organization (PSO), 163, 204–205
congestive heart failure (CHF), 48, 167
Consulting Remedy, LLC, 159
continuous survey readiness (CSR), 125, *126*
control charts, 62–66
    described, 62
    ER visits, *65*
    ER visits outlier, *66*
    normal distribution and, *62–63*, 62–64, *64*, *65*
    standard deviation formula, *63*
    templates for, 65
    trending data used in, 66
convergence, 32–33
coronary artery bypass graft (CABG), 14
corrective action form, 137, *138*
Covey, Stephen, 32, 56
COVID-19 pandemic
    CMS reporting requirements, 159–160, *160*
    National Healthcare Safety Network (NHSN) reports on, 153, 159
    trending data and, 60, 61–62
Creating a Lean Culture (Mann), 4–5

D

daily operations, 140–142
data
    defined, 45
    example, *46*
data-information-knowledge-wisdom (DIKW), 44, *45*, *46*, *47*
    data, defined, 45
    data example, *46*
    information, defined, 45

information example, *47*
knowledge, defined, 46
knowledge example, *46*
triangle, *46*
wisdom, defined, 46
wisdom example, *46*
deeming process, 9
department director report-outs, template for, 38, *40*
department of health (DOH) scenario, 188–190
DMAIC process model, 86–87, 89
DNV accreditation, 9
  ISO 9001 standards, 88
  QM.6 system requirements, 30
  requirements, 149, *150*
  requirements oversight, 127
  standards, classification of, 12, 123
Drive: The Surprising Truth about What Motivates Us (Pink), 104

E

Eckes, George, 97
Einstein, Albert, 89
electrocardiogram (EKG), 58, 59, 72, 78
electronic clinical quality measures (eCQM), 156, 158
electronic medical record expert, 130
The Elegant Solution (May), 110
email notification, action item, *122*
emergency department care, 16
emergency medical condition (EMC), 18
Emergency Medical Treatment and Active Labor Act (EMTALA), 18–20, *20*, *21*, 152
employee engagement, 103–107
  current state of, assessing, 106–107, *107*
  motivation and, 103–105, *103*
EMResource, 160
EMR subject matter expert, 196
external reporting, 153–160
  COVID-19 reporting, 159–160, *160*
  Hospital Consumer Assessment of Healthcare Providers and Systems (HCAHPS), 154–155
  National Healthcare Safety Network (NHSN), 153
  QualityNet/HARP (CMS) portal, 155–159
extrinsic motivation, 103–104

F

fall rate, 56, 59
Federal Aviation Administration (FAA), 142
five-foot rule, 105–106
five-star quality rating system, *13*, 13–17
  categories in, *57*
  diagnoses codes, 14–15
  Hospital Consumer Assessment of Healthcare – Provider and Systems (HCAHPS) data, 15, 153, 154–155
  MEDPAR data, 13, *13*, 14

mortality rates, 167
National Healthcare Safety Network9 (NHSN), 17, 153
patient survey rating, *154*
QualityNet/HARP data, 15–17, 18, *155*, 155–158, *159*
scorecard example, *70*
SMART goal model for attaining, 55, 69
five whys, 95
follow-up, in job instruction, 112
follow-up care, 17

G

G4 Beijing-Hong Kong-Macau Expressway traffic jam, 31–32
gap analysis, 127, *127*, 137
governing board, 41
  report-out example, *42*
Graben, Mark, 86
Graupp, Patrick, 112

H

hand hygiene standard work, 112, *113*
harms, *see* hospital-acquired conditions (HAC) and harms
HARP, *see* QualityNet/HARP
Harrington, H. James, 47
HCQIS access roles and profile (HARP), *see* QualityNet/HARP
Health Insurance Marketplace, 8
Health Insurance Portability and Accountability Act (HIPAA), 21–22, 152
heart attack care, 16
heart failure (HF), 14
high reliable organizations (HRO), 143
Hogan, Michael, 86
hospital-acquired conditions (HAC) and harms, 171–174
  criteria defined by the CDC, 165
  present on admission flag (POAF), 171–172, *172*, 173
  preventable adverse events, 142–143
  process for reviewing, 172–173
  role of quality professionals in, 171–173
hospital-acquired infections (HAI), 156, 164, 165
Hospital Consumer Assessment of Healthcare Providers and Systems (HCAHPS), 157
  accessing and understanding survey results, 154–155
  goals, 153, 154
  questions utilized for five-star criteria, 15, 154, 191–192
hospital inpatient measure sets, 157
hospital inpatient quality program measures, 157
hospital quality reporting (HQR), *158*, *159*
Hospital readmission reduction program (HRRP), 157
hospital value-based purchasing (HVBP), 157

hospital-wide readmissions (HWR), 14, 157
huddle meetings, 181–184, *182–184*

I

iatrogenic pneumothorax, 14
ImageTrend, 160
information
    defined, 45
    example, *46*
in-hospital fall with hip fracture, 14
Inpatient Prospective Payment System (IPPS), 155
inpatient quality reporting (IQR), 5, 155, 157
in-process measures, 57–59, *58–59*
interviews, 175
intrinsic motivation, 103, 104
Ishikawa fishbone diagram, 94
ISO 9001 standards, 89, 187

J

job descriptions for survey readiness, 194–199
    admin assistant, 194
    command room champion, 194
    command room communication specialist, 195
    committee charter example, 198–199
    EMR subject matter expert, 196
    subject matter expert, 197
    survey commander, 195
    survey escort, 196
    survey scribe, 197
job instruction, 111–112
Joint Commission
    criteria involving data and analytics, 80
    sentinel event (SE), 165, 206–210
Joint Commission accreditation, 9
    criteria, in quality oversight scorecard, 74
    for deemed status purposes, 29
    measurement and analytics, 47, 48, 80
    requirements, 149, *150*
    requirements oversight, 127
    standards, classification of, 11–12, 123
Juvare, 160

K

Kalvin, Lord, 47
knowledge
    defined, 45
    example, *46*

L

leader, defined, 118
leadership commitment, 125–126
Lean Hospitals (Graben), 86

Lean methodology, 26, 85–86, 89, 92, 99
    basic principles of, 85
    certification, 187
    goal and outcomes of, 85
    in Graben's *Lean Hospitals*, 86
    learning and applying the concepts of, 86
    in Mann's *Creating a Lean Culture*, 4–5
    overview of, 85
    quality plan and, 151
Leapfrog Group, 18
left ventricular assist device (LVAD) certification, 123

M

Magnet American Nurses Credentialing Center, 18
Making Six Sigma Last (Eckes), 97
manager accountability, 126
Mann, David, 4–5
mastery, in intrinsic motivation, 104
Maxwell, John C., 116
May, Matthew E., 110
McKnight, William, 105
Medicaid, *see* Centers for Medicare and Medicaid
    Services (CMS)
medical executive committee (MEC), 40–41
    report-out example, *41*
medical imaging, 16
medical screening examination (MSE), 18, 19
Medicare, *see* Centers for Medicare and Medicaid Services
    (CMS)
Medicare Provider Analysis and Review (MEDPAR), 13,
    13, 14
Medicare spending per beneficiary (MSPB), 14, 157
methicillin-resistant staphylococcus aureus (MRSA), 17, 74
methodology, in quality plan, 151
Microsoft Excel
    as action item tracking tool, 119–120, *120*
    control chart created in, 64
    Pareto chart created in, 66
    quality oversight scorecard created in, 73, 74, 79
    spreadsheet for CMS five-star scorecard, 69, *70*
    square root calculation and, 62
    standard deviation and, 62, 193
minutes, 39, *41*
    quality committee minutes, template for, 39, 40, *40*
    review schedule, 38, 39, *39*
mortality rates, 14, 58, 69, 72, 78, 79, 167, 173
mortality reviews, 167–169
    forms, 211–216
    Level-1 review, 168, 169, *169*, 211
    Level-2 review, 168–169, 212–215
    mortality review log, 169, *169*
    process of, 167–168, *167*, 169
motivation, 103–106, *104*
    carrot-and-stick management style and, 103, *104*
    defining ideal behaviors and, 105–106

extrinsic, 103–104
formal/informal conversations and, 106
intrinsic, 103, 104

N

National Healthcare Safety Network (NHSN), 17, 153, 160
National Quality Forum (NQF), 164–165
near misses, 142–143
never events (NE), 164, 165
Next Generation StrengthsFinder 2.0 (Rath), 178
non-participating providers, 10
normal distribution, 62–64, *64*
    in change management, 96–97, *97*
    class grades, *62*
    control chart ER visits, *65*
    control chart ER visits outlier, *66*
    in control charts, *62–63*, 62–64, *64*, *65*
    defined, 62
    ER visits, *64*
    ER visits sideways, *65*
    principle of, 63
not present on admission (NPOA) indicator,
    171–172, 173

O

Ohno, Taichi, 109
one-on-one meetings, 179–182, *180*
One Question (Coleman), 102
onsite survey activities, *see* survey audits
open-door policy, 179
opt-out providers, 10
organization, in quality plan, 150, *151*
organizational alignment, 32–33
organizational assessment, 128
outcome measures, 57–59, *58–59*
oversight, in quality plan, 151, *151*
ownership
    defined, 84
    quality improvement and, *83*, 84, *84*
    quality professional in training and, 108

P

Pareto chart, 66–68, *67–68*
Pareto principle, 66
participating providers, 10
patient safety, 17
Patient Safety and Quality Improvement Act
    (PSQIA), 161
patient safety indicators (PSI), 152, 164, 165
patient safety organization (PSO), 161–163, *162*
    benefits of, 162
    confidentiality agreement, 163, 204–205
    creation of, 161

documentation for patient safety work product
    (PSWP), 163
file storage for patient safety work product (PSWP), 163
importance of, 161
list of, on AHRQ website, 162
policy, 162–163
reporting patient safety work product (PSWP), 163
requirements of, 162
seal, *162*
patient safety work product (PSWP)
    documentation for, 163
    file storage for, 163
    reporting, 163
payment standardization, 157
percutaneous coronary intervention (PCI), 59, 78
performance improvement projects, in quality plan, 152
perioperative hemorrhage or hematoma, 14
perioperative pulmonary embolism or deep vein
    thrombosis, 14
personality assessment, 177–178
Pink, Daniel, 104
plan-do-study-act (PDSA), 26, 54, 85, 89–96
    "act" in, 92
    action items, 116, 120
    cycle iterations, 91, *91*
    cycle questions, 89–91, *90*, 102
    in daily operations, 150
    "do" in, 92
    employee engagement and, 103
    overview of, 89
    in patient safety organization (PSO), 162, 166
    "plan" in, 91
    in quality plan, 151
    in root-cause analysis (RCA), 94–96
    in sample scenario, 188, 190
    steps of, 91–94
    "study" in, 92
    template, *93*
    tools, *92*
pneumonia, 14–15, 165, 167, 171
postoperative acute kidney injury requiring dialysis, 14
postoperative respiratory failure, 14
postoperative wound dehiscence, 14
post-survey activities, 137
pregnancy and delivery care, 16
prepare the worker, in job instruction, 112
present on admission flag (POAF), 171–172, *172*, 173
present the operation, in job instruction, 112
pressure ulcer, 14, 108, 152, 171
pre-survey activities, 137
preventative care, 16
process improvement, 84, 85–96
    ISO 9001, 89
    Lean methodology, 85–86
    plan-do-study-act (PDSA), 89–95, *90*, *91*, *92*, *95*
    root-cause analysis, 94–96, *95*

selling, *83*
Six Sigma (6σ), 86–89
proficiency, 143
project management, 115–122
    action item standard work, 120, *121–122*
    action item tracking tool, 119–120, *120*
    asking questions of people to get to an action
        item, 119
    collecting action items, 118, *119*
    communication in, 116
    creating action items, 119
    follow-up and follow-through, 116
    in quality, 115–119
    rules of, 116–118, *117*
    techniques for, 116
    variables within your control, 118, *118*
project management professional (PMP), 187
psychiatric unit services, 16–17
purpose, in intrinsic motivation, 105
Purrier, Martha, 112

Q

quality
    CMS quality penalties, 5–6
    creation of, 27
    culture, 4–5
    defining, 3–4
    examples of, 4
    improving, 27–29
    poor, cost of, 5–7
    project management in, 115–119
    regulation (*see* regulation)
    sustaining (*see* sustaining quality)
quality assessment and performance improvement
        (QAPI), 29, 30, 33, 34–40, 149
quality committee, 34–40
    creating, 35
    meeting (*see* quality committee meeting)
    other names for, 34
    roles of, 34–35
    structure, 35–40
quality committee meeting, 36–40
    agenda, 35–36, *36*
    attendance structure, 35
    department director report-outs, template for, 39, *40*
    minutes, 39, *41*
    minutes review schedule, 38, 39, *39*
    presentation schedule, *38*
    quality committee minutes, template for, 39, 40, *40*
    standard meeting agenda template, 36
    standard meeting time, 36
quality director, 25–29
    defined by job descriptions, 25–27
    quality management and, 25–29
    in sustaining quality, 140
    top priorities for, *28*, 28–29

quality director standard work, 143–147
    daily, *144*
    key elements in, 143, 147
    monthly, *146*
    weekly, *145*
quality governance structure, 29–34
    DNV, 30
    Joint Commission accreditation, 29
    QAPI program, 29
    roles and responsibilities, 31, 33–34, *34*
quality improvement, 82–100
    accountability and ownership, *83*, 84
    change management, *96–97*, 96–99, *99*
    example quality improvement plan, 199–204
    overview of, 82–83
    process improvement, *83*, 84, 85–96
    program elements, in quality plan, 151, 152
    sustainability, 82–83
    transparency, *83*, 84
    transparency-ownership-process improvement
        timeline, *84*
quality incident comparison checklist, 206–210
    care management events, 207–208
    environmental events, 208–209
    patient protection events, 206–207
    potential criminal events, 209–210
    product or device events, 206
    radiologic events, 209
    surgical or invasive procedure events, 206
quality incident events, 163–165
    event classification guide, *166*
    hospital-acquired conditions (HAC), 164
    hospital-acquired infections (HAI), 164, 165
    never events (NE), 164, 165
    patient safety indicators (PSI), 164, 165
    quality incident summary, 165–166
    sentinel events (SE), 164, 165
    serious reportable events (SRE), 164–165
    state reportable safety events (SRSE), 164
    terms, *164*, 164–165
quality incident summary, 165–166
quality management, 24–44
    governing board, 41, *42*
    medical executive committee (MEC),
        40–41, *41*
    mission of, 25
    quality committee, 30, 33, 34–40
    quality director, 25–29
    quality governance structure, 29–34
    red flags, 24
quality measurement, 45–81
    accreditation criteria under the Joint Commission,
        47, 48
    analytics and, 47, 48–49
    basics of, 45–46
    cascading measures, 68–72, *69*, *70–71*, *72*
    control charts, *62–63*, 62–66, *64*, *65–66*

data-information-knowledge-wisdom (DIKW), 45, *45, 46, 48*
  exercise, 49–54
  in-process *versus* outcome measures, 57–59
  Pareto chart, 66–68, *67–68*
  quality oversight scorecard, 72–79, *75–77*
  role of, in improving quality, 47
  SMART goals, *54,* 54–57
  trending data, *60–61,* 60–62
QualityNet/HARP, 15–17, 18, 155–158
  categories of data in, 156–157
  HARP, overview of, 155
  psychiatric unit services, 16–17
  QualityNet, overview of, 155–156
  QualityNet home page, *155*
  readmissions, 156, *156*
  terminology, 155
  timely and effective care, 15–16
  updating information in, 18, 157, 158, *159*
  venders used for, 157–158
  Vendor Management page, 157–158, *158*
quality oversight scorecard, 72–79, *75–77*
  cover page, *75*
  department template, *76*
  process for developing, 73–74
  program data, 72–73
  program scope, 72
  quality measures for each department, 78
  tabs, *75*
  unit example, *77*
  updating, 78–79
quality plan, 149–152
  accreditation requirements, 149, *149*
  approval, 152
  authority, 150
  communication, 151
  components of, 150–152
  elements of, 149, 150
  methodology, 151
  organization, 150, *151*
  oversight, 151, *151*
  performance improvement projects, 152
  purpose, 149, 150
  quality improvement program elements, 151, 152
  required by CMS conditions of participation (CoP) regulation, 149
  scope, 150
quality professional
  in sustaining quality, 140
  in training, role of, 101–103, *102*
quality team, 175–185
  assign primary and secondary owners, 179, 180
  calendar for reporting, 184–185, *185*
  developing, 175–180
  huddle meetings, 181–184, *183–184*
  interviews, 175
  key themes, *176,* 176–177, *177*
  one-on-one meetings, 179–181, *180*
  outline the work of the department, 179, *179*
  personality assessment, 177–179
  support, 186
quality training, 101–114
  catch-ball sessions, 107–109, *109*
  employee engagement, 103–107, *104, 107*
  hand hygiene standard work, 112, *113*
  high-level patient process quality involvement, *102*
  role of the quality professional, 101–103, *102*
  simplifying the message, 102
  standard work, 109–111
  training within industry (TWI), 111–112, *113*
  turning each moment into a teaching moment, 102

R

Rath, Tom, 178
readiness assessment dashboard, 128, *128*
readmission rates, 14, 58, 60, 69, 156
regulation, 8–23
  benchmarking agencies, 18
  Centers for Disease Control and Prevention (CDC), 8
  Centers for Medicare and Medicaid Services (CMS), 8–18
  Clinical Laboratory Improvement Amendments (CLIA), 22
  distribution of healthcare expenditure, *10*
  Health Insurance Portability and Accountability Act (HIPAA), 21–22
  other regulations important to quality departments, 18–21
  US Department of Health and Human Services (HHS), 8, *9*
report-outs, 39, *40, 41, 42*
requirements oversight, 127
root-cause analysis (RCA), 94–96, *95,* 143
run charts, *60–61,* 60–62

S

scope, in quality plan, 150
sentinel events (SE), 164, 165, 206–210
sepsis, 14, 15, 29, 59, 73
serious reportable events (SRE), 164–165
Shingo, Shingeo, 5
Shingo Institute, 5
Shingo Model, 5, 7, 32
Six Sigma (6σ), 86–88, 89, 92, 99
  analyze phase of, 87
  certification, 187
  change management assessment and, 97–98
  control phase of, 88
  define phase of, 87
  DMAIC process model used in, 86–87, 88
  improve phase of, 87–88
  measure phase of, 87
  overview of, 86

in quality plan, 151
timelines for, 88
SMART goals, *54*, 54–57
  exercise, 55–56
  five-star status and, 55
  individual tasks and, 57
  key elements, 54–55
The Speed of Trust (Covey), 56
staff
  education, 128–129
  recognition, 137, 138
standard deviation, 62–64
  formula for, *63*
  MS Excel to obtain, 62, 193
  principle of normal distribution and, 63
  Six Sigma and, 86
standardized infection ratio (SIR), 102, 153
standard operating procedures (SOPs), 19, 110
standard work, 109–111
  action item, 120, *121–122*
State Children's Health Insurance Program, 8
state reportable safety events (SRSE), 164
StrengthsFinder, Clifton's, 177–179, *178*
stroke, 14, 16, 73, 123, 167
stroke management certification, 123
subject matter expert, 130, 197
substance use treatment, 16
Summit, Pat, 102
surgical site infections (SSI), 165
survey action plans, managing, 125
survey audits, 129–136
  communicate and obtain approvals, 135, 136
  contact list, 134–135
  create job descriptions, 130, 131
  develop a communication plan, 130, *130*
  identify the people who will need to be part of the survey, 129–130
  set up the process and structure for the survey, 132–135
  survey badges, 132, *132*
  survey briefing agenda, 133, 134, *134*
  survey command center white board, 132, 133, *133*
  survey job description template, 130, *131*
  survey organizational chart, 130, *130*
  survey ready box, *134*, 135, *135*
survey commander, 129, 195
survey command room champion, 129, 194
survey escort, 130, 196
survey procedure planning, *see* survey audits
survey readiness and preparation, 125–136, *see also* job descriptions for survey readiness
  continuous survey readiness, 125, *126*
  corrective action form, 137, *138*
  gap analysis, 127, *127*
  leadership commitment, 125–126
  manager accountability, 126

onsite survey activities (*see* survey audits)
organizational assessment, 127, 128
post-survey activities, 137
pre-survey activities, 137
readiness assessment dashboard, 128, *128*
requirements oversight, 127
sample case study, 136–138
staff education, 128–129
staff recognition, 137, 138
survey procedure planning (*see* survey audits)
survey readiness oversight, 126–127
survey readiness oversight, 126–127
survey scribe, 130, 197
sustaining quality, 140–148
  daily operations, 140–142
  near misses, 142–143
  quality director standard work, 143–147, *144–146*
  quality professional in, role of, 140

T

Thompson, William, 47
timely and effective care, 15–16
To Err is Human, 82
total hip replacement (THA), 14, 157
total knee arthroplasty (TKA), 14, 157
total quality management (TQM), 92
tracers, 127
tracking tool, action item, 119–120, *120*
training programs, 187
training within industry (TWI), 111–112, *113*
transparency
  defining quality and, 4
  five-star quality rating system and, 13
  HCAHPS and, 154, 155
  quality improvement and, *83*, 84, *84*
  quality measurement and, 54
  quality oversight scorecard and, 73
trending data, *60–61*, 60–62, *see also* control charts
tryout performance, in job instruction, 112
20% time, 105

U

US Department of Health and Human Services (HHS)
  Clinical Laboratory Improvement Amendments (CLIA) and, 22
  COVID-19 reporting, 159
  HIPAA privacy rule, 22
  office of the secretary (OS), 8
  organization, 8, *9*
  Patient Safety and Quality Improvement Act (PSQIA) and, 161
US Public Health Service, 8
"unknown" indicator, 171, 172, 173

unplanned readmission, 17
unrecognized abdominopelvic accidental puncture or
    laceration, 14

V

ventilator-associated pneumonia (VAP), 165

W

wisdom
    defined, 46
    example, *47*
World Health Organization, 142
www.Innovate2Accelerate.com, 49, 64

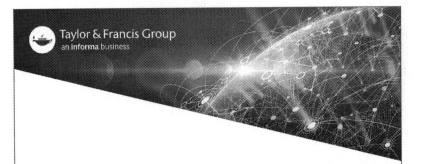

Printed in the United States
by Baker & Taylor Publisher Services